A LIFE IN PIECES

A LIFE
IN PIECES

The Making and Unmaking

of

Binjamin Wilkomirski

BLAKE ESKIN

W. W. Norton & Company

NEW YORK / LONDON

Copyright © 2002 by Blake Eskin

All rights reserved
Printed in the United States of America
First Edition

Photograph on page 39 courtesy of Schocken Books.
Photograph on page 173 courtesy of Max Grosjean.
The other photographs are provided courtesy of the author.

For information about permission to reproduce selections from this
book, write to Permissions, W. W. Norton & Company, Inc.,
500 Fifth Avenue, New York, NY 10110

The text of this book is composed in Stemple Garamond
with the display set in Manticore Titling
Composition by A. W. Bennett, Inc.
Manufacturing by Quebecor Fairfield
Book design by Brooke Koven
Production manager: Julia Druskin

Library of Congress Cataloging-in-Publication Data

Eskin, Blake.
A life in pieces : the making and unmaking of
Binjamin Wilkomirski / by Blake Eskin.
p. cm.
ISBN-393-04871-3
1. Wilkomirski, Binjamin. Bruchstücke. 2. Holocaust, Jewish
(1939–1945), in literature. 3. Authors, German—20th century—
Biography. 4. Impostors and imposture—Germany—Biography.
I. Title.

PT2685.I383 785 2002
833'.914—dc21   2001044705

W. W. Norton & Comp any, Inc.,
500 Fifth Avenue, New York, N.Y. 10110
www.wwnorton.com

W. W. Norton & Company Ltd.,
Castle House, 75/76 Wells Street, London W1T 3QT

1 2 3 4 5 6 7 8 9 0

To my family

SEÑORA: . . . He must know the truth. Which of us is going to tell him?

TEACHER: I will. I'll tell him.

SEÑORA: And will you tell them?

TEACHER: Yes, I'll tell them that he is my son, our son, their own flesh and blood.

SEÑORA: Why don't you go now and tell them?

TEACHER: And suppose they don't want the truth?

—MAX FRISCH, *Andorra*

I never would have thought that you would be taken in by all this talk about Benjamin. What did you see in him?

—MENDELE MOYKHER SFORIM,
The Brief Travels of Benjamin the Third

The choice for Jews as for non-Jews is not whether or not to have a past, but rather—what kind of past shall one have.

—YOSEF HAYIM YERUSHALMI,
Zakhor: Jewish History and Jewish Memory

CONTENTS

Prologue   15

Hope   19

Certainty   41

Doubt   66

Phantom Siblings   86

Character Assassination   104

Auschwitz, Switzerland   123

The Second Holocaust   139

Other People's Shoes   154

The Wilkomirskis of Riga   171

Annual Meeting   191

California Split   208

Conspiracy Theories   226

Epilogue   243

ACKNOWLEDGMENTS

This book evolved out of assignments for the *Forward* newspaper and the public-radio program *This American Life*. The munificence of the Forward Foundation and the sustained encouragement of Seth Lipsky, Jonathan Rosen, and the erstwhile *redaktzia* of the *Forward* enabled me to venture as far as I did. Julie Snyder and Ira Glass of *This American Life* took a crucial early interest in Wilkomirskis other than Binjamin. John Hodgman's enthusiasm for this project has outlasted his career as an agent, and Simon Lipskar has done a yeoman's job in long relief. Undeterred by the many unknowns involved, Jill Bialosky made a commitment to this project, and she has been a sympathetic and perceptive editor. I appreciate the efforts of Deirdre O'Dwyer and the rest of the Norton team.

I am grateful to the child survivors who took the time to speak with me and to the Wilburs who shared their knowledge and thoughts about our family history. Linda Kulman and Ralph Alswang, Ralph and Elisabeth Weingarten, Susann Wilbur and Phoebus Tongas, Ellen Wilbur and Henry Katz, and Elissa Gootman extended their hospitality when I was reporting far from home. The Millay Colony for the Arts provided a much needed month of refuge for revisions. For reasons too diverse to enumerate here, I am indebted to Derth Adams, Shamma Boyarin, Lore and Morris Dickstein, Julie Eisenberg, Simon Erlanger, Devra Eskin, Eva Fogelman, Daniel Ganzfried, Robert Krell, Stefan Maechler, Jonathan Mahler, Daisy Miller, Monika Muggli, Bob and Gretchen Passantino, Robert Schonberg, Aviva Slesin, Leon Stabinsky, Ilan Stavans, Amy Tübke-

Davidson, Irina Veinberga, and the staff of the New York Public Library.

My mother, Eden Force Eskin, instilled in me a love of stories and trusted me to tell ours. My father, Robert Eskin, does not figure prominently in this plot, but his support behind the scenes was indispensable. And without you, Rachel, neither this book nor my life would have found its proper shape.

A LIFE IN PIECES

PROLOGUE

September 28, 1997

It is two o'clock on a Sunday at the end of September, and my parents' living room is full of Wilburs. There are about twenty of us. Some of them I've never met before and a couple of the Orthodox ones I've never even heard of until this afternoon, but all are my cousins. My last name has always been Eskin, my mother was called Force before she met my father, and her mother was a Stein before she married my grandfather. But *her* mother, my great-grandmother, was once known as Anna Wilbur.

It is not so much our common cognomen that led so many Wilburs to gather in Manhattan on this autumn afternoon as a curiosity about what came before it. Like many American surnames, Wilbur is an invention, a distortion, an Anglicized revision of the family name. Anna's oldest brother led the way to New York at the beginning of the twentieth century, and the siblings who followed him adopted the name when they arrived in the United States. On the ocean they were still Wilkomirskis, as they were in Riga, a city of hundreds of thousands of souls on the eastern coast of the Baltic Sea.

The stranger from Europe was also called Wilkomirski, an uncommon name no more intrinsically Jewish than Wilbur, and his story also begins in Riga, but from there it diverges from ours. While the

Wilburs followed various paths in an American climate of peace and opportunity, back in Europe young Binjamin Wilkomirski struggled with dislocation and identity loss in the wake of the Second World War. He has retrieved enough of his past to write an incomplete memoir. He is looking for more of it, which is why, he says, he is coming to see us.

The Wilburs have gathered to tell our story, to hear more of his story, to explore whether they are parts of the same story. Is his history ours? When he walks through the door, the answer will turn murky. Sometime after that, the murk will deepen profoundly, and then all will become quite clear. But none of this has happened yet; it is two o'clock on a Sunday afternoon and we do not even know that the stranger has other names. He is late, and as we wait we enjoy a prolonged moment in which everything we imagine, and everything we imagine he imagines, is possible. A rupture can be healed, a childhood can be restored, a family can be reunited, history can be rewritten, fate can be outwitted, miracles can happen to ordinary people, the world can be made whole again. Our guest is late, and for the time being everything will be perfect.

As I WAIT in the living room to meet Binjamin Wilkomirski, I anticipate a second windfall, one that no other Wilbur will share: a promising feature story told from an insider's perspective. About to fall into my lap is a double portion of manna, a personal history that will help me understand where I come from and a public tale that can edify and astound others. It seems almost too good to be true, and it might be, if our visitor hadn't already transformed himself and amazed the public with his own retrieved past. The story of how I found my own past through his search would be but a faint echo of his extraordinary discoveries, of course, but with his cooperation it would still be quite powerful.

When Binjamin Wilkomirski arrives I will greet him with open arms and, in one hand, a microphone. To do both is tough, I will discover, at times impossible. After he leaves I will wish I could have felt more of a cousin's warmth; after a year's silence is broken, I will come to regret that I did not express enough of the journalist's skepticism.

A great effort has gone into convincing people that the lost soul on his way to my parents' apartment is Binjamin Wilkomirski, child survivor of the Holocaust. Later, once he was widely accepted as Binjamin, prying that identity away from him would become a messy and prolonged struggle, conducted on public and private fronts, among the many individuals around the world whose own lives and sense of history had become entwined in his. Why roll the ball up the hill and let it tumble down again? Why revisit the parlor game that is about to begin in my parents' apartment on the East Side of Manhattan? Why reprise the larger, parallel drama of masquerade and exposure in which my own experiences play a tangential part? To some, it might seem painful or embarrassing, and others might find it upsetting to reexamine the scars of a wounded man or objectionable to risk hurting him again. It would be easy enough to ignore his mistakes, easier still to forget how we—and this includes publishers, scholars, critics, journalists, psychologists, and other accredited and self-styled experts as well as hopeful relatives and friends—were misled, how we misled others, and how some of us misled ourselves. But there is much to be learned from the tale of Binjamin Wilkomirski, even if he is unable to appreciate it. His story can reveal something about the world that wanted so much for it to be true, for him to be real.

REPORTAGE, LIKE testimony, requires trust. The teller must convince the listener that he is credible, and the listener must believe in the storyteller if he wants to derive the intended meaning of the story being told. When the listener discovers that his trust has been abused, he becomes disoriented. Like the victim of a confidence game, he must scramble to make sense of the information scattered before him. He must separate facts from falsehoods while reevaluating the long-held presuppositions that did not protect him from being duped.

A reporter is both listener and teller, and when he gets ensnared by a hoax, he carries the burden of being an unreliable narrator in addition to his confusion. Recounting that hoax can be a way of boasting of your cleverness to the degree you smelled a rat, a method of papering over your own gullibility to whatever degree you didn't, a step toward restoring the credibility you think you have lost, a form of revenge against the artful storyteller who seduced you.

The hopes aroused that day in my parents' living room—the desire to know my own history better and to enlighten others with it—did not diminish when I learned that Binjamin Wilkomirski might be an impostor. On the contrary, they became stronger. He was still a good story, and I wanted another whack at it, a second chance to get it right.

HOPE

———

It was the Wilburs who sought out Binjamin Wilkomirski, not the other way around.

I was the first to come across him. One day I was flipping through book catalogs to see what items of interest might appear in the coming season. In the glossy brochure of Schocken Books, the venerable Jewish imprint that introduced America to Franz Kafka and Gershom Scholem, I found a notice for *Fragments: Memories of a Wartime Childhood* by one Binjamin Wilkomirski.

The author's name was enough to make me stop and take a closer look. The name Wilkomirski reminded me of the bedtime stories my mother would tell me when I was a child, stories from her own early years about her expansive, close-knit extended family. For most of her childhood, my mother shared an apartment in the Bronx with her sister and parents, her grandfather Izzy, grandmother Anna, and Anna's unmarried sister, Rebecca. Anna and Rebecca were both Wilburs, and countless other Wilburs, it seemed, lived in the same predominantly Jewish Bronx neighborhood. Another colony of Wilburs, a more religiously observant branch of the family which seemed somewhat estranged from hers, lived a subway ride away in Brooklyn.

Again and again my mother would tell me that the Wilburs came from Riga, and in Riga their name was Wilkomirski. That nobody in the family used the name Wilkomirski anymore made it seem all the more important that I remember it. As I grew older, I would ask my mother more and more questions about the Wilkomirskis. I wanted to know how Anna and Rebecca lived back in Riga, but a detailed description of their day-to-day existence there was beyond my mother's formidable command of family lore.

It is these stories, and not religious practice or communal involvement or even my own infrequent encounters with various Wilburs who have long since left that corner of the Bronx and dispersed around the United States, that provide me with a sense of my roots. For me, the name Wilkomirski has always stood not only for these ancestors from Riga but more broadly for the world my forebears left behind. I was born in America, but for me Wilkomirski represented who I was before I became an American. This heritage was unknown and perhaps unknowable, but seemed essential and was something I still carried with me. When I was little, I had blond hair and fair skin, unlike either my mother or my father. To explain why I didn't resemble either of them, my mother would tell me how much I looked like her grandmother Anna and how I must have inherited these recessive traits from the Wilkomirskis.

Based on the few sentences in the Schocken catalog and what I knew of my own family history, I could not see how the author of *Fragments* had anything to do with us. Though Wilkomirski was an unusual surname, it was hardly unique to the Wilburs' ancestors. It referred to the Lithuanian town where, we believed, they once lived. Wilkomirski was not a generations-old marker of our identity. It was, like Wilbur, a form of camouflage in a multiethnic society in which Jews were a significant minority. Moreover, *Fragments* had been translated from the German, but the Wilburs from Riga spoke Yiddish, not German.

Perhaps the most important reason I felt at a remove from *Fragments* was that the promotional copy described it as the memoir of a man born in Europe on the eve of the Holocaust. Many American Jewish families have a specific, acute, and still painful awareness of who and what was taken from them in the Holocaust, but I do not come from one of them. My great-grandfather Samuel Eskin sailed into New York Harbor in 1904, and on all sides my family has been in the United States for four generations. Up to now, I'd never heard of any particular Wilbur—or, for that matter, of any ancestor—who had died or disappeared during the Second World War. As far as I knew, nobody needed to be found. My great-grandmother Anna had been joined in America by her brothers and sisters, their spouses, and their children. The last Wilburs arrived in 1929, before Hitler came to power and long before he posed an obvious threat to the Jews of Riga. There were so many Wilburs in New York by 1929 that it seemed everyone had emigrated.

As large as the Holocaust looms in the historical consciousness of every American Jew, unless one is mourning a particular loss any attempt to understand its impact on a personal level necessarily requires abstraction and speculation. If Great-grandfather hadn't been prescient enough to leave Russia when he did, the family probably would have been killed when the Germans invaded the Soviet Union. If Hitler had defeated the Allies and crossed the Atlantic, I might not be here today. Finding *Fragments* led to such a conjecture: if Anna Wilbur had kin who stayed in Latvia, perhaps some of them were named Wilkomirski, and maybe this Binjamin was one of them.

So I called my mother to tell her about *Fragments*. Over the years, she has persuaded elderly Wilburs to sit down with her and tell her names, dates, and places, which she began compiling into a family tree, and to pass down their Old World photographs. Mom had never heard of a Binjamin, but she did remember her grandmother Anna searching for relatives at the end of the war. For whom exactly she wasn't sure, since my mother was seven when the war ended in Europe, and her parents and grandparents insulated her as best they could from the disturbing news reports, cutting off discussion when she came into the room. Such things were not spoken of in front of the children. All my mother knew was that Anna's search did not have a happy ending.

Mom said she would ask Aunt Miriam, who is her mother's first cousin and the matriarch of the Brooklyn-based, religiously observant wing of the family. Miriam was born in Riga and was one of the last group of Wilkomirskis to leave it. If anyone would know whether there was a Binjamin unaccounted for, it would be Miriam.

According to Miriam, our family was the only Jewish family called Wilkomirski in Riga, and some of them indeed remained in Europe. Anna had two siblings who stayed behind: a sister who'd died before Miriam emigrated, and a brother named Avram. Avram and his wife had a son, but his name wasn't Binjamin. Avram hadn't been heard from since the mid-1930s, however, and it was possible that Avram later had other sons she didn't know about. In any case, Miriam assumed they were all dead.

A few months later, the New York Times Book Review endorsed Fragments as an "extraordinary memoir." "Born to a Jewish family in Latvia," the review said, Binjamin Wilkomirski "was not much more than a toddler when he saw his father killed, was separated from his family and was sent to live in camps where filth and sadism ruled." The review mentioned several examples of the horrors he witnessed: watching rats emerge from the belly of a dead woman's body, seeing babies have their skulls bashed in by uniformed adults. Reviewer Julie Salamon compared the memoir's loose, associative structure to her two-year-old son's descriptions of his night terrors. Fragments represented the nightmarish experiences of a child caught up in the Holocaust in content and also in form.

Depictions of sadistic violence give my mother nightmares whether or not they have to do with the Holocaust. She avoids movies with high body counts. But because the author's name was Binjamin Wilkomirski and he was born to a Jewish family in Latvia, she picked up Fragments.

The earliest scene in Fragments, which re-creates the first memorable trauma in the life of its author-protagonist, unfolds in Riga. It describes a full-grown man wearing a hat, a coat, and a smile. The man's name is not given, and the reader must guess at his relationship to the narrator, who seems quite attached to him. Uniformed members of the Latvian militia pluck the man from a bare room, drag him into the barricaded streets, and prop him against a wall. The confused boy crawls downstairs after him, ending up by his side. The boy experiences "the feeling of deathly terror in my chest and throat." A military vehicle rushes toward the man and boy. The man's head falls back. A dark stream erupts from his neck as the soldiers ram him into the wall. The boy is unharmed, but he feels sadness, fear, abandonment. "All at once I realize: From now on I have to manage without you, I'm alone," he says.

Rendered more like a rough charcoal sketch than a photograph, the episode is told from a child's perspective. The narrator omits any historical context he might have absorbed over the years. Without a history book handy, the reader doesn't know when the Germans reached Riga or how quickly they disposed of the Jews there. The ice in the streets tells us it's winter, the walled-off thoroughfare suggests a ghetto, the boy's crawling indicates his age. In an introduction, the author has already warned us that he doesn't know exactly how old he is. He explains that his own memories are "mostly a chaotic jumble, with very little chronological fit." As he relates the story of his early life, he doesn't seem to have a much better sense of it than his readers do. Like us, he is forced to interpret the clues he has. He guesses, for example, that the man's fond smiles in the boy's direction mean that he was "maybe my father."

The boy in *Fragments* is unsure of his parentage, his native language, and even his name. Only two people in *Fragments* call him by name during the war. One is a gray-uniformed official at Majdanek, who takes Binjamin—she does not mention a last name—to see a woman he is told is his mother. He doesn't recognize the woman, and she doesn't call him by name. The other person who names him is a woman imprisoned with him at a second concentration camp near Krakow. (The flyleaf identifies it as Auschwitz, but the narrator never does.) As they are being liberated, this woman calls out to Binjamin, who says he all but forgot he had a name. The woman takes him to a Krakow synagogue, where she gives him over to a rabbi with the words, "I'm bringing you the little Wilkomirski boy, Binjamin Wilkomirski." How she knows the little Wilkomirski boy is never explained.

MY MOTHER is a quick and ardent reader; not only does she love literature but she is a writer and editor by profession. But *Fragments,* which reaches 155 pages with the help of large print, wide margins, and plentiful white space between the lines, took her a couple of weeks. She could stomach only a few pages per sitting. *Fragments* wastes few words, and it is packed with cruelty.

As she was making her way through *Fragments*, my mother sent the following letter to its author:

> Dear Mr. Wilkomirski:
>
> Although I had promised myself to read no more books about the Holocaust, I read your book *Fragments* with great interest. It was very moving, and clearly painful to read about the ghastly experiences you were forced to undergo as a young child and how the rules you learned in the concentration camp survived in your subsequent life.
>
> I initially read the book because the name Wilkomirski is a name from my own family. . . .
>
> The name Wilkomirski was adopted by my grandmother's grandfather when he was a young boy in an effort to avoid being captured by Russian soldiers who kidnapped young Jewish boys. He and his sons continued to use the name. When the family came to America, all its members adopted a new surname.
>
> In your book you indicate that you are not certain that your last name is really Wilkomirski. If it is, then there is a possibility of a family connection. . . . There are many descendants in the United States of the Wilkomirskis who came here, and they are my favorite relatives.
>
> If you have any interest in exploring this possibility, I would very much like to hear from you.

Since she is writing to a total stranger, my mother is careful not to divulge too much information. For instance, she avoids mentioning the family's Americanized surname. She also simplifies matters by telling Binjamin only one version of how the family came to be called Wilkomirski. As a boy, I heard several, and many more emerged since we came upon *Fragments*. They all involve a young man called to serve in the Russian imperial army. Nobody quite knows who first took the name; it may have been Anna Wilbur's father, or his father, or someone else. In some versions, the boy changes his name to something less conspicuously Jewish as he skips out on military service; in others he has served his ten or twenty or twenty-five years and, having been separated from his family for so long, takes a new name. Perhaps he came from the Lithuanian town of Wilkomir, now known as Ukmerge, or maybe that was where he was stationed. Some Wilburs insist that, before Wilkomirski, the family was called Levin or Levine. Others say with equal assurance that the family was called Berliner.

The ambiguity of our own origins only serves to feed our interest in the author of *Fragments*, and increase our identification with him as we anticipate learning more about him. The difference in our situations is vast, of course. Alone in the world, he experienced an abrupt break with his past—no parents, no papers—whereas our collective knowledge, solid and well documented in America, fades only at the distant European horizon. But somehow we think we can understand him, because just as he doesn't know his real name or where he comes from, we can't be certain, once we look far back enough, of who we are.

Two months later, my mother received a reply from Switzerland. It began, as many letters do, with an apology for the delay in responding. Binjamin explained he had been on the road since my mother's letter arrived, kept busy, he said, by his "two professions." His dual vocation was spelled out in his letterhead:

BINJAMIN WILKOMIRSKI

✡ BWJ-Archive ✡
    Special aspects of modern Jewish history in Europe and the Near East
    Holocaust library and documentation
    Research project on Polish/Jewish children of the Shoah
    Visiting lecturer, University of Ostrava, Czech Republic

Musician and Atelier for Building Clarinets
    Restoration of historic clarinets, intonation correction, special French
    and German mouthpieces, special reeds for German mouthpieces

"I was really thrilled by your letter," he wrote. His enthusiasm was reinforced by a liberal use of exclamation points. In 1994, he explained, he went to Riga to research his past, and what he found there "seems to have some connections with the information You gave me about Your family!

"After wandering a few hours through the town, I could identify the house in the former 'Big Ghetto' in which I was in November 1941 as a [sic] approximately three years old boy," he said. Though he couldn't determine who the smiling man was ("either my father or an uncle—certainly somebody very close"), Binjamin pinpointed the spot on the south end of Katolu Street where he watched the man die. With the assistance of a local Jewish historian, Binjamin said he found that "a few houses more south of this place, in the direction of the river Daugava, in Moskva-Street 80, there lived until 1926 the only family Wilkomirski (or Wolkomirski in Russian pronunciation) in Riga! A couple named Rucha (Rahel) and Avram!" A local directory described Avram as a silversmith.

Binjamin also mentioned meeting three old men at Riga synagogue. They had grown up in Riga and attended a Jewish school, the Cheder Metukan. They remembered a boy named Wilkomirski in their class; unfortunately they could not remember his first name. They told him that the Wilkomirski boy left school in 1926, when the family moved away.

The researcher-musician went on to tell a few other stories he had collected in his quest. He repeated the story from *Fragments* of the woman who helped him leave Auschwitz, adding that she rescued him on January 22, 1945. "She knew my name and called me Binjamin Wilkomirski," he wrote. Another former prisoner, he added, "told me she was an intelligent women [sic] and he thinks she really recognised me." Binjamin also mentioned a Mordechai Wilkomirski who came from the Baltic and died in Israel in 1978; perhaps he was Binjamin's oldest brother. In addition, an unnamed elderly Jew in Germany told the author of *Fragments* he remembered a Wilkomirski from the Baltic states at Majdanek. This Wilkomirski had a nephew named Binjamin, who had also been deported to the camp.

Based on all this information, Binjamin said, "I am pretty shure [sic], Wilkomirski is my real name."

. . .

MOM SHARED Binjamin's reply with Aunt Miriam. Miriam remembered the house at Moskva Street, number 80. She herself lived there in 1926 with her mother, Rucha; two younger brothers; and her bachelor uncle, Avram. Miriam remembered Avram and other Wilkomirski relatives making their living as silversmiths. And the Cheder Metukan was the state-sponsored Hebrew-language school where Miriam's brothers studied. The three old men at the synagogue were around the same age as her younger brothers, and quite possibly the men remembered one of them. Although Binjamin drew some flawed conclusions—that Avram was Rucha's brother-in-law, not her husband—the information he found jibed with Miriam's memory.

The tidbits Binjamin offered about our Riga ancestors reminded us of our own authenticity. It's strange to admit that authenticity was something we craved; if we wanted authenticity, that means we felt a lack of it. At the remove of an ocean and several generations, however, it becomes difficult to have an authentic sense of one's own past. Much as I felt a strong connection to the world my ancestors inhabited, I couldn't quite imagine it. What indistinct notions I did have came filtered through my mother's vision of life in Riga, which was itself already a fantasy.

My mother has made her living by editing dictionaries, writing encyclopedia entries, and updating history and geography textbooks, among other things, so she values careful and accurate research. The information Binjamin unearthed about various Wilkomirskis in Riga apparently won her over. In her next letter, she provided him with a chart with the names of the emigrant Wilkomirskis and their children, and she told him that the family name was now Wilbur.

"Several of my cousins have read your book and have been struck by the possibility of a family connection," she told Binjamin. "I shall start looking for family photographs to copy so that you can determine if you perceive a family resemblance. . . . I plan to send a letter to all my first and second cousins telling them about our correspondence and asking for more information about the family. When I know more, I will write to you."

The Wilbur family survey did not yield much significant infor-

mation—nobody told her more than Miriam knew—but as my
mother was waiting for the results she spoke to Binjamin on the
phone a couple of times, and her optimistic caution evolved into a
wholehearted embrace. At the Passover seder, she worked a reference
to Binjamin into the story of the oppression, exile, and liberation of
the Jews of ancient Egypt. If he was a long-lost relative, it would
mean that, though her beloved grandmother was long dead, Anna's
postwar searches would not have been all for naught.

My mother's next letter began:

> Dear Cousin Binjamin,
>   I take the liberty of calling you cousin because I believe that
> you are probably my second cousin. If you are Avram's grand-
> son, then our grandparents were brother and sister. If you pre-
> fer to leave open the question of relationship, please let me
> know. . . .

Binjamin's reply did not address the question of his relationship
to the Wilburs. It was a short note containing the news that the
United States Holocaust Memorial Museum, in Washington, D.C.,
had invited him to America for a speaking tour in the fall. The Holocaust Museum's tour would take him through six cities including
New York. "I hope there will be an opportunity to meet You and
other members of Your family," he wrote.

Now that I might be meeting Binjamin Wilkomirski, I resolved
to read *Fragments*. I took it with me on vacation. I have a higher tolerance for brutality on the page than my mother does, so rather than
dipping my toes, I dove in. From the very beginning, there was
something so immediate about the violence, something so primal
about the memoirist's disjointed sense of himself, that I was riveted.
Riveted with horror: his memories really did feel like they had, as
he put it, "hard knife-sharp edges, which still cut flesh if touched
today." I kept reading, afraid of putting the book down or even of
looking up at my surroundings, the wind stirring up the lake and the
clouds moving across the Adirondack Mountains. If I stepped out of

the world in which Binjamin Wilkomirski seemed to still be trapped, I would have a hard time getting myself to reenter it, to handle those sharp-edged fragments once more. I would have read the whole thing in one sitting, in fact, but I had promised I would go out on a hike. Along the trail, I couldn't get *Fragments* out of my head; I thought of poor Binjamin, surrounded by the natural paradise of the Swiss Alps and feeling like he was still in Majdanek. I was eager to return to him.

Before *Fragments*, I had read my share of literature about the Holocaust and seen quite a few films about it, but with its astonishing, unfamiliar perspective, Binjamin's story struck deeper. Long ago I had read Anne Frank's diary, which ends just before she is taken away. It's possible to visualize her life from deportation to death, but impossible to have her describe it. I had read Jerzy Kosinski's *The Painted Bird*, about a child caught up in the Holocaust. I had found it compelling and disturbing in many of the same ways *Fragments* was, but it differed in two key respects. The boy in *The Painted Bird* does not set foot inside a concentration camp. And while Kosinski teased his readers with hints that *The Painted Bird* was autobiographical, it is labeled as fiction, whereas *Fragments* was a memoir that protested its own artlessness: "I'm not a poet or a writer. I can only try to use words to draw as exactly as possible what happened, what I saw." I'd never been able as a reader to get inside the thoughts of someone so young—he was no more than seven at war's end—who had seen so much of the war and lived to tell.

Of course, what Binjamin Wilkomirski could tell had its limits because of his age. His story is episodic and often unsure of itself. "Did I have four brothers or five, which seems righter?" he wonders at one point. When he describes a hiding place, he remembers the routine he followed there, but not how long he stayed. "Was it a few days, a few weeks, a month, longer? I have no idea." Many scenes have more unknowns than specific details when it comes to duration, location, action. There are few proper nouns. Characters materialize out of nowhere; exits, if noted, are rarely explained. At times Binjamin recalls having trouble comprehending that he has a mother, that he has a name, that there is a world beyond the concentration camps. Binjamin says he can only describe what he saw as a child through the eyes of a child. "If I'm going to write about it, I have to give up on the ordering logic of grown-ups," he says.

The book invites us to do the same. Making sense of *Fragments* requires a certain level of involvement, and if you suspend your tendency to apply logic, you must use your imagination. The impressionistic descriptions often use a part to represent the whole: when his child's eye notices a menacing boot or a gray uniform, the reader must rely on his prior knowledge of the Holocaust to fill in the rest of the malevolent Nazi wearing it. The episodic, nonlinear narrative works the same way, requiring us to connect the dots to create his biography.

The dots connect more or less like this: After the death of his perhaps-father in the ghetto, Binjamin flees Riga by boat with a woman and several older boys. They travel by boat, then board a train headed for Lvov, in western Ukraine, but they do not make it that far. The woman disappears, and Binjamin and his brothers end up at a farmhouse, in the care of a sturdy Polish woman with "big arms and heavy hands, who embodied absolute power over us children." They hide in the house by day; when it turns dark, they sneak over to a nearby hut for a bowl of soup. One day the woman tosses Binjamin in the cellar as a punishment. Nobody lets him out the next morning, and by the time he frees himself the house is empty. A few days later, another woman, this one in uniform, spots Binjamin. She promises to take him to "Majdan Lublin—Majdanek." His brothers are there, she assures him, and he will be able to play there.

He quickly discovers that "Majdanek is no playground." He does not find his brothers there. Instead he finds an older boy named Jankl, who brings him food and teaches him how to ration it out to himself. Binjamin loses his shoes, and Jankl teaches the younger boy to tie rags around his feet to protect him in the snow. Binjamin is in good hands until Jankl dies.

At Majdanek, Binjamin survives a series of acts of arbitrary cruelty. A camp guard tosses him into a kennel, where he spends a night fighting off rats and crawling insects and awaiting the return of the vicious watchdogs. Another guard gives Binjamin a ride on his shoulders, then flings him headfirst into a stone wall. Yet another guard hurls a heavy ball at the head of another little boy, who is killed by the impact. When a boy new to the barracks needs to relieve himself in the middle of the night, Binjamin tells him to go right there in the straw bed. The next day the guards kill the boy, and Binjamin feels responsible. The suffering continues when there are no guards present; Binjamin sees a pair of babies so hungry they nibble their frostbitten fingers down to the bone.

One morning after the roll call, Binjamin is loaded onto a transport. "I'm not even sure whether it was a truck or a railcar," he says. "All I remember is the end of the journey." Pressed among a sea of legs and stomachs, he panics. He is on a forced march. The air is smoky, and he steps on naked corpses.

Binjamin then finds himself in a different concentration camp. Women hide him behind a plank, cover him with their skirts, and let him conceal himself in a huge pile of clothes; they bring him food each day until a pair of babies hidden elsewhere in the rag pile are found and killed. Binjamin returns to the barracks; the population of children dwindles.

At last, he sees groups of inmates leaving the boundaries of the camp. One of them recognizes Binjamin and calls out to him. She brings him to Sandomierz, a city about one hundred miles to the northeast, then back to Krakow, to a Jewish orphanage. He stays in Krakow, sometimes begging in the streets. Shortly after a pogrom hits the city, a woman named Frau Grosz appears and invites him to come with her to Basel. "Switzerland is a beautiful country," she says. Similar assurances had lured him to Majdanek, but he sees no other choice but to follow her.

By the time Binjamin arrives in Switzerland, Frau Grosz has disappeared. He is given a new identity and ends up in a Swiss orphanage. He has escaped the physical boundaries of the camps, but the survivalist mind-set of wartime has become ingrained. He is caught hoarding cheese rinds. When he refuses to take bread from one of the nurses there, he remembers that his "mother" in the camp gave him a piece of dry, stale bread. When his shoes disappear, he remembers Jankl and the rags. When two boys arrive speaking Yiddish, he fears that they know he helped kill the boy who relieved himself in bed.

With each misstep, Binjamin receives a gentle rebuke, but he still expects a fatal punishment. Likewise, after Binjamin moves in with a foster family, their apple cellar and coal furnace look too much like the barracks and ovens he saw in the death camps. When shown a picture in school of William Tell, he sees an SS officer targeting a child. Forced to board a ski lift, he fears it is a Nazi killing machine. His foster parents tell him to forget the bad dream that was his past, but he cannot. When his first child is born, he sees its hairy head emerging and thinks of a corpse he saw in Auschwitz, a woman with a rat circling around in her womb. "Nobody ever told me that the camp was over, finally, definitely over," he says.

THE FEW pages of *Fragments* set in Riga contained no names or any other clues that would establish my blood relationship to Binjamin Wilkomirski. Nor did anything that followed. I had no idea whether he came from a working-class family like ours or a well-off one, whether he received a religious education, like my Riga ancestors, or a secular one. On the other hand, I noticed nothing that would make his kinship impossible. Just as I could envision Binjamin having four brothers or five and being transported from Majdanek either by truck or by train, his indeterminate origins enabled me to see him as a relative or not, whichever seemed righter.

As much as I kept reminding myself that I had no way of knowing that Binjamin's story had anything to do with mine, I could not help but identify strongly with him. For one thing, I could not help but see him as a hero. The boy described in *Fragments* is the antithesis of a hero in the classic sense. He is never the agent of change in the story; he is naïve, passive, and helpless during the war and much the same in Switzerland afterward. He is ashamed of the few instances when he does remember taking action, and in his descriptions of them he splits in two—into the person who acted and the person who felt it was wrong to act. When Frau Grosz asks him if he wants to go to Switzerland, he tries to scream that he doesn't, but to no avail: "I heard the unmistakable sound of my own voice, as if it was someone else's, loud and clear: 'Yes, I'm coming too.'" The same thing happens when he condemns the boy to death by telling him to relieve himself in bed: "With horror I realized that I'd said right out loud, really loud, what I was only thinking."

Binjamin Wilkomirski's heroism reveals itself not in his wartime tribulations or his postwar adjustment but only much later in his life, in the framing story of his adult rediscovery and retelling of his past. For years, he could not come to terms with his memories or convince anyone of their significance, but in the end he reassembles them to the extent that he can and he publishes the story. By testifying to what he experienced and witnessed, he triumphs over his silent suffering.

But the main reason I identified with Binjamin had nothing to do with his latter-day heroics. It had to do with his coming from the place where my ancestors lived and his persecution due to his Jewish background. If he really was our cousin, I would have a personal connection to my family's European past. Brought closer to the Holocaust, I would think less about statistics or Anne Frank's diary. I would approach it through the story of the likely murder of my missing uncle and the improbable survival of my cousin now living in Switzerland.

EXCITING AS the possibilities were, I wasn't ready to call anyone Cousin Binjamin, as my mother had done. Before he arrived, I wanted to learn more about him. I searched through online newspaper databases to see what else had been written about Binjamin Wilkomirski. Mostly I found reviews, all full of praise. In the *Washington Times,* Arnost Lustig, himself a survivor and author, wrote, "It makes you feel, perceive and understand and, in so doing, makes you spiritually richer. The book is destined to become one of the five or 10 lasting books about the Holocaust." Lustig was hardly alone in elevating *Fragments* to the top shelf of Holocaust literature. One British critic placed *Fragments* above the memoirs of Bruno Bettelheim and Primo Levi in terms of its emotional power; several reviewers mentioned it in the same breath as Elie Wiesel's *Night.* The respect readers had for *Fragments* bordered on the kind of awe one exhibits before the sacred. Jonathan Kozol, known for his compassionate writing about underprivileged children, wrote in *The Nation* that *Fragments* was "so profoundly moving, so morally important and so free from literary artifice of any kind at all that I wondered if I even had the right to try to offer praise." Schocken put Kozol's quote on the back cover of the paperback edition.

This hesitant reverence, which I feel a bit of myself, is also apparent in the few profiles of Binjamin Wilkomirski I found. "What will the voice of a man who has endured so much sound like?" a reporter for the *Los Angeles Times* worries as Binjamin comes to the phone. She is relieved to discover that "it is soft and kind, vulnerable and urgent."

The profiles cover much of the same ground as *Fragments,* although Binjamin explains a bit more about how his story came together into a book. In a Jewish weekly newspaper, he talks about making drawings from memory and showing them to Holocaust historians, who told Binjamin he had drawn a barrack at Majdanek and a fixture at Auschwitz. He tells a reporter for the *South China Morning Post* about his daily practice of "concentration training," which involves focusing on a single memory in the hope that a fuller version of that memory will come to him later. The *Los Angeles Times* writer asks him whether his memoir is the outgrowth of recovered-memory techniques, and he insists it is not. "I never lost my memory or had to work to get it back," he said.

Binjamin told the *South China Morning Post* about the couple he found in Riga. "He believes that they were his grandparents," the newspaper reported months before my mother first wrote to him. Binjamin explained that they were metalworkers, and that he felt close to them when he was shaping clarinets.

BEFORE MEETING Binjamin, I also wanted to learn more about my own family, so I tagged along with my mother on a fact-finding visit to Aunt Miriam's apartment on Ocean Parkway in Brooklyn. Miriam I knew mainly from my mother's stories, and we'd met only when I was too small to remember her. I wouldn't have recognized Miriam if I'd passed her on the street. She is scarcely five feet tall and, in her late eighties, moves much slower than she no doubt once did. She has a round, attentive face, and she covers her head with a cloth turban. My mother is as fond of Miriam as she is baffled by her strict religious lifestyle.

Miriam brings out a plate of fruit and an unfrosted white cake she baked for the occasion. She asks after my grandfather, my father, my sister, my first cousins. There seems to be an order to this litany, which makes sense for a woman who has several dozen great-grandchildren. She speaks with the throaty *r*s, the clipped vowels, and the occasionally alien grammar that she brought over from Riga as a teenage girl. Her end of the conversation arrives in short, matter-of-fact bursts.

After a few minutes, Miriam's son drops off her two brothers, Hyman and Louis. They all know my mother. Miriam's son used to run a summer camp, and my mother worked for him when she was in college. Every once in a while, my mother gets invited to an Orthodox wedding, and they usually notify her when one of the observant Wilburs dies. None of them know me. In my generation, there is hardly any interaction between the observant and assimilated sides of the family.

Miriam's brothers both wear heavy horn-rimmed glasses. They are a few years younger than she and speak with less of an accent, but their minds are no longer as sharp as hers, if they ever were. They are here to help out, but mostly just to visit with us. Miriam will be our main informant.

"When did the name become Wilkomirski?" my mother asks.

"It was the great-grandfather," Miriam says. I'm not sure whose great-grandfather she means, and she doesn't clarify.

"So you all lived at Moskva Street?" my mother asks Miriam and her brothers.

"Eighty Moskva Street," Miriam says. "A big apartment house. Six floors. We lived on the first floor. On the back was the river."

"Give them the name of the river," one brother says.

"The Dvina," Miriam calls it; in Latvian it is known as the Daugava. Her memory of the city where she spent her youth is precise, but if she feels nostalgia for Riga she keeps it to herself. Where someone else might set the scene—my brothers shared a bed by the window, the curtains were lacy, the neighbors made too much noise,

I would watch the boats float along the Dvina—Miriam keeps to the basics.

"Did Avram ever come here?" Mom asks.

"He didn't, because my grandma, they never let her in America." According to Miriam, her uncle Avram married around the time of his mother's death, in 1927. "Avram married very late," Miriam adds.

My mother pulls out a pile of photographs she inherited from her grandmother and other Wilburs. Soon they come to a picture of five adults in the courtyard of a building, posed around an outdoor worktable covered with animal pelts. The man on the right is wearing a bloody smock and holding a bundled fur.

AVRAM WILKOMIRSKI (RIGHT) AND CO-WORKERS, RIGA.

"I think this is Avram," Miriam says, pointing to the man on the right.

"And he had a son?" my mother asks.

"I'll show the picture," Miriam says.

Next to Avram's portrait is a picture postcard showing a little boy of two or three. He is wearing a dark shirt, darker knickers, white kneesocks, and sandals. His brown hair droops almost to his

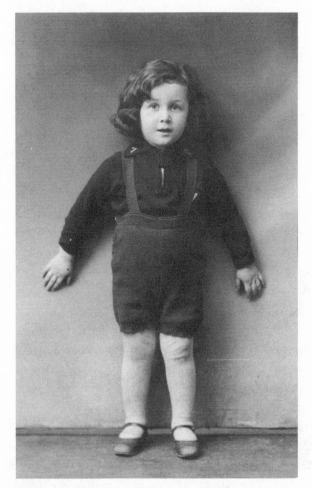

SIMA WILKOMIRSKI, RIGA, 1933.

shoulders before curling around at the ends. Arms at his sides, he presses his tiny hands against the wall behind him. He stares up at the camera, openmouthed.

"That's the boy," says Miriam. The picture, embossed with the name and address of a photographer's studio in Riga and dated 1933, was a gift to my great-grandmother Anna and her family. "*Zum Andenken. Fon Sima Volkomirsky. Riga, 18/VI/33*," it says. A memento from Sima Wilkomirski, Avram's son.

Sima's picture is passed around the room. "Is this the man who wrote the book?" one of Miriam's brothers asks as he looks at it. My mother explains that it can't be; Binjamin would be a decade younger than Sima.

"I have a picture when he was smaller," Miriam says as she sends her son to retrieve her photo album. "I may also have a picture when he was bigger."

The oxblood leather album has a silver plaque with an engraved message in Hebrew lettering. It was a gift from her classmates at the yeshiva in Riga. The crumbling cardboard pages have come loose from the binding and the glue holding the pictures on the black pages is losing its adhesion, but Miriam's connection to the people in the pictures remains strong. The album has some of the same photographs as in my mother's pile and many unfamiliar ones, too, like the series from a holiday outing Miriam took with a Jewish youth group from Riga. The pictures may stir Miriam's memories of the day, but for us she simply points out her friends, sometimes adding, "She was taken by Hitler." As were most of the girls who gave Miriam the photo album: fewer than one out of ten Latvian Jews survived the war.

Turning back to family matters, my mother asks about the Wilkomirski sister who died in Riga.

Her name was Hinda, Miriam says. "I was about eight years old, maybe a little less. My parents cried and cried. I said, 'What is it?' They told me she died. All of this was right after the war." She means World War I, the one she lived through. "She had the sugar, I guess—diabetes—because they had to remove her leg."

"Do you remember her husband's name?" Mom asks.

"I don't know the first name. He remained with the four children," Miriam says. "One of the boys was in my class. And the oldest girl, she always used to come to us. And the other, Sora was her name. And the boys, one of them was Moishe. And they had another boy, I think Shmuel?" She asks her brothers, but they do not remember. In any case, their last name would not have been Wilkomirski.

"Did they ever come here?" my mother asks.

"No, no. Hitler took them," Miriam says. She points to the fruit and cake on the table. "Take something," she tells my mother, then gets up to go into the kitchen. "I have tuna casserole. You want tuna casserole?" We do not, but Miriam goes to fetch it.

Whether Binjamin is a cousin or a total stranger, I realize I don't have to look so hard for a familial connection to the Holocaust. Miriam might not want to talk about it, and her brothers might not remember much about the people they left behind, but the connection is there.

SINCE I WANTED to write about Binjamin, I asked Schocken to send me a current photograph of him. The only photograph in *Fragments* shows Binjamin Wilkomirski as a ten-year-old. His straight hair is precisely parted, and he wears a neat sweater vest over his white collared shirt. The picture is tightly cropped, but from the looks of the suit jacket to one side and the row of buttons to the other, he seems to be surrounded by two adults. There is a disembodied hand resting awkwardly on his left shoulder, and the unsmiling boy looks uncomfortable.

From the current picture, he seems to have aged better than I

PUBLICITY PHOTO OF BINJAMIN WILKOMIRSKI, 1996.

expected for someone with his troubled history. He is illuminated from above, and the light shines most intensely on his high forehead and broad nose. Other parts of his face—his deep-set eyes hidden behind a pair of large, rounded glasses, his furrowed brow, and the drooping corners of his mouth—lie in shadow. He has a loose, curly head of hair and modest sideburns. He grips his chin and looks down and to the side. His eyes avoid the lens, and he seems to be staring into oblivion.

I bring the picture to my mother's house to show it to her. She takes a long look. "A typical Wilbur face," she says.

CERTAINTY

At the end of his memoir, the author of *Fragments* explains why he began looking for meaning in traumatic, contextless images from his childhood, why he tried to reconcile these troubling memories with the historical record. "I wanted my own certainty back," he says.

After all Binjamin has lost, it seems like a modest request, but it is not entirely clear what he is asking for, since certainty can be one of two things. A certainty is an established and irrefutable truth, but the word also describes a state of mind: that of feeling sure whatever the facts may be. One is an assertion of factuality, the other an expression of belief.

The author of *Fragments* yearns for certainty on both counts. He can't document who he is or where he comes from, and he's been encouraged to dismiss his memories of childhood trauma as bad dreams. The former sort of certainty looks impossible for him to attain, but a sense of sureness may be in reach. Emotional certainty is unstable, however, and ultimately dependent on the factual kind when it pertains to something as concrete as an identity.

It's hard for someone who has not lived with such profound uncertainty as the author of *Fragments* to comprehend his predicament. But uncertainty spreads once it is in the air, and when I thought about my own roots, I realized I was also relying more on sureness than on proof. For Miriam, who grew up in Riga, this isn't the case, but for my mother and her cousins, for all of us who never saw the family in its previous habitat, the history of the Wilkomirskis is oral and imprecise. It is told in multiple ways. We assume that at least the core of it is true and demonstrable, but have never documented it. We think we know who we are, but we can't be certain.

THE LINCHPIN of the family reunion is almost a half hour late, and the twenty Wilburs in my parents' living room are getting impatient. Everyone seems less worried that Binjamin won't show up than that they'll have to keep making conversation with the unfamiliar relatives waiting with them. We aren't quite the random sampling a statistician might choose, but nonetheless we suggest the diversity of the Wilbur clan, which, because of the fruitfulness of the assimilated as well as the observant, number in the hundreds. Missing are the cousins who wear black fedoras over their black yarmulkes and the relatives who have embraced hip-hop and Buddhism. Yet one finds in this living room representatives of the Old World and the New, the insular and the intermixed, and, running beneath these differences, a curiosity about one's opposites and perhaps even a muted resentment at sharing the same label—the family name, though it might also be our status as Jewish Americans—with others who seem so different. I chat with a woman I've never met before, a shy third cousin from Brooklyn who is a few years younger than me. She wears a long-sleeved blouse with ruffled cuffs and a skirt that goes down to her ankles. She will marry soon, a doctor. Despite the proximity in age, we find little to keep the conversation going. All we have in common, it seems, is our curiosity about Binjamin. When the doorbell rings, the room falls silent, and the air of anticipation mixes with a palpable sense of relief.

THE MONOCHROME publicity portrait of Binjamin Wilkomirski has inadequately prepared us for our colorful guest. The author of *Fragments* wears a mustard-colored dress shirt and dark pants. Around his neck he has knotted a fringed silk scarf, and two golden medallions hang in full view. One takes the form of the Hebrew letters *chet-yod*, which spell *chai*, or life; the other is a box containing the *tefilat ha-derekh*, a Jewish prayer for travelers. His light brown hair is loosely curled, expansive, and unruly. So are his bold sideburns, which, though not as full as muttonchops, almost meet at the chin. Extralong whiskers wouldn't have shocked me on a student experimenting with his newfound hirsuteness, but I'd never seen anything like it on a man his age.

From head to toe, Binjamin looks like nobody I'd seen before. In my mind I cast him as the Cowardly Lion in a klezmer reworking of *The Wiz*. It's not just the golden color scheme but the way he holds himself. He has the feral eyes of an animal confronting an unfamiliar domesticity, but his broad, strained smile conveys some eagerness to balance his uneasiness. He is rail thin and looks worried he might collapse, if not physically then emotionally. His gait is weak and wary.

Binjamin told us he would be bringing his wife, and he is followed into the room by a tall, solid woman in a businesslike suit with dark, curly hair and round glasses. Verena Piller looks as sturdy as he seems shaky. Accompanying the couple are two chaperones from the United States Holocaust Memorial Museum.

After kissing my mother at the door, Binjamin makes his way around the living room to embrace the rest of the familial delegation. Introductions are as necessary for the Wilburs as they are for our guests. When Binjamin reaches me, I can't help but notice he reeks of stale cigarettes.

My mother has saved him a seat near Miriam and her brothers so they can discuss Riga. Before he can get there, however, two unfamiliar cousins home in on the celebrated writer. One of them is carrying a copy of *Fragments* in a plastic bag, a Ziploc. He takes out a pen, breaks the seal of the bag, and asks Binjamin to sign the book. Binjamin accepts the pen and turns to the title page. He listens to the spelling of my cousin's name and signs his autograph. My cousin takes his copy of *Fragments* back from Binjamin, slips it in the Ziploc bag, and presses the air out, sealing the relic inside.

My mother finally manages to seat Binjamin next to Miriam, who is wearing a smart purple suit with a white and purple turban. Verena stays by Binjamin's side. I sit nearby with a tape recorder and microphone. Miriam extracts her photo album from a noisy plastic bag and opens it on a folding table. My mother's pictures are also there.

Mom steers Binjamin to the picture of Avram's son Sima at two or three, and he examines the back of it first. "Interesting, the writing is 'Volkomirsky.' It's important to know, when we check old archives, we must check WI- and VO-."

"Different people spell it differently," Miriam says. "But it's Wilkomirski."

Binjamin studies the face carefully. "Do you know when he was born?" he asks.

"I know it was in the thirties," Miriam says.

"Because my oldest brother, I remember, he must have been about twelve in Majdanek." In *Fragments,* he calls the oldest of his four or five brothers Motti, short for Mordechai. "He was probably five, six years older than I was."

"Well, in '29, they didn't have any children," Miriam says.

Binjamin asks Miriam about Avram's other children.

THE AUTHOR OF *Fragments,* HYMAN WILBUR, AND
MIRIAM VIM, NEW YORK, 1997.

She doesn't know that he had any, she says. "My father, he was the writer."

"We know that they lived at Moskva, 80, in 1927," Binjamin says to Miriam, who also lived at Moskva, 80, in 1927. "But people in Riga said they moved outside, and outside the town there were no registers in the countryside in the 1940s." Without documentation, Avram and his family could be dead or alive, and Binjamin, who thinks he may be one of them, is hopeful.

"But from people, what I hear, the Nazis destroyed the Jews when they came in," Miriam says. The doorbell rings, and another Wilbur arrives. "I'll have a cold drink, a seltzer," Miriam says.

Next Binjamin asks us about other Wilkomirski names he's come across. "In Majdanek, when I was in the *Kinderquarantäne,* there was in Sector Five, Barrack Nine, in the beginning of May a Helenka Wilkomirska." Helenka is presumably a product of his research, rather than a name he remembers. He repeats her name. "Helenka. Like Rucha, but the Polish made Helenka out of it."

None of the Wilburs quite follow what Binjamin is saying. Rucha Wilkomirski—at least the one who lived at Moskva, 80, in 1927—is Miriam's mother. She immigrated to America in 1929 and died here. Rucha could not have been in Sector Five, Barrack Nine, of Majdanek. The thread is dropped, and Binjamin mentions another Wilkomirski, named Sonia.

"Was she from Riga?" Miriam asks.

"Sonia was in the ghetto in Vilna. And I know that in Vilna other Wilkomirskis, about four people, were killed."

"From our family we didn't have anybody there," Miriam declares. Back in Brooklyn, Miriam had mentioned that we had a Wilkomirski cousin in Riga named Sora. Talk of Sonia Wilkomirski has prompted two of my cousins to try to blend them into one person—"Sora, Sonia. Sonia, Sora. Maybe like a nickname?"—but the mixture won't take. We have a few pieces of a jigsaw puzzle, and Binjamin is holding other pieces, but we can't manage to attach the Wilburs' thick forest to Binjamin's cloudy sky. If only we had the whole picture, we could see how it all fit together, or we would at least know we were working with two different puzzles.

"This," Miriam says, pointing to her album, "this I could tell you who it is. This is my grandmother, Liba Raiza."

Miriam moves steadily through her pictures. "This is my younger brother Louis, by Haim's bar mitzvah, and that's me." Binjamin notices something familiar in the bar mitzvah boy's face, and he mutters something in German to Verena about it. They become animated until they figure out that the man in the photograph is Miriam's brother, who waves at them from his seat nearby.

"This is already after the first war. Latvia they were nice, the city paid for, they let open a Jews' school. But it was a coed. And that's me when I started in that school. This is my brother, they tutored him. That's a friend.

"That's a picture from Riga to send to my father. That's my husband, that's my sister-in-law, my mother-in-law. That's the picture we took.

"This, when I was here, my friend sent me. That's my friend's baby. Hitler took them.

"This is my brother, he sent us pictures from Israel. He was wounded from the Arabs in '29, so he sent us a picture." It is an oval portrait of a man looking over his shoulder. A long scar can be seen on his bare back.

Binjamin, who had been drifting off a bit, perks up. "Who is the Wilkomirski from Israel?" he asks.

"My brother lived there for five years," Miriam explains. The brother she is referring to is not one of the two men in the room, but a third brother, now dead, who left for America not long after he was stabbed.

"In '79 in Israel died a man with the name Mordechai Wilkomirski, the same name I remember as my older brother," says Binjamin. He tells us how this Mordechai escaped from the Baltic to Palestine. Miriam doesn't remember a Mordechai Wilkomirski in our family.

By now Binjamin seems to have exhausted what he knows about the Wilkomirskis. Still, he trots out a couple more stray clues. "We hear that still now, there is a woman in Riga with another name who was born Wilkomirski," he says. "She must be rather old today, late seventies or eighty. You can't imagine who that could be?"

"Not what I know," Miriam says. "It's alright."

Miriam seems to be reassuring Binjamin not so much that he'll find something one of these days, as that it's alright if he doesn't. She pages through her photo album, and Binjamin scans face after face after face. He seems tired and restless, his attention comes and goes. He is like an actor playing a crime victim on a cop show, looking through a mug book of thieves without expecting to find his man. He does not seem hopeful or despairing, but resigned, as if he has done this before and is used to not finding any familiar faces.

"Alright," Miriam says. "Here's the picture I want to show you, what we think is of Avram. This is the uncle."

Binjamin looks momentarily at Avram, but another photograph lying on the table captures his attention instead. "Who's this?" he asks breathlessly. "His face, that strikes me. The shape is like my first son."

My mother says she's not sure, but she promises to make Binjamin a copy.

BINJAMIN WANTS to take a break; he needs a cigarette. Miriam and her brothers are also worn out. They wish Binjamin luck and head back to Brooklyn.

There is no smoking in my parents' home, so I volunteer to show Binjamin up to the roof and keep him company. Although I don't smoke, I could use a break, and I'd also like a chance to be alone with Binjamin for a few minutes. On the roof I can introduce myself in a more relaxed setting without a tape recorder and try to gain his trust.

Binjamin has a hard time lighting up in the wind. I point out the spire of the Empire State Building to the northwest and the river to the east. When I run out of landmarks, I point out the playground ten stories below where I played as a toddler. As soon as the words come out of my mouth, I fear that I have made a mistake. I didn't mean to flaunt the stability of my childhood before someone who did not have the luxury of thinking about anything other than survival. But he just listens politely and sucks on his cigarette.

I explain to Binjamin that I have been taping his visit because I would like to write a story about his encounter with the Wilburs, something for the radio, if it's okay with him. If it's not, then the tapes will stay within the family. Keep taping, he says, and he'll let me know how he feels.

Gingerly, I ask Binjamin about what's been on my mind all along: DNA testing. I don't know much about how DNA tests work, but the idea appeals to me because it seems like the easiest and perhaps the only way to establish our kinship with any degree of certainty.

Binjamin takes a drag of his cigarette and tells me he's taken a DNA test before, with the man he calls Father Yakov. Father Yakov is not mentioned in *Fragments,* nor did the name come up in any of the articles I'd read. Binjamin is offering me a fresh angle, exactly what I was looking for when I offered to take Binjamin for a smoke, and I listen carefully.

IT TURNS OUT that the story of Binjamin and Father Yakov had already been told on Israeli television, since it was through the Israeli news program *Second Look* that Father Yakov found the man who he believed was his son.

In 1994 *Second Look* broadcast an hour-long documentary titled *Wanda's Lists.* The film, with a title riffing on Steven Spielberg's 1993 film *Schindler's List,* was a collaboration between producer Vered Berman and Lea Balint, the widow of a Jerusalem attorney who specialized in Holocaust reparations claims. As a child during the war, Balint was hidden in a Polish convent, and decades later she began researching "children without identity," by which she meant Jewish children who, for whatever reason, were separated from their families during the Holocaust and no longer knew their real names or hometowns. Balint created a computer database of some 2,400 Jewish children orphaned during World War II.

Balint, who took an extension course in filmmaking with Berman, introduced the veteran producer to several children without identity (who were then in their fifties and sixties) and to Wanda Sokolowska. As a young woman in wartime Poland, Wanda helped the underground funnel Jewish children out of the Warsaw ghetto and into non-Jewish homes or institutions under false identities. Wanda kept a list of the children she helped and the families who hid them. Using this list and several others not belonging to Wanda, Berman and Balint tried to identify children without identity.

Like the author of *Fragments,* these children without identity have been tormented by their mysterious origins. "People tell me to let the past be and concentrate on the future," a woman called Erela says in the film. "I can't move forward without those four lost years of the past. I can't say I haven't lived; I did marry and raise a fine family. But there are always those questions in the background: Who am I? Why don't I have a name? Why don't I know where I came from?" By the end of the hour, Balint and Berman take Erela to Zakopane, Poland, for a reunion with the family who sheltered her during the war. The family gives Erela her mother's identity card, which will lead to the discovery of her real name.

Berman and Balint reclaim other identities and engineer other reunions in the course of *Wanda's Lists.* Not appearing on any of Wanda's lists but included in the film nonetheless is a man from Switzerland identified as Bruno Wilkomirski. "Before, I was called Binjamin, and others called me Bronek," he explains. Balint met Bruno at a 1993 reunion of child survivors who knew each other from a Polish orphanage after the war. The reunion wasn't much help to him since Bruno had been in Krakow and the other survivors were all from Lodz, but he was a child without identity and Balint began helping him.

In *Wanda's Lists,* Bruno can be seen poring over microfilm records and photographs with the help of an old friend. "Six, seven years ago, he told me that he dreams that he's in a room and hears noises, children's cries, and gunfire," the friend, psychologist Elitsur Bernstein, says. "He asked me what I would say about it as a psychologist. I told him that I'm with him, I'm not a psychologist. Then we began talking. Many things that I had known earlier, all kinds of fine details and hints, began to coalesce into a clearer picture."

When Balint and Berman went to Poland with Erela, Bruno tagged along, paying his own way. In one scene, he visits the Institute of Jewish History in Warsaw to look through old photographs from the orphanages. Balint asks him whether he found anyone, and he says no. He also meets an old teacher from the children's home. They do not remember each other, but Bruno says he remembers the building, which has been torn down. He takes the camera crew to the spot on Augustianska Street where it once stood. "On this side where the trees are," he says, "was a sort of playground for children." (Berman thought Bruno might be playing up his emotions for the camera, but she decided to include the footage anyway.) Back in Israel, Bruno finds Julius Loewinger, a documented Krakow orphan, who remembers the playground Bruno describes.

Wanda's Lists also includes some home movies shot by Bruno. There is a clip of him visiting the spot in Riga where his perhaps-father died and also a scene at Majdanek. As he points to the barrack where he was held, he says, "Maybe it's strange to say so, but for me it's like coming home."

At the end of *Wanda's Lists*, Berman and Balint asked anyone with information about Bruno Wilkomirski or other children without identity on the show to call their telephone hotline. "The whole story about Riga sounded a little fishy," Berman recalled. "But I said, 'What the hell, maybe somebody would know about it.'"

WHEN *Wanda's Lists* aired, the past was weighing heavily on Yakov Maroko, an elderly Orthodox man living in the religious neighborhood of Bnei Brak. At the beginning of World War II, Maroko lived in Warsaw with his wife and their son, an infant named Michael Benjamin. The Marokos were confined in the Warsaw ghetto, and had several brushes with danger. At one point a German soldier descended upon them and asked if they had any valuables. Yakov said no, but the soldier found a watch in Yakov's pocket. As Maroko tells the story in his self-published autobiography, *Shaagat Meuneh* (*The Tortured Cry*), he and his wife were ordered to lean against the wall with their hands in the air, and Michael Benjamin was thrown to the ground like a ball. Yakov cried out in pain, and a miraculous change came over the soldier, who said he didn't want to hurt anybody and wished someone would just kill Hitler. Take your child and run away, the soldier said.

The Marokos did not run, and in 1943 they were shipped to Majdanek. The first night, they slept on the ground together. Yakov gave his coat to his wife and Michael Benjamin. In the morning the Nazis announced that coffee was available a short walk away. It made no sense for all three to go, so Yakov volunteered to get it.

Instead of hot coffee, Yakov Maroko received a whipping at the hands of the SS and an order to march around naked in the cold rain. Yakov never saw his wife or Michael Benjamin again. "This part is the hardest in my life. It is hidden in my heart. The reader will forgive me for not sharing my pain," he wrote in his memoir.

After the war, Yakov went looking for his family. In Lodz he finds a cousin and they go into business together selling the belongings of dead Jews. Yakov becomes rich and remarries, but he is often in despair, asking himself, "If my wife and child wouldn't come back to me after those terrible days, why should I live at all?" He leaves for Sweden, where his brother has taken refuge, but when the state of Israel comes into existence he decides to emigrate and live among Jews. He and his second wife have three children, and as he looks at the playgrounds of Jerusalem, he wishes he could see Michael Benjamin playing with them. When his second wife dies, he marries again and embraces his new wife's children as well as his own. But even a large family is no replacement for Michael Benjamin.

A pious man, Maroko avoided television, so he did not see *Wanda's Lists*. His first wife's sister did, however, and when he calls her out of the blue shortly after the broadcast she assumes it has to do with the boy who had been in Majdanek and was once called Binjamin. The sister-in-law detected a certain resemblance between this Bruno Wilkomirski and Maroko's first wife. It has been fifty-two years since Maroko has seen his Michael Benjamin, so he is skeptical, but he also wonders what inspired him to call his sister-in-law that day.

A wary Yakov Maroko goes to meet Elitsur Bernstein, Bruno's psychologist friend, in his Tel Aviv office. As they watch a videotape of Bruno, it all starts to come back to Maroko: the joy he once felt kissing his little Michael Benjamin, the coffee trick at Majdanek, the pain he felt when they did not return to Warsaw. Then Maroko describes the incident in the ghetto when the soldier had him put his hands up against the wall, and Bernstein's wife says it is just like Bruno's first memory: looking up at his father, against a wall with hands held high. Maroko has a feeling that Bruno Wilkomirski is his son and he wants to talk to him. Never mind that the two scenes unfolded hundreds of miles away, one in Riga and the other in Warsaw; never mind that in *Wanda's Lists* Bruno talks about being the youngest of five or six brothers while Michael Benjamin was an only child. Bernstein puts them in touch, and Maroko calls Bruno in Switzerland. Bruno is overcome by emotion and can hardly speak. Maroko invites him to visit at Passover.

A few hours later, Maroko receives a fax signed "Binjamin" on the archive/clarinet shop letterhead. "I do not yet know exactly what to say—my feelings are so indescribable!" he wrote. "For more than 50 years I have lived without parents, and now—could it be that I have found you, my father? Has He made a miracle?" In his letter, he wrote that scientific tests were "not so important"; what mattered was the many connections between them. "You were also in Majdanek. I have lists of over a thousand Jewish children from Poland who were hidden or survived the camps, and the name Benjamin does not come up once. It appears that, at that time in Poland, it was then a very rare name. It is therefore highly improbable that in 1943 there were two different Benjamins. Some of the things you told Elitsur [Bernstein] correspond to my own memories."

The language in Maroko's reply is like a love letter. When their eyes meet, he says, "I will be yours, and you mine, so dear angel. Then I will open my . . . heart to you for ever." He quotes a verse of Psalm 126: "They that sow in tears shall reap in joy." He asks Bruno to "please inform me if you remember anything about your mother. When do you see her the last time, and what happened then."

VERED BERMAN and Lea Balint quarreled over *Wanda's Lists,* and when Berman began working on a follow-up program, she went ahead alone. With Elitsur Bernstein's help, the filmmaker collected DNA samples from both men. She watched as Maroko gave blood. "The only sure response is a negative one," the phlebotomist explains to Maroko as Berman and her crew look on. "If it's no, then it's one hundred percent no."

Four weeks later, the cameras return as a doctor tells Maroko, "He can't be your son. It's absolutely impossible, because there's a certain incompatibility that makes it biologically impossible." Berman asks Maroko for his reaction. "I just want to send regards to Bruno," he says, fighting off tears.

The Passover visit went ahead as scheduled. On April 18, 1995, Yakov Maroko, his family and friends, and a bevy of journalists went to Ben-Gurion Airport. "Bruno is my son," Maroko told Berman at the airport. "I appealed to rabbis, and they told me, one after another, as people who can be trusted, that this is my son." One of Germany's best-respected newspapers was also persuaded of their kinship. "Blood tests and DNA tests of both men yielded no decisive result, but no negative result, either," the *Süddeutsche Zeitung* reported. "After both Morocco [sic] and Wilkomirski had been independently interviewed by rabbis, their relationship was definitively established." Another German newspaper trumpeted the reunion of Maroko and his son "Dr. Bruno Wilkomarski [sic]."

Bruno Wilkomirski walks into the arrivals hall wearing an open-necked shirt, a yarmulke, and a scarf draped over his shoulders. He smiles and moves quickly toward Yakov, who was so nervous about seeing his son he took a sedative. The two men hold on to each other and weep. "This is your brother," Yakov says to one of his sons as he embraces Bruno. "Your brother!" In his memoir, Yakov writes that their meeting reminded him of the moment in Genesis when Joseph is reunited with his brothers and with his father, Jacob, who thought that his favorite son was dead.

The Maroko family set off to spend Passover at a vacation spot not far from Jerusalem. Bruno is full of questions about his childhood and about the unfamiliar religious rituals performed by the Maroko clan. Yakov interprets his curiosity as a good sign. "They have stolen his body, but not the Jewish spark," Maroko wrote. "They couldn't remove that."

After Yakov Maroko's death, his widow would tell a reporter that he understood that Bruno Wilkomirski was not his beloved Michael Benjamin, but his memoir gives the opposite impression. "It was enough to look at his face and see the color of his hair, which was identical to that of his late mother. And it was enough to compare his hands to mine to know that he is indeed my son."

For Bruno, however, the question never seemed relevant. "The

most important thing," he tells Vered Berman at the end of the follow-up to *Wanda's Lists,* "is that we met. We were in the same situation, at the same places. We found out now that we have so many
memories, the same memories of the time. It's a very strong feeling,
not only of solidarity, but really the feeling that we belong together.
The biological thing is in the background; the important feeling is the
human feeling you have."

IN HIS ROOFTOP retelling of the story of Father Yakov, Binjamin
provides me with few details. He leaves out Yakov's last name, his
own alternate first name, his psychologist friend Bernstein, and so
on. As he smokes his cigarette, I get a rough outline: Father Yakov
lost his son in the war just as Binjamin had lost his father; Father
Yakov found Binjamin on Israeli television; the DNA test was
negative, but it did not stop them from developing a father-son
relationship.

Anyway, Binjamin says his reluctance to take a DNA test has less
to do with Father Yakov than with his long-standing dislike of the
medical profession. He confesses he had been experimented upon
by Nazi doctors—it wasn't only twins who had been subjected to
that, he says—and the experiments made him very sick. When he left
Krakow he was supposed to go to Palestine. He wasn't well enough
to make the journey, so instead he was smuggled into Switzerland,
where he was cared for by a doctor and his wife. His foster father
viewed him mainly as a medical curiosity, and expected Binjamin to
grow up to be a doctor and care for other unfortunates as his foster
father had cared for him. But Binjamin rebelled, turning away from
medicine and entering into a time he calls his "terrorist period," when
he was so troubled he felt capable of anything. Instead of becoming
a doctor, he turned to the study of music and history.

BACK IN THE apartment, Binjamin tells me he discovered he had
leukemia when he was about forty. "Of those young child survivors
I met until now, everyone has undergone some medical experiments.
And many of them had later similar diseases in a much higher per-

centage than the rest of the population. I was for ten years very ill, it was due to Verena that I survived that. And since then I have heard that other child survivors had the very same experiences."

I ask Binjamin about his sense of Jewish identity. It comes up in the wartime episodes in *Fragments* only in a few metaphors. His brothers are candles in a row, suggesting a menorah; he thinks of King David as he rides the shoulders of the Nazi officer who later smashes his head into a wall. He doesn't know how observant his family in Riga was, so I ask about his foster family. He told me they weren't Jewish, which surprised me, since I thought that after the war Jewish orphans as a rule ended up with Jewish guardians.

"There were about 153 or something like that who did not have a chance to end up in a Jewish family," he says. And in Switzerland it was more difficult than elsewhere. "After the war, they still had laws blocking Jewish orphan children from entering the country until 1950. So until then you had to smuggle them in."

"So then you had to pretend you weren't Jewish."

"No, we learned that already in Krakow before, when we had to change names, that we never tell the original name and never tell the country we come from, and then they could never send us back."

I ask him whether he's begun to practice Judaism since figuring out who he was.

"Yes, I feel religious, but I'm not Orthodox. But since I'm with Verena together for fifteen years I didn't miss one shabbas. We have our traveling set, we never miss the kiddush"—the prayer over the wine. "And I feel, among religious people and also among Hasidic people, I feel very good. I feel I have some connection with this world."

"So Verena is Jewish too?"

"She has Jewish ancestors, but she was not raised that way. But she got involved, and with me she learned the prayers. She cooks challah, and she makes gefilte fish, wonderful gefilte fish. And we have many friends from the liberal side, and in the Orthodox group too. For me, I have no difficulty to switch from one group to the other. For me, all are Jews, and I am thankful for every Jew who says 'I am a Jew' and doesn't hide it."

I ask Binjamin what he makes of us, considering that we have too little information to establish definitively whether we are related.

"But all the Wilkomirskis are somehow connected," he says. "Maybe you have to go very far back, but there is a feeling. I just heard from somebody the Wilkomirskis had also some cousins in Lithuania, but they didn't know them. And I met a woman who looks like a Wilkomirski, but from a Lithuanian-Warsaw branch. It's the same genes exactly." He then talks about a musician named Wanda Wilkomirska who lived in Poland during the war. "They came originally from Wilkomir in Lithuania. One part went north to Latvia and other parts stayed or went south to Poland." He does not allow for the possibility that two unrelated families adopted the name independently. It is as if the Wilkomirskis are a dispersed clan, a lost tribe of Israel.

"So you're pretty sure that there's a connection."

"I'm absolutely sure," he says. "It's not so important to know which generation back you are related. The human feeling is at the end the only important thing in life."

With that, Binjamin gets up to say goodbye until tomorrow. Before he leaves, I hand him an article I published in anticipation of his visit, describing his uncertain past and the Wilburs' excitement at discovering him.

By this time most of the Wilburs have gone home. The few of us remaining try to digest the long afternoon. We still don't know who Binjamin is, or what exactly he has to do with us. His research is confusing, his methods perplexing. His identity hinges on one moment at Auschwitz fifty years ago, when a woman recognized him as Binjamin Wilkomirski. Even if his memory is good, what if she was mistaken? If we didn't know about his book, one cousin says, we might not have believed him at all.

Whatever the truth may be, Binjamin's history does not contain enough facts to link it to our story. That connection can be built only with emotion, with a leap of faith. Aunt Miriam doesn't voice an opinion, but she seems unmoved, and doesn't seem to accept him as a long-lost relative. My mother, on the other hand, had already made the leap before he arrived, perhaps in hopes of completing her grandmother's search. After today's meeting, she revises her earlier hypothesis that Cousin Binjamin is Avram's grandson. She proposes alternate theories explaining why the old woman at Auschwitz would have called him the little Wilkomirski boy. He could be a cousin from Avram's sister's family or his wife's family. He could be a neighbor's boy. He could have been living with Avram for any number of reasons; it was wartime. Under some scenarios, a negative DNA test wouldn't rule out a connection between Binjamin and the Wilburs.

I come down much closer to Miriam's position. I don't want to trample anyone's feelings—my mother's, my cousins', or Binjamin's—but I wish I knew more of the facts.

In the middle of our conversation, the phone rings. My mother answers. Verena is calling from the hotel, looking for me. I come to the phone, and Verena puts Binjamin on. He tells me he read my article as soon as he got back to the hotel. He knows he will see me tomorrow, but he wants to call me now to tell me how touched he was. Other reporters had misunderstood him, but I had captured him perfectly. I ask him if I can keep recording for my radio story. He says yes.

THE NEXT DAY Binjamin is the guest of honor at a benefit luncheon and reading sponsored by the Holocaust Museum at the Hotel Carlyle on the Upper East Side. The price of admission is $150 per plate, which goes to the museum's education and remembrance fund, but the museum provides the Wilburs with an entire table at no charge. Our presence, it would seem, is part of the message they want to send to donors: that the Holocaust remains relevant; that the pain it caused is still being felt; that every once in a while, in spite of the overwhelming destruction, the fabric of Jewish life can be rewoven; and that the museum is responsible for one such instance of repair. In its press release about his New York visit, the museum mentioned "a New York family who are very likely long-lost relatives."

Neither pork nor shellfish is served at lunch, but the event at the Carlyle is not sufficiently kosher for the Orthodox Wilburs. Our table is filled mostly with my mother's first cousins and their children, third- and fourth-generation Americans who are meeting Binjamin for the first time. Some have not read *Fragments,* and some know little more about Binjamin than what my mother has told them. One Wilbur present didn't know the name Wilkomirski before my mother told her about the book.

"It went right through me to the floor to see that name on the back of faces that were familiar to me," my mother's cousin Sherry says. On the non-Wilbur side of her family, only two relatives left in Poland survived the Holocaust, and she had wondered what had become of the Wilkomirskis. "This is almost romantic, in a sad way. This is beautiful. It's goose-pimple time."

Sherry says she sees the Wilburs' future in Binjamin. "He not only survived, but he survived in a spectacular fashion, to make this kind of life, and to connect. Which means it's going to keep on going. It makes the link between us stronger." She echoes Binjamin's sentiments of the previous day when she says, "You know, if it turns out that a Wilkomirski isn't a blood Wilkomirski but part of a greater community of Wilkomirskis, that's family, too."

My mother's cousin Susann, who flew in from Los Angeles for Binjamin's visit, is standing with Judy, another cousin of their generation. My mother thinks Judy and her brother bear the closest resemblance to Binjamin. According to Mom, you can see similarities between them in the line of the mouth, the contours of the lips, the shape of the nostrils. She pays attention to these details because she sculpts.

"I read the book and I thought: I would not have survived," says Susann. "Whether or not he's related, it somehow seems immaterial."

"This is a contemporary," Judy says.

"This is a cousin," Susann says.

"And if he's not a cousin, we make him a cousin," Judy says.

Susann says that when she read *Fragments,* she wanted to tell Binjamin, "'You're lost, we have the same name, you belong here.' When I heard the connections with the house on Moskva Street and Avram, for me that was it. I didn't need any more. I feel like he's a cousin, I'm feeling it more and more. I don't know that I really need definitive proof, I don't know that it's possible we'll ever find it, but that's fine."

Judy concurs. "You want to embrace him and bring him into the family no matter what the outcome is."

"We're a pretty good family, aren't we?" Susann says.

"Yes, we are. We are warm and loving," Judy says.

In the end, what is most important is the human feeling.

"IT'S MY PLEASURE to welcome you to this very special luncheon today," our host, a member of the Holocaust Museum's board, says as we take our seats. "Fifty years have passed since the end of World War II. Today there are still victims, witnesses, and survivors among us. But soon they will pass from our midst. Then, only the documents and artifacts still being collected around the world will be able to serve as silent witnesses. The United States Holocaust Memorial Museum must continue to collect, preserve, and conserve these precious remnants of a world gone, for our children and our children's children."

"Before we start, I'd like to acknowledge just a couple of people in the room," he says. He mentions Binjamin; Joan Ringelheim, who runs the museum's oral history archive and education programs; and the two Schindler Jews in attendance, Abe Zuckerman and Murray Pantirer. "Our author Mr. Wilkomirski's family also is here," the board member says. "They are all sitting at Table 11."

"Ten," my mother blurts out, loud enough for the whole room to hear. We are, in fact, sitting at Table 10. As a rule, my mother is a stickler for accuracy in matters large and small, and she is rarely shy about correcting people in positions of authority. So it strikes me as odd that she does not announce to the room that we might not actually be Binjamin's family. I think about saying something, but I don't because I came as a reporter and consider myself more an observer than a participant. As it is, I feel conspicuous enough. I am standing like the Statue of Liberty on a nicely upholstered chair and holding a microphone up to a speaker embedded in the ceiling, all so I can get a broadcast-quality recording.

After the opening remarks, Joan Ringelheim, who interviewed Binjamin for the museum's video archive when he was in Washington, steps up to say a few words about the role of individual testimony in telling the history of the Holocaust. "It's in these stories that one can connect with the personal, with the individual, because nobody lived through this as a mass," she says. "Every survivor and every victim lived through their own torment, their own difficulties, their own tragedy, and it's very important not to encapsulate it as massive figures, because I think most of us can't quite understand it that way. And it's the story that we have to know, because it's in the story that the 'unbearable sequence of sheer happenings,' as Hannah Arendt said, are transformed into potential meanings. Events otherwise are like dots on a page with no connections.

"You know, there are times when we meet individuals who break through what it is we think we understand about a historical event, and I've studied this event a long time. And I think Binjamin is just such a person. For me he's broken through what I understand about children, what I understand about memory. He was told that children don't have memories, that children forget. But not only that, that children *should* forget. Well, not only didn't he, but he *won't*. And with that I introduce a man who has given us a great gift."

"Shalom," says Binjamin, who is wearing an outfit similar to yesterday's—collared shirt, scarf, pants—plus a yarmulke. "In the last years I met many, many child survivors and I worked with important clinical psychologists who work in this field. And we saw that the development of the memory of a child in a war situation, in a situation of constant threat against his life, that such a memory develops in a completely different way than the memory of a child growing up in a peaceful situation. We must remember that a little child, a baby, develops almost animal-like instincts, a very clear visual memory, what we call a body memory of emotions, and an incredible sense of orientation. A baby who grows up in a peaceful situation loses that when, at four or five years old, the intellect starts to lead him. But in situations of war, it is essential that little children, as I was, keep and develop these instincts. So children who couldn't make that development had a poor chance to survive, and only those children who developed a very good sense of orientation, a very good sense of body feeling and a very good visual memory, they could cope with situations and take a chance to survive if the chance was given. Even children who were only about one year old, born in a camp and liberated after one year—later, when they learned to speak, they could remember exactly what happened in the barracks. One-year-old babies could remember what was going on around them. It's something incredible for those who grew up in a peaceful situation."

"For those who aren't familiar with my biography," he says, "I'll give a short outline and read a small passage. I don't know where I was born, but it must have been in the vicinity of Riga. . . ." Apologies for his English notwithstanding, Binjamin is dynamic and smooth here at the end of his American tour, as skillful a storyteller in person as he is on the page. He reads one scene from *Fragments,* the one in which the babies gnaw their frostbitten fingers to the bone. "It's a sickness called hunger," Binjamin reads as his audience at the Carlyle sits over what remains of the cold salmon entrée.

In the course of his talk, he reveals a few additional facts about himself. He says that when he was picked up from the Polish farmhouse in the spring of 1943, he was probably near Zamosc, where Poles and Jews alike were rounded up and sent to Majdanek. He also talks about how he "belonged to a pool of children who could make medical experiments," he says. "These doctors were so arrogant."

Binjamin also talks about his work as a historian. With a psychologist he knows, he has developed a new therapy for children without identity. "It's possible from the smallest piece of memory of a child to tell the whole story, because a good historian knows where to search," he says. They will share their therapeutic approach with psychologists in Bosnia and other war-torn places, so the orphaned and lost child survivors of these wars will avoid the fate of children who lived through the Holocaust only to end up in mental institutions. "We have no idea how big the number of child survivors is who disappeared in such homes," he says.

Our emcee from the museum thanks Binjamin and makes a plea for donations. "Think about this for a minute," he says. "If your parents or your grandparents had decided to stay instead of go, you might not be here today. And that's why the museum is so important, because we must never forget, and when we're all gone, the people that come after us must never forget. Please remember that the capital campaign built the museum, the education and remembrance fund pays for programs like the one you heard today."

After the speeches, I ask my mother why she didn't correct the host about our being Binjamin's family. "My own feeling is that it's not proven whether we are or not," she says. "I feel that I'm willing to consider him family if he's willing to consider us family. I don't want to claim kinship to somebody who doesn't want to claim it in return, but I have very warm feelings toward him and his wife. And if it helps the Holocaust Museum to call us newly discovered family, that's fine with me."

BINJAMIN SEEMS relieved when the luncheon ends—it is the end of his two-week tour—and I am, too. I am tired of standing like Lady Liberty and switching positions when the blood drains out of the arm holding the microphone. But I'm exhausted more by the mental contortions I've been going through as I listen to Binjamin tell his life story. Hearing it again allows me to analyze it a bit more, to think more and feel less than when I read the book. I believe that Binjamin believes that *Fragments* is his life story, but I question whether Binjamin can remember anything from such a young age, whether he can reconstruct so specifically what happened to him with so little data and after such a long interval, whether he is such a good historian. A careful historian always knows when to admit what he doesn't know, what can't be known. Can he really know which sector of Majdanek he was in when no records show that a Binjamin Wilkomirski was there at all? When he went to Riga in 1994, did he will himself into identifying the south end of Katolu Street as the starting point of his wartime troubles?

My doubts prevent me from pulling Binjamin closer and making him a cousin, as the other Wilburs at the lunch are doing. Without a DNA test or some tangible evidence, I don't see how I can think of our visitor other than as one of the children without identity he mentioned in his lecture. I'm inclined to think of *Fragments* as the fruit of research mixed with the wishes that developed around a seed of real trauma, but I felt uneasy about slicing open the fruit to find out how big the seed was. After all, he was a Holocaust survivor, he'd suffered terribly, and as much as he'd exposed himself, I held back from asking questions that I fear would hurt him.

Yet as my doubts fester, I have a growing affection for Binjamin. He has been friendly with my mother and her cousins, respectful of Miriam and her brothers, and as cooperative with my journalistic project as I could hope. I was flattered and relieved by his response to my article; you never know how your writing will be received. I may not accept human feeling as the only thing that matters in the end, but it does matter. I'd like to treat him like a cousin without making him one, if that's possible.

BINJAMIN AND Verena spend a few days in New York after the museum tour, and he asks to see us socially. My parents invite them for a dim sum brunch and a walk through lower Manhattan. They explain to Verena how to get from the hotel by subway, but she tells my parents Binjamin won't ride on trains because of bad associations from wartime.

Later in the week, I dine with Binjamin and Verena. Despite his bout with leukemia, Binjamin remains an avid smoker, and it takes a while to find a restaurant to accommodate him, but we eventually settle into an Italian place not far from their Lexington Avenue hotel. It is a pleasant, off-the-record dinner, the sort of meal you have with distant cousins when they come to town. It begins with polite, informational conversation, and all parties hope to find enough to talk about to make it through to coffee without too many awkward silences. I ask Binjamin for his impressions of Atlanta and Chicago and Boca Raton. They ask me about my sister, my entry-level editorial job, my marital status. It is the second day of Rosh Hashana, and I confess that I do not care much for religious ritual; Binjamin admits that he does not go to synagogue often. Binjamin and Verena talk about their work as musicians. She is a classical soprano, and they hold chamber concerts at their farmhouse in Amlikon, outside Zurich. They invite me, should I ever come to Switzerland, to stay with them in Amlikon and to use Binjamin's files on the Wilkomirskis there.

At the beginning of the evening, Binjamin said I could interview him again after dinner if he felt up to it. He does, so we drop off Verena at their hotel and cross the street to the Waldorf-Astoria. Binjamin and I settle in a couple of comfortable chairs in the lobby not far from the big clock. I return to the question of DNA testing, and he begins talking again about Father Yakov.

"You know, you have to wait a certain time for the results, and in this time, it was about four weeks, we exchanged letters, faxes, and called each other. For me, it was very strange. I realized suddenly that during all the last decades I never thought that I had a father. I was always completely fixated on the idea that I must try somehow to re-create a picture of the woman in Majdanek people told me was my mother, and I couldn't get this picture back. In a way that blocked me completely, I never thought about a father. And that was the first time in my life I thought, Of course, I must have a father. And this man was so kind, so warm, so nice. A week before the results of the test were coming, he called me and said last shabbas he had the whole family at his house. He explained the situation to the family, and said he had feelings like a father for a son toward me. And he felt it really wasn't so important if we really were genetically related; he still has a father's love toward his son, he has still this to give. And I'm looking for somebody like a father, and he just offers to me to be someone like a father. And if I'm ready to accept that, he's ready to accept me in his home.

"So we went to Israel and met his family and him, and through this contact a really wonderful friendship developed. I really felt he was a person I could really trust. The test results, we saw later, were negative, but during a certain period of time we were at the same places in Majdanek."

I ask whether Father Yakov is the first person he's met who he thought might really be a relative.

"I never really thought he can be my father," Binjamin says, "because some memories I had were against this possibility." But for the first time, "I had the feeling that I could absolutely trust a man. I never had that feeling before, I was always suspicious. But here, it was something completely natural, and that was something important for me, because I always had this serious problem for me. That's the problem of guilt. And that's because I was involved in events that led to the death of the boy in my barrack"—the boy who soiled the bed—"and felt very guilty for that."

Six months after they first met, Binjamin returned to Bnei Brak to see Father Yakov and ask him what halacha, or Jewish law, says about his responsibility for the young boy's death. "That was very important for my inner peace," he says. Yakov took him to see rabbis and other wise men, and they told him that he was not culpable. "When that happened I was four and a half or five. At that moment I had the feeling I was something that didn't feel right. But Yakov explained that the halacha says that a child really cannot be responsible for that unless the child learned the law." Binjamin sighs. "I profit a lot from his wisdom," he says.

Binjamin may never have thought Yakov was his father, but with the Wilburs, "that's much more concrete, and I'm convinced that somehow, far away, we are relatives. For me, it's no question. The question is, of course, whether it's possible to reconstruct the whole family history and all the branches of the family."

DNA testing isn't the answer, however. Binjamin says his doctors told him he's too old for DNA tests. "Most of these tests are designed for father-and-children relations when the child is up to about ten years, not more. And also several kinds of illnesses you have during your life can modify the whole picture, and among those are blood cancer and blood diseases, and I had leukemia for a long time and other forms of cancer. So they said it's not absolutely sure. So I tend more to try to find more historical details about the family history."

"Maybe it's research that never ends. I want to emphasize that, not only as a historian but as a person, I will never stop looking for new information." As if on cue, the clock in the hotel lobby strikes eleven, underscoring the urgency of his eleventh-hour quest. "More information, it calms you. And every small piece of information gives you back a small part of your identity. And that's the most important thing."

I tell Binjamin that his visit may have given the Wilburs a piece of our identity.

"Everything new you get into your mind, it changes you," he says. "You're not the same anymore as before."

DOUBT

───────────

In preparing my public-radio story about Binjamin, I tried to verify independently some of the information he'd shared with me. For instance, I looked for a reference to the law he'd mentioned barring Jewish refugee children from entering Switzerland before 1950. The prohibition wasn't in any book I could find, so I called the Swiss consulate for help. I was given the names of three Swiss lawyers based in New York, but after conferring with their colleagues at home, none of them could confirm it for me. Their nonsuccess struck me as strange; one would think a postwar ban on Jewish immigration would not only be noted but notorious. On the other hand, the law Binjamin described was in keeping with Switzerland's xenophobic reputation, which had only been reinforced for me by his book.

The Jewish-refugee ban explained a key piece of Binjamin's biography: why he had to be smuggled into Switzerland. I didn't want to bother Binjamin by asking him for a legal citation; perhaps I didn't want him to know I didn't accept everything he said at face value. Any small inconsistency in a story should make a reporter ask larger, more fundamental questions about its integrity, but in the end I decided to gloss over that part of his life. After all, this legal footnote was peripheral to the main drama of Binjamin meeting the Wilburs.

On *This American Life,* I talked about my family's reactions to Binjamin, which ranged from "making him a cousin" to Aunt Miriam's wary indifference. I also discussed the epistemological problems in Binjamin's life story, the central one being that his identity was contingent upon one moment half a century earlier when a woman at Auschwitz recognized him as Binjamin Wilkomirski. I said I wasn't certain he was Binjamin Wilkomirski and wondered aloud whether he could really remember the spot in Riga where his perhaps-father died. I pointed out that wishful thinking flourished on both sides of the encounter. Expressing my skepticism about Binjamin probably wasn't the kindest thing to do to a relative, but I wasn't sure he was one. On the other hand, I had committed myself to regarding him as a relative, so I tried to doubt him gently.

I sent Binjamin a cassette with my story. This time he didn't call to share his impressions. He was in contact with my mother, who was sending him photographs and exchanging information about various Wilkomirskis with him.

About a month after my story aired, Mom sent him a letter:

Dear Binjamin,

As I listen again to Blake's radio program, I hear his doubts about whether you are in fact a relative. I do not share those doubts. The main difference between the way Blake thinks and the way I think is this: I will continue to believe we are related unless somebody proves to me that we are not. Blake demands undeniable proof that you are related. Most of my cousins share my perspective, not Blake's.

Susann is still pursuing discussions with the 79-year-old man who was the boy in the photo that looks like your son. His name is Lester. . . .

In the long run, I don't know if any of this matters. As I said, as far as I am concerned, you are a cousin. Please consider yourself a cousin and keep in touch.

More than once I have asked my mother what prompted her to send this letter. What did Binjamin say to her? Was he angry, disappointed, hurt by what I said? She insists he said nothing; her letter was not an apologetic reply but a preemptive act of reassurance. Perhaps she was reflexively protecting her family. I recognized the impulse. I can't count the number of times it has sheltered me over the years, although this time I was on the other end of it, and I wasn't particularly happy about it. If I had wanted to tell Binjamin directly that I doubted he was our cousin, I would have done it myself.

The only person who didn't seem particularly upset was Binjamin. In his next letter to my mother, he said nothing about my doubts, and he asked her to pass along his regards to me.

THE BELIEVABILITY of Holocaust testimony has been a source of anxiety for its victims even before they knew whether they would survive to tell their stories. In *The Drowned and the Saved*, Primo Levi writes that during the war, "both parties, victims and oppressors, had a keen awareness of the enormity and therefore the noncredibility of what took place in the Lagers." The Nazis did their best to keep the camps a secret from the outside world, and since they expected to win the war, they told Jewish inmates that the evidence of the Final Solution would be destroyed once their murderous plan was complete. As for the prisoners, Levi describes a common dream in the camps: "They had returned home and with passion and relief were describing their past sufferings, addressing themselves to a loved one, and were not believed, indeed were not even listened to." To this day, many Holocaust survivors, in their memoirs and recorded oral testimonies, express a deep anxiety that for someone who did not endure the unimaginable horrors they did, their stories are fundamentally unbelievable.

If doubt troubled the author of *Fragments*, it didn't necessarily stop him from asserting himself, even when the doubt came from an authoritative source. He told one journalist that the historian's office at Majdanek disputed his memories of the barracks there. "They really tried to make a fool of me," he said. "And I said, 'I was there, not you.'"

Binjamin inoculates himself against doubt by making it an essential element of his story. By setting aside "the ordering logic of grown-ups" at the outset of *Fragments,* by calling attention to his own uncertainty throughout the book, he gets his readers to accept their confusion rather than follow up on it.

Of course, Binjamin's testimony is meant not just to tell his own story of survival but to stand for the stories of the multitudes of young children who died and to bolster those children without identity too cowed by their own uncertainty to go public with their stories. "Perhaps other people in the same situation would find the necessary support and strength to cry out their traumatic childhood memories, so that they too could learn that there really are people today who will take them seriously," he writes in *Fragments.*

Binjamin Wilkomirski was taken very seriously. The Jewish Book Council gave *Fragments* its 1996 National Jewish Book Award for Autobiography/Memoir. The book received similar prizes on the other side of the Atlantic: the Prix Mémoire de la Shoah in France, the Jewish Quarterly Literary Prize in England. Professors of Holocaust courses added *Fragments* to their syllabi, school groups in Zurich and organizations abroad invited Binjamin to speak. Rosie O'Donnell held up a copy of *Fragments* and recommended it to the viewers of her daytime television show. The BBC invited Binjamin to be the celebrity guest on the classical-music show *Private Passions,* and he chose the hour's playlist: the scherzo from Mahler's First Symphony, an aria from *The Magic Flute,* a track from *Songs of the Ghetto: A Jewish Child of Poland* performed by Sarah Gorby. Newspapers quoted him as an authority on matters concerning the Holocaust. When Swedish poet Barbro Karlén came to Switzerland to promote a memoir in which she claimed to be Anne Frank reincarnate, Binjamin condemned her book as nonsense. "It is a fraud in a moral sense," he told a Swiss newspaper, adding that the blame lay not with her but with the people making money off her. Karlén, he said, "is simply disturbed."

Binjamin Wilkomirski did not have the reputation of Anne Frank, Elie Wiesel, or the Schindler Jews, but he was, as Joan Ringelheim of the Holocaust Museum put it, one of those uncommon individuals who can "break through what it is we think we understand about a historical event." When a person becomes an exemplar, questioning his story seems to challenge more than the integrity of that particular individual. Holocaust deniers have been trying since the late 1950s to impugn the authenticity of Anne Frank's diary, the idea being that if this eloquent but in many ways ordinary girl was your point of entry to seeing the human face of Nazi atrocities, the invalidation of her story could erode your trust in other parts of the historical record. Had the diary been forged, of course, it wouldn't alter the fact that the Holocaust happened, but as a bulwark against this pseudoscientific campaign, literary scholars, historians, and scientists undertook multiple studies of Anne Frank's manuscript and have affirmed not only the integrity of the text and authenticity of the handwriting but the contemporaneity of the paper and ink she used. In the end, the Netherlands State Institute for War Documentation issued a critical edition of the diary, a much weightier tome than the mass-market paperback, to aid scholars in their work but also to ward off nefarious propagandists seeking to distort Holocaust history.

As much as I doubted that the author of *Fragments* was a relative and indeed whether he was really Binjamin Wilkomirski, I did not seriously consider the possibility that this man with the imprimatur of a reputable publisher and the United States Holocaust Memorial Museum might not be a Holocaust survivor at all. I do not remember such a thought occurring to me. What in the world could make a person represent himself as a Holocaust survivor when he wasn't one? And how could he persuade seasoned editors and scholars? No, he must be a Holocaust survivor. To think otherwise would be despicable. I would have dismissed such a notion as soon as it came into my head.

THE STORY OF Binjamin Wilkomirski goes far beyond his relationship with me and the Wilburs, however, and others had their own reasons for being suspicious.

When word got out in Zurich that the clarinetist known around town as Bruno Doessekker would be publishing a Holocaust memoir, those who had known him since childhood were puzzled. As far as they knew, the boy who from the age of four had lived in the well-appointed, Protestant home of Dr. Kurt and Martha Doessekker was not a Jewish child orphaned in the Holocaust. Someone, probably from Zurich's musical circles, tipped off Hanno Helbling, a former cultural editor of the *Neue Zürcher Zeitung*. In February 1995 Helbling, then living in Rome, wrote to Siegfried Unseld, the head of the German publishing concern Suhrkamp-Verlag, to warn him that his company had a phony memoir on its hands. "I had been told that these memories are not authentic and were more or less a fiction," Helbling recalled. "I didn't do any research, I just told him what I had heard."

Helbling's letter caught Suhrkamp-Verlag, which was planning to publish *Fragments,* and Eva Koralnik, Binjamin Wilkomirski's literary agent, off-guard. Both had estimable literary credentials; Suhrkamp is one of Germany's most respected presses, and Koralnik, who herself came to Switzerland as a Jewish child refugee, represents many living Holocaust authors as well as the estate of Anne Frank. Unseld suspended publication of *Fragments* and put Thomas Sparr, the head of Suhrkamp's Jewish imprint, in charge of an inquiry. Sparr asked the author of *Fragments* for a birth certificate, adoption records, and any papers supporting the story told in his memoirs.

Instead of documents, Sparr received testimonials from psychologist Elitsur Bernstein, who said he'd known of his friend's search for his identity since the early eighties and even accompanied him on fact-finding missions to Poland and Riga, and from psychotherapist Monika Matta, who assured Sparr that *Fragments* described the actual memories of her patient of two and a half years. Sparr and Koralnik then journeyed to Jerusalem, where they met with children-without-identity researcher Lea Balint, who offered further assurances, and with Julius Loewinger, the man who corroborated Binjamin's description of the playground at the Krakow orphanage. Also coming forward was the interpreter of Binjamin's conversation with Polish Holocaust historian Ewa Kurik-Lesik. He remembered that Kurik-Lesik said the scene in *Fragments,* in which Binjamin is smuggled in to visit his mother in another sector of Majdanek, has historical precedents; and if he hadn't been moved, the boy would surely have died in Sector Five. The witnesses all affirmed the plausibility of *Fragments,* but none could definitively corroborate the author's identity.

When Binjamin had recovered from the shock of doubt, he offered to show Sparr his adoption papers, but warned him that they indicated the wrong birth mother, a woman from the French-speaking part of Switzerland. Binjamin said he'd already begun a legal procedure to have them amended. He proposed adding a brief afterword to *Fragments* that would explain the discrepancy between his papers and his memories. Suhrkamp wrote back to Helbling informing him that the dubious story in fact checked out and they were going ahead with publication.

"As a child, I also received a new identity, another name, another date and place of birth," Binjamin writes in the afterword, which comes off more like an organic conclusion than an appended caveat. Like the rest of the book, the afterword wraps a few bits of data in a tissue of uncertainty and emotion. If there is one difference, it is that while the larger events of the war happening around Binjamin can be researched in any decent library, details of the author's personal circumstances, protected by stringent Swiss privacy laws, lie beyond the grasp of his readers. Binjamin does not specify his other name or birthplace. The date of birth, February 12, 1941, he says, comes from "a makeshift summary, no actual birth certificate," and "has nothing to do with either the history of this century or my personal history." For a child such as himself, he says, having an "imposed identity" is nothing unusual; hundreds of other children without identity were "furnished with false names and often with false papers too," their real identities untraceable. "Legally accredited truth is one thing—the truth of a life another," he writes.

The imposed identity was described in a bit more detail by Klara Obermüller, a friend of Eva Koralnik and a critic for *Die Weltwoche*, a liberal Zurich weekly newspaper. Obermüller published the first review of *Fragments* on August 31, 1995, just as it was coming out in Switzerland. "According to official information, he was born in Biel on February 12, 1941, spent the first years of his life in an orphanage and from there was given to a foster family that later adopted him," Obermüller wrote. "Today, he is called Bruno instead of Binjamin." She explains that Binjamin Wilkomirski is something of a provisional identity, that he himself is unsure of his own story and aware that he will probably never have a watertight explanation of his past.

Nevertheless, he had published a book "whose literary standing is not to be doubted."

That year, Obermüller chaired the jury of Zurich's literary commission, which gave Binjamin Wilkomirski one of its annual prizes for *Fragments*. The fragmentary memories in the book, the commission said as they awarded the 6,000-franc (about $4,000) prize, were "too little for the reconstruction of a reliable biography, but enough for a book, the high literary rank of which silences the doubts about its authenticity."

DOUBTS ABOUT its authenticity also emerged in isolated pockets outside of Zurich. These doubts came not from any prior knowledge of the author, but from reactions to his testimony. Gary Mokotoff, the New Jersey-based head of a Jewish genealogical publishing concern called Avotaynu and a member of the Jewish Book Council, read *Fragments* after it won the council's National Jewish Book Award.

"Put this letter in your hold file," Mokotoff wrote to the council's president, Arthur Kurzweil, on December 6, 1996. "I must tell you that after reading Wilkomirski's book the facts surrounding his survival do not add up; that the book might be historical fiction rather than fact." Latvian Jews, he wrote, were deported to Stutthof, not Majdanek. Mokotoff found it "inconceivable" that a child of three or four would have lasted in one forced-labor camp for more than a few days, let alone that the Nazis would bother to transport him to a second camp. And while selfishness plays a key role in many survivor accounts, Binjamin Wilkomirski only describes acts of altruism.

"If you take each of the events he described, they seem to be the sum of the experience of all survivors," Mokotoff wrote. "In the brief, two-year period, he was hidden by Christians, saw his family killed, attempted to flee the Germans, [was] deported to camps, witnessed Germans bashing in the heads of children (but not him), was packed on deportation trains, survived by playing dead on a pile of corpses, visited briefly with his mother at Majdanek (even though he claims he did not know he had a mother), the seeming friendliness and then barbarity of Germans toward children. And on and on and on." *Fragments,* Mokotoff noted, "is very well written. I wonder if Schocken was so caught up in the content of the book, that they wanted to believe that it really happened."

The Wilkomirski book reminded Mokotoff of *For Those I Loved* by Martin Gray, a Polish Jew who survived the Holocaust and settled in France. In his book, which was ghostwritten by Max Gallo, Gray describes his black-market activities as a teenager in the Warsaw ghetto, his deportation to and escape from Treblinka, his activity as a partisan fighter, and his vengeful search for Martin Bormann and other Nazi war criminals after the war.

For Those I Loved first appeared in 1971 in France, and Gray sold 250,000 copies. The book became an international sensation. It was translated into eighteen other languages, and plans for a movie were under way. The English-language edition of Gray's book was also expected to be a success. Large first printings were planned on both sides of the Atlantic. "Certainly stranger and wilder, than all but the most extravagant novels of our time," wrote one board member of Book of the Month Club, which offered Gray's book to its members. "Hemingway to plot it, Faulkner to imagine the weirder episodes, Isaac Bashevis Singer to give the tone of melancholy, humorous, heroic Judaism: these unlikely collaborators might have produced something like *For Those I Loved*. But even then, it would not have had the same ring of truth."

On the eve of its publication in England, *The Sunday Times* of London published an investigation suggesting that Gray, who made a fortune after the war by manufacturing period furniture and peddling it overseas as antique, had unscrupulously crafted his autobiography in much the same way, particularly the section about Treblinka. While attempts to escape Treblinka were frequent, they were rarely successful, and of the 870,000 people brought to the death camp between the summer of 1942 and the spring of 1943, only a handful survived. *The Sunday Times* sought out those survivors and asked the ones they found about Gray's book. Their recollections of the camp, which were consistent with testimony given earlier by SS officers and survivors at public trials, did not jibe with *For Those I Loved*. For example, Gray said he arrived at an elaborate train station, almost like a stage set, at Treblinka in September of 1942. But written records of the camp and the testimony of other survivors indicated that the mock station house was not constructed until months later. "It was impossible to see the things Gray said he saw in Treblinka in the autumn of 1942," one survivor of the camp told *The Sunday Times*.

When confronted by *The Sunday Times*, Gray insisted he had a "splendid memory" and provided additional information about Treblinka, some of which also contradicted descriptions given by other survivors. Gray also gave the paper the name of a Treblinka survivor who "remembers me very well," but when contacted, the man did not remember Gray, nor could he corroborate his story. Gray fired back with threats of legal action. "Let me repeat what the book makes clear: that I was in Treblinka 30 years ago, as a frightened 16-year-old, for a period of between two or three weeks," he wrote to *The Sunday Times*. "What I set down, driven by personal needs to tell my story many years later, was not intended to be a researched 'history,' but my memories and impressions, still indelibly vivid, as they came to me." He called *The Sunday Times* investigation "distasteful," and dared them to say he had not been in Treblinka.

Meanwhile, other parts of *For Those I Loved* came under scrutiny. *The New Statesman* interviewed survivors of the Warsaw ghetto uprising, who found similar fault with Gray's description of that event. Mokotoff, who publishes books on Jewish genealogy, couldn't understand why a Christian racketeer in Gray's story would be called Mokotow the Tomb, since Mokotow is "a uniquely Jewish name."

A representative of Editions Robert Laffont, Gray's French publisher, said verification was expensive and unnecessary: "It is not customary in France to carry out elaborate research into books of this kind." The German publisher of Gray's book halted publication pending an investigation, but the American and British publishers left the book in print and proceeded with paperback editions. In time, Gray succeeded in turning *For Those I Loved* into a feature film.

For Those I Loved is no longer in print, and, as Mokotoff pointed out in his letter, in recent years it has been more or less forgotten by everyone except those Holocaust "revisionists" who invoke it as an example of the unreliability of first-person accounts of the Holocaust. Gary Mokotoff worried that *Fragments* would also draw their attention.

MOTOKOFF'S CONCERNS about *Fragments* remained private. The first public doubts about Binjamin Wilkomirski were aired in March of 1998, in a review on the Amazon online bookstore. Michael Mills, a reader from Canberra, Australia, was troubled by similarities between *Fragments* and what he'd read about Buchenwald. There was a children's barrack at Buchenwald, and from there children were shipped to Auschwitz. Mills cites the case of one four-year-old boy hidden under floorboards at Buchenwald who spoke a multilingual gibberish at war's end, much like the "Babel-babble of an assortment of children's barracks" which Binjamin describes on the first page of *Fragments*.

Where another reader might have taken such details about another camp as corroboration—if such things happened at Buchenwald, why not at Majdanek?—Mills thought Binjamin Wilkomirski might have conflated research with his remembered tale. "If Wilkomirski's memories of childhood concentration camp experiences are indeed genuine," Mills wrote, "it is most probable that they are to be located at Buchenwald rather than at Majdanek."

Mills's comments were hardly typical of the others posted on Amazon. Like their professional counterparts, the lay reviewers called *Fragments* a "masterpiece" of Holocaust literature, a "must read" for mental health professionals working with troubled children. "Anyone who reads this book cannot help but become a better and more knowledgeable person," one reader wrote. Two admitted to crying over Binjamin's story.

Jon Blair, a British filmmaker interested in making a documentary about Binjamin, was intrigued by Mills's dissenting opinion and asked Mills to elaborate on his suspicions. Mills explained in an e-mail that he read *Fragments* against standard histories by the likes of Lucjan Dobroszycki, Gerald Reitlinger, and Raul Hilberg, and found troubling inaccuracies in Binjamin's personal history. For instance, Mills questioned whether Binjamin could have seen "a gray black monster with a round lid that was standing open" near the

Polish farmhouse. If he saw his perhaps-father die in the Riga ghetto in late 1941, he would have arrived in Poland too late to see Hitler's tanks barrel through, and if he'd been sent to Majdanek, he would have left the farmhouse too early to witness the Red Army's counteroffensive two and a half years later.

Mills's messages contain a progression of conditional phrases: "If he was imprisoned in a camp in a barrack with many other children . . ."; "If Wilkomirski's father was in fact killed in Riga . . ."; "If Wilkomirski's memory of the killing of his father is genuine . . ."; "If he was indeed a member of a Jewish family . . ." Mills wonders whether the author of *Fragments* might be a gentile because "it is not clear from his book how he was identified as a Jewish child, and his sole self-identification in the context of his fragments of memory seems to be as a child surrounded by malevolent adults, both at the camp and afterwards." The text of *Fragments* bears out this point. Binjamin seems entirely unaware during the war that he is being persecuted because he is a Jew. Circumcision is never an issue, and anti-Semitism plays no part in his descriptions of Riga, the Polish farmhouse, or his time at Majdanek ("the children's camp," "no playground") and Auschwitz. After the war, Binjamin describes being the target of anti-Semitism in Switzerland, but for him the Holocaust remains a campaign against children. At the Swiss orphanage, he cannot imagine why there are white porcelain dishes "for children" rather than the usual dull tin. In his adoptive home, the fruit cellar and coal furnace look like "wooden bunks for children, oven doors for children." And though the English translation of *Fragments* has Binjamin's schoolmates teasing him by singing "Beggar kid, beggar kid. / There's never enough for the yid," the taunting rhyme contains no anti-Semitic slur in the German original.

Blair was impressed by Mills's analysis. "Since you appear to be something of a considerable expert on the period," Blair wrote, "are you an academic or specialist of some sort?"

"I am not an expert or an academic, just a petty bureaucrat who has an interest in this topic, and has read widely," wrote Mills, who works for Australia's Department of Finance and Administration. "It seems to me that, because of the growing interest in the history of the Jews during the Second World War, a very large number of books on this topic has recently been produced, of varying quality. I have noted historical errors in some of them, and I like to make readers aware of them where possible."

Mills neglected to mention that one place where he had noted historical errors was on the web site of the Committee for Open Debate on the Holocaust. In addition to maintaining a web site, the committee buys advertisements in college newspapers calling for "open debate" between its proprietor, Bradley Smith, and a representative of the Anti-Defamation League on questions such as "Is the Diary of Anne Frank an authentic personal diary or a 'literary' concoction?" and "Were 'gas chambers' used during WWII by Germans to kill millions of Jews as part of a program of 'genocide'?" Mills also participated in the alt.revisionism newsgroup on the Internet.

MILLS HAD another reason for questioning the authenticity of *Fragments*. "I understand that this book is based on repressed childhood memories 'recovered' by the author with the help of a psychiatrist," he wrote in his Amazon review. "So-called recovered memories are extremely controversial."

The debate over the reliability of memories of early-childhood abuse goes back at least as far as Sigmund Freud. Early on in his investigations of the psyche, Freud hypothesized that each of his hysterical patients had been seduced in early childhood by an adult. He believed that, from the fragmentary memories and telling silences revealed in analysis, he could determine what infantile sexual trauma each of his patients had suffered. By the late 1890s, however, Freud stopped believing that every neurotic (himself included) had actually been molested in early childhood, and he no longer thought himself capable of distinguishing between descriptions of actual infantile trauma and fantasies. Some of his patients' stories, he concluded, must be vivid but false recollections that represent their wishes or fears. Freud stopped reconstructing these sexual traumas and abandoned the seduction theory.

Mills's mention on the Amazon web site of recovered memories caught the eye of Mark Pendergrast, the author of *Victims of Memory: Sex Abuse Accusations and Shattered Lives* (1995), an empiricist's look at the epidemic of unverifiable reports of abuse in American society. Pendergrast dates the upsurge in reports of long-forgotten abuse to the late 1980s, when books like Ellen Bass and Laura Davis's *The Courage to Heal* and Lauren Stratford's *Satan's Underground* first enjoyed success and abuse survivors and their therapists became fixtures on daytime television.

Pendergrast identifies unscrupulous therapists who hypnotized their patients and dispensed suggestion-inducing drugs, but for many individuals it was enough simply to treat every troubling thought as a clue to past abuse, synthesizing them in private journals and therapy sessions until a story emerged. Many cases seem to have been the result of contagious hysteria spread by a legion of well-meaning counselors who, like the early Sigmund Freud, were too eager to believe that their patients had been abused and too quick to explain exactly what had happened. But these memories of abuse had real consequences. As recovered-memory therapy entered the mainstream, people were accused and occasionally convicted of sex crimes without any evidence beyond the newfound memories of their accusers and the expert testimony of therapists. Even when the unprovable accusations had no legal ramifications, they tore families in half, including Pendergrast's. (Both of his adult daughters shunned him after making what he calls "vague, unspecified accusations" that he sexually abused them as children; he denies their allegations.) Pendergrast writes of two pairs of Holocaust-survivor parents accused by their children of abuse. They told him that "losing their children was worse than what they had endured in the concentration camps." Pendergrast says he pressed the parents to consider whether they really meant what they had said, and in both cases they assured him that they did.

In *Victims of Memory*, Pendergrast calls on experimental psychology to debunk many abuse claims. Psychologists like Elizabeth Loftus of the University of Washington have conducted experiments demonstrating how easy it is to plant memories of events that didn't happen. Pendergrast also discusses infantile amnesia, a concept dating back to psychologist Jean Piaget and borne out by experiments. "Very few people remember much before the age of five," he writes. Although he mentions one experimentalist who thinks some individuals can have memories going back to age two, "the reality of infantile amnesia would appear to be beyond dispute."

When Pendergrast read *Fragments,* he found much of the story implausible. Binjamin's description of being hurled headfirst into a stone wall seemed like a textbook recovered memory. A little child could not survive such violence, Pendergrast thought, let alone remember it.

From his home in Vermont, Pendergrast wrote to three New England Holocaust scholars to alert them to the problems he saw with *Fragments.* In a letter dated April 20, 1998, he wrote to the University of Vermont's Raul Hilberg, who wrote the landmark documentary history *The Destruction of the European Jews;* Lawrence Langer of Simmons College, known for his studies of Holocaust testimony and fiction; and Elie Wiesel, winner of the Nobel Peace Prize, who holds a chair in the religion department at Boston University.

"It seems quite clear, even from a cursory look through the book, that it is a work of fiction rather than non-fiction," Pendergrast wrote. "The book quite possibly contains a mixture of real and confabulated memory, but most of it appears to be confabulated." He says that, judging by Wilkomirski's 1941 birth date, "he would be subject to the period of infantile amnesia during most of the time he purportedly recalls here in fragments. . . . I would very much appreciate it if you would have a look at the book and render your opinion."

A FEW DAYS after Raul Hilberg received Pendergrast's note, he was seated next to Lawrence Langer on a flight to Indiana. The two scholars had been invited to the University of Notre Dame to speak at a conference titled "Humanity at the Limit: The Impact of the Holocaust Experience on Jews and Christians." Organized with the help of the United States Holocaust Memorial Museum, "Humanity at the Limit" included artists, anthropologists, historians, literary critics, theologians, and other scholars from America, Israel, and Europe. Even the Vatican sent a representative.

Langer and Hilberg are leading figures in the field of Holocaust studies, but for the husband-and-wife team who planned the Notre Dame conference, perhaps the biggest coup was getting Binjamin Wilkomirski to speak. Betty Signer says she spent six months pursuing the author of *Fragments* before he finally committed to coming. "He is a very big name now in terms of his book and writing," she boasted to a campus newspaper. Binjamin represented the conference's mission to highlight the increasing consideration accorded to survivor memory in Holocaust studies. "Statistics don't adequately represent what happened," Rabbi Michael Signer told the *South Bend Tribune*. Many of the distinguished participants were themselves survivors or refugees, but none of them would embody humanity at the limit better than Binjamin Wilkomirski.

On the plane to South Bend, Langer turned to ask Hilberg whether he had read *Fragments*. It was an open question, since for Hilberg Holocaust history is synonymous with archival research. Documents are "texts which contain a great deal of what we call history," he wrote in his memoir, *The Politics of Memory*. A document is "first of all an artifact, immediately recognizable as a relic. It is the original paper that was once upon a time handled by a bureaucrat and signed or initialed by him. More than that, the words on that paper constituted an *action:* the performance of a function. If the paper was an order, it signified the *entire* action of its originator."

Constructed largely from German documents captured by the Allies, Hilberg's *The Destruction of the European Jews* systematically delineates the Nazis' methods of expropriation, concentration, deportation, and annihilation. The 1961 edition, which ran to 800 pages, was the underacknowledged source for much of Hannah Arendt's *Eichmann in Jerusalem*. Hilberg has spent the better part of four decades researching, writing, refining, and revising his magnum opus. "I knew even as the original version went to press that inevitably I would become aware of errors, that there were gaps in the story, and that analytical statements or conclusions would some day strike me as incomplete or imprecise," Hilberg writes in the preface to the three-volume third edition, published in 1985. "I knew that to achieve greater accuracy, balance and clarity, I would have to make use of more documents."

For years, *The Destruction of the European Jews* has been criticized for its reverence for documents, particularly those of the Nazi
perpetrators, and its indifference to Jewish sources, especially survivor accounts. Hilberg, a Jewish refugee from Austria, has also been
condemned for his view that Jews were often complicit in their
demise.

Hilberg is unyielding in the face of such complaints. Unlike
Rabbi Signer and many others involved in Holocaust studies, Hilberg is confident that statistics, properly explained and contextual-
ized, can adequately represent what happened. Besides, in the many
survivor testimonies he has read, "only one fact is always revealed
clearly and completely. It is the self-portrait of the survivors, their
psychological makeup, and what it took to survive," he writes in *The
Politics of Memory*. Survivor accounts lack the sort of data—names,
dates, places—that Hilberg regards as the necessary building blocks
for history. Survivors describe what is important to them, but they
rarely choose to record what the historian would. "I tried to glimpse
the Jewish community," he writes. "I searched for the dead. Most
often, however, I had to remind myself that what I most wanted from
them they could not give me, no matter how much they said."

Hilberg admitted he hadn't read *Fragments,* and asked Langer
what he thought of it. Langer has spent more than two decades
studying how the Holocaust is retold in testimony, fiction, and art,
and he can be a harsh critic of what he considers inadequate or
undignified treatments of the subject. In Langer's view, Holocaust
fiction doesn't gives a storyteller much more leeway than a memoirist. "When the Holocaust is the theme, history imposes limita-
tions on the supposed flexibility of artistic license," Langer wrote in
a 1990 essay called "Fictional Facts and Factual Fictions: History in
Holocaust Literature." Langer wrote that this restriction is largely a
function of our age. "The urgency of the historical event continues
to exert its mysterious power over modern consciousness," he
writes. When that urgency dissipates, "the boundaries separating the
historical moment from its imaginative rendition will be blurred, and
it will no longer matter so much whether fictional facts, tied to the
actual deeds of history, have become factual fictions, monuments to
artistic vision that require no defense or justification, but stand or

fall on the strength of their aesthetic mastery of the material." When Auschwitz recedes from the collective memory as the battlefields of the Napoleonic Wars and World War I did, a future Tolstoy or Hemingway can render the camp with his full imaginative powers, Langer wrote. But not before.

Langer told Hilberg that *Fragments* was "one of the best Holocaust novels I've ever read." From his reading of the book he was confident that, though labeled a memoir, it was in fact a historical fiction built around its author's life. *Fragments* was going to be one of the books Langer planned to discuss when he spoke at the conference.

At a dinner in South Bend hosted by the Signers, Langer met Binjamin. He and Verena told Langer that *Fragments* was strictly nonfiction. The perplexed professor didn't argue, and left it out of his talk at the panel.

When Hilberg met Binjamin, he decided to talk to him in German to see if he could determine Binjamin's background from his accent, but Hilberg says his hearing isn't so good anymore and he couldn't really tell. He quizzed Binjamin about Riga, and Binjamin gave correct answers, but nothing one couldn't find in a book.

Binjamin's presentation to "Humanity at the Limit" began with some of the same stories he'd told at the Hotel Carlyle, about the babies who devoured their own fingers. This was an academic conference, however, so he decided to give a scholarly paper about the new therapeutic approach he had developed with his psychologist friend Elitsur Bernstein. His Notre Dame talk was not the debut of their "Concept for Cooperation Between Psychotherapist and Historian in Therapy for 'Holocaust Child-Survivors Without Identity'"; they had already presented it at the Institute for Applied Psychology in Zurich, where Bernstein had an affiliation, and at a Viennese treatment center for Holocaust survivors and other sufferers of post-traumatic stress disorder. (The announcement for the Vienna event identified him as "Dr. Benjamin Wilkomirski" of the University of Ostrava.) *Werkblatt,* a Vienna psychoanalytic journal, had published it in German.

Many children without identity, who were only now, due to old age and the collapse of the Iron Curtain, emerging, were afflicted with "psychopathological and highly complex somatic disorders," Binjamin said, but traditional psychotherapy was of limited value to them if their goal was regaining their identity. A person "can only gain this knowledge by close cooperation with a specialist historian who is willing to take an active part in reconstruction therapy," he said. Binjamin recommended other deviations from therapeutic practices: waiving the rigid fifty-minute time limit, leaving behind the couch for a walk in the park, honoring "a client's spontaneous request to bring with him a 'fellow sufferer'—a friend who experienced the same traumas as himself, who can help complete those memory fragments which he finds difficulty in bringing to the surface or reconstructing by himself."

The Wilkomirski-Bernstein approach treats fragments of memory as clues not only to a person's "inner reality," the normal purview of psychotherapy, but to their "external reality" as well. Even the earliest preverbal memories, whether in the form of images, smells, or body memories, can be keys to this external reality. The historian must be attuned to tiny details: bits of what Binjamin calls *Krematoriumsesperanto,* or concentration-camp jargon; sketched physical details; sensations of heat or motion from a particular traumatic moment. This approach is based on discussions with "large numbers" of survivors who described traumatic events from the first two years of life and had their memories corroborated by adult eyewitnesses. "We were witness to the fact that when some of our clients were given special exercises in concentration and memory (meditation and/or Eriksonian techniques), they were able to achieve total and clear recall of successive events that in the past appeared to have been completely repressed," Binjamin said.

Binjamin supplies three anonymous case histories to illustrate their method. One patient remembers an ornate belt buckle and a green uniform, and through this costume, which belongs to a policeman, identifies his own hometown. In another scenario, memories of railroad tracks and the direction of the sunlight hitting the patient's eyes helps him identify "with a great degree of likelihood" a massacre he survived. The third case comes "at the end of a year in therapy, during which one of our clients had undergone constant guidance in special exercises in concentration aimed at focusing his memory on a

specific occurrence that repeated itself again and again in his dreams."
The recurring dream involved a man being shot against a wall, and it
was followed by memories of a waterborne escape, of a cold and wet
feeling, of a skyline at daybreak. The dreamer travels to Riga, which
he immediately recognizes as "the city with its church towers that
was imprinted in his memory," Binjamin said as if he could be talking about someone other than himself. Meanwhile, "the historian
looks down the list of inhabitants of the town from 1927 and finds
the name of a family with that very name who had lived there in the
vicinity of the places the client has been talking about from his memories. As a result of this turn of events, our client ceases to suffer from
the terrible migraines he has endured for so many years."

Although the three histories all seem to come from Binjamin's
case, he claims that "more than 50 candidates" have signed up for treatment. "During the course of therapy, many of our clients experienced
significant relief from physiological and psychological maladies," Binjamin concludes. "Some of the symptoms even disappeared completely when a concrete connection to their origins was reached."

Binjamin received a nearly unanimous standing ovation from his
international and interdisciplinary audience at Notre Dame. Raul
Hilberg sat on his hands.

PHANTOM
SIBLINGS

On his way to the "Humanity at the Limit" conference, Binjamin made a side trip to California. In Los Angeles he had breakfast with my cousin Susann, who had been in my parents' living room and at the Hotel Carlyle six months earlier, but the main purpose of his West Coast trip was to visit with another kind of extended family.

"When I'm together with young child survivors like me—four, five years old—we immediately feel we can speak without words," Binjamin had told me back in New York. Through glances and gestures, they understand one another because of the experiences they have in common. "Unconditional solidarity still exists among us."

Their solidarity can now be found in local support groups on six continents and at yearly conferences sponsored by the Federation of Jewish Child Survivors of the Holocaust and the Hidden Child Foundation, but twenty years ago they had no institutional network. And, as the author of *Fragments* was fond of pointing out, children got short shrift in the first four decades of Holocaust studies. "In the infinitely many books I read about the Shoah," Binjamin told a roomful of students during a guest lecture at the University of Ostrava, "the children were always mentioned in one sentence:

'Children were the first to be killed because they could not work.' And that was it."

While Anne Frank and the child protagonist of *The Painted Bird* evolved into popular emblems of the indefensible violence against Jews of all ages during the Holocaust, there is ample truth in Binjamin's statement. Although an estimated one and a half million of the six million Jews killed in the Holocaust were children, scholarly accounts of the period have long treated children as a "peripheral concern," as historian Debórah Dwork wrote in *Children with a Star: Jewish Youth in Nazi Europe* (1991). "They were not old enough to be explicit objects of policy, and they therefore never became part of the recorded history." The Nazis didn't keep many files on these children, whom they saw as an impediment to their forced-labor machine, and the few people who tried to save Jewish children didn't keep many records for fear that they would fall into Nazi hands.

The exact number of child survivors of the Holocaust is impossible to determine. According to Dwork, 11 percent of the European Jewish children alive in 1939 lived to see the end of the war. These approximately 175,000 children were a fraction of the multitudes of orphans of various nationalities and religious backgrounds drifting through postwar Europe: children of combatants killed in action, children of dead civilians, displaced Baltic and Polish children separated from their families as they fled the advancing Communist forces, non-German children with Aryan features who were put into German homes, children of Gypsies, Serbs, and Jews were all looking for what was left of their homes, families, and communities. Whether in reaction to the Nazi emphasis on false racial categories or in recognition of the continent-wide crisis, there was little press coverage specifically about Jewish orphans. David (Chim) Seymour, a Polish Jew and one of the founders of the Magnum photo agency, undertook a project on "Children of War" in memory of his parents, who perished in the Warsaw ghetto, but Chim focused on more than just Jewish children.

Of course, Jews found themselves in a different situation from other European war orphans, and the eradication of entire communities required extraordinary solutions. The Youth Aliya movement shipped 15,000 children, many of them orphans, to kibbutzim in Palestine between the end of the war and the declaration of the state of Israel. The American Jewish Joint Distribution Committee (the Joint for short) collected surviving Jewish children and tried to reunite them with parents, older siblings, or more distant relations. The Joint's postwar relief operations housed 35,000 Jewish orphans and cared for another 50,000, according to Paul Friedman, a psychiatrist dispatched by the Joint to assess the mental health of Jewish children in orphanages and displaced-persons camps. Most of the children in the Joint's care survived in hiding, but according to Friedman, about 4,000 children under eighteen emerged alive from concentration camps. Child survivors from camps tended to be older males capable of labor; hidden children tended to be younger and were more likely to be girls, since a circumcised boy was ultimately unable to conceal his Jewish identity.

DOCTOR FINDS AFFECTION CHIEF NEED OF ORPHANS SURVIVING NAZI RULE was the rosy headline the *New York Times* ran over its February 11, 1947, story on Friedman's research, which was tucked below the day's food news and recipes on page 33. Friedman spoke more soberly in the report he published the next year in *Commentary*. He admitted approaching his assignment with dread and was surprised to find that Europe was not the "huge, unattended hospital for neurotics, psychotics, and the hopelessly insane" he expected. Most survivors, Friedman observed, recovered quickly from the privations and terrors of the war. Children in particular exhibited an "amazing vitality and eagerness to build useful, happy lives."

It was not as if they emerged unscathed, however. Children had an "overwhelming need for a sense of identity, of family," Friedman wrote, and those who had been in Christian foster homes didn't always understand why they were being uprooted again. In addition, all of the hundreds of children he interviewed told him "the most tragic and bloody stories in a tone of the utmost detachment, even nonchalance, as though they were telling me about some very unimportant event, something that had happened long ago and to someone they hardly knew." He tells the story of one girl who was about five when her parents left her with a Ukrainian peasant family. Several days later, a local boy showed the girl her father's photo identity card; the boy had picked it up at the site where local Jews were massacred. "I wanted to cry, but I was afraid to cry because he would have known that I was a Jewish girl," she told Friedman. The boy took her to an open pit, where she saw the corpses of her family and other Jews from their town. Again she did not cry. "I was afraid they might kill me," she said. Four and a half years later, she was still unable to cry.

At first Friedman thought the abnormally matter-of-fact descriptions were indicative of schizophrenia, but he quickly discarded that theory. "Almost all the children I saw," he wrote, "had lost the ability to respond with spontaneous emotion to life." In those rare instances when they did break down, they reminded Friedman of soldiers suffering from combat fatigue. Since the children had suffered in various ways, it was impossible to apply a universal diagnosis or develop a unified psychological profile, other than to say that "there was one common denominator that, to a greater or lesser degree, existed for all DP's, adults and children alike: emotional numbness or shallowness."

For those children unable to return to their own families, it was crucial to foster loving, secure, structured environments where creativity and independence were encouraged. This was a challenge in DP camps where orphans lived under conditions Friedman said were in many ways "reminiscent of the German concentration camp," but even in these camps a few sensitive youth leaders succeeded in instilling a sense of stability and community in their large, makeshift broods.

Friedman's ideas about child development ran parallel to those of Alice Goldberger, who ran group homes in the English countryside for two dozen young Jewish orphans brought over from the Continent. Some had been in Terezin or Auschwitz, others hidden in children's homes or with families. The youngest of the children in her care was three years old. During World War II, Goldberger, a German refugee, had run a school on the Isle of Man for enemy-alien children and then joined the staff of the Hampstead War Nurseries, where she was trained by Anna Freud. At the postwar group homes, Goldberger and her staff provided the children with plentiful food, new clothes, schooling, practice in English, and lots of love and attention. When the children had difficulties, Goldberger intervened gently; in more serious cases Anna Freud provided psychoanalytic referrals.

In 1951 Freud published "An Experiment in Group Upbringing," a case history of six children who arrived at a country estate in Lingfield, Surrey, from Terezin at age three. Each child had been separated from its mother before turning one, and they had all lived together at the concentration camp. From the anomalous circumstances of their early lives, Freud tries to draw general conclusions about child development. Melanie Klein, Freud's foremost rival, postulated that a child's prolonged separation from its mother in early life caused catastrophic and irreversible damage, but the Terezin toddlers seemed to refute Klein's theory. In England the children exhibited an acute fear of dogs, vans, and feathers, but Freud thought they exhibited fewer anxieties than children raised in comfortable, peacetime surroundings. Having never been raised by natural or surrogate parents, the children formed their primary relationships among themselves, looking out for one another and displaying an unusual sense of loyalty and fairness. They directed their aggression less at each other than at adults and outsiders. The orphans in Alice Goldberger's care were "hypersensitive, restless, aggressive, difficult to handle," Freud wrote. "But they were neither deficient, delinquent, nor psychotic."

Resources were limited, and homes like Alice Goldberger's, places with the nurturance prescribed by Paul Friedman, were an exception rather than the rule. In Israel the Youth Aliya orphans received basic necessities, but their new kibbutznik compatriots, much like those individuals described in *Fragments* who know Binjamin only in a Swiss milieu, didn't know what to do when children played concentration camp. These children may have shown early signs of what the author of *Fragments* described at Notre Dame as "psychopathological and highly complex somatic disorders"; the Youth Aliya files "yield a picture of melancholy and depression, problems in developing personal relationships, loneliness, learning difficulties, nightmares, anxieties, stuttering, bed-wetting, nail biting, mistreatment of kittens, and other signs of anguish," journalist-historian Tom Segev wrote in his history of Israel's relationship to the Holocaust, *The Seventh Million* (1993). Other children found varying levels of material and emotional support, and their new guardians hoped, as Binjamin says his foster parents did, that they would simply leave their traumatic early experiences behind them. "The kibbutzim tried to help the Holocaust children in the only way they knew: they made an effort to erase the children's past," says Segev. According to psychiatrist Judith Kestenberg, co-author of *The Last Witness: The Child Survivor of the Holocaust* (1996), immigrants to America fared little better. "It is disturbing that after the Holocaust, when these children came to the United States and Palestine, no one listened to them," she wrote.

JUDITH KESTENBERG was one of a handful of psychiatrists who took an early interest in child survivors and the long-term effects of their trauma. Their work predates and prefigures *Fragments*. Kestenberg first came to the subject in the early 1960s, when her husband Milton, a lawyer, began helping Holocaust survivors apply for compensation to the Conference on Jewish Material Claims Against Germany. The Kestenbergs found that, beyond the obstacles every applicant to the Claims Conference faced—unsympathetic German-speaking physicians, parsimonious adjudicators, an unforgiving process in which a meaningless typo could forever invalidate a claim—child survivors had additional difficulties. Orphans eligible for educational subsidies found out about them too late. Parents decided to forgo claims for their children, and by the time the children could apply themselves, deadlines had passed. Applications from those too young to remember every detail of their persecution would be rejected for being too vague. Psychiatrists argued that children couldn't be permanently disabled by what they had suffered in the first years of life because they were too young to remember what happened.

The Kestenbergs, on the contrary, believed that being hunted by the Nazis left an "indelible influence" on even the youngest children, and in 1981 they founded the International Study of the Organized Persecution of Children "to expand understanding of effects on the development of those who suffered from child persecution and those who witnessed it as children during the Nazi era." They formed an international network of affiliates to collect testimony and other data. They developed techniques for facilitating the emergence of unspoken childhood memories by focusing on child survivors' sense memories of sounds, textures, and motion.

In Holland, psychiatrist Hans Keilson looked at more than two thousand cases of Jewish children orphaned during the war. In his longitudinal study, published in 1979 as *Sequential Traumatization in Children,* Keilson found a correlation between the age at which children lost their parents and the psychiatric diagnoses made on them a quarter century later. Those who were separated as adolescents tended to be more susceptible to depression triggered by stressful events, while children a few years younger were more likely to show signs of anxiety. Keilson also found that the children with brutal wartime experiences who landed in nurturing postwar environments tended to fare better than those children who had an easier time during the war but a difficult foster situation afterward.

Another pioneer in the child-survivor field was psychologist Sarah Moskovitz. In 1977 Moskovitz met Alice Goldberger at a party. When Goldberger explained about the children she had cared for three decades earlier, Moskovitz wanted to know what had happened to them. Though they had scattered around the world, Goldberger was still a surrogate mother to many of them, and most kept in touch with her.

Moskovitz traveled from her home in Los Angeles to Sacramento, New Orleans, London, Brussels, Cologne, Haifa, and Sydney to interview Goldberger's former wards, publishing her findings in 1983 as *Love Despite Hate: Child Survivors of the Holocaust and Their Adult Lives.* Some, but not all, of the children had been adopted after leaving the group home, Moskovitz reports. Some had easier adult lives than others. Some were professionally successful, others less so. One woman lived in a mental institution. Some were observant Jews, others were secular, and a couple became evangelical Christians. Some were married, others not. Some were more comfortable discussing their childhood than others. About half kept a German shepherd or a Doberman pinscher as a pet.

Moskovitz found that, despite their individual differences, these child survivors shared "a hunger for some link with the past through family connections destroyed or distorted, for traces of themselves buried in childhoods they dare not remember." Their backgrounds were riddled with uncertainty. "Even the clear pain of loss can be clouded by gnawing doubt: is the woman of my earliest memory my mother or someone else?" she noted. At the same time, thanks to the efforts of Alice Goldberger, the traumatized orphans had become compassionate adults and responsible parents. "Despite the persistence of problems and the ashes of the past, what we note in the Lingfield lives are endurance, resilience, and great individual adaptability," Moskovitz concludes, reinforcing the findings of Anna Freud. "Contrary to previously accepted notions, we learn powerfully from these lives that lifelong emotional disability does not automatically follow early trauma, even such devastating, pervasive trauma as experienced here."

As SHE WAS putting together *Love Despite Hate,* Moskovitz began seeking out child survivors in the Los Angeles area. In the early 1980s she began collecting their oral histories for the pioneering video archive founded in New Haven, Connecticut, in 1979 by television producer Laurel Vlock and psychiatrist and survivor Dori Laub. With a social worker, Moskovitz organized a couple of short-term therapy groups for child survivors. When the therapy groups ran their course, Moskovitz brought together about three dozen people at the University of Judaism for the first meeting of the Child Holocaust Survivors Group of Los Angeles.

It was a propitious moment for them to come together. The child survivors who came to the meetings were in their late forties or fifties, more of them women than men. Many had busy careers. If they had raised families, their children were growing up and moving out of the home, and for the first time they had the bittersweet luxury of time to think about the past. Initially, the child survivors didn't gel—they couldn't quite see the purpose of such a group—so Moskovitz, who lost relatives in the Holocaust but grew up in America, invited one of their own to address them.

"The older survivor possesses a memory, a memory of family and tradition," Robert Krell, a hidden child from Holland working as a psychiatrist in Vancouver, told the Los Angeles child survivors. Back in 1983, Krell used some of the same phrases and concepts that would turn up in Binjamin's memoir more than a decade later. "The child or adolescent survivor frequently has only fragments of memory. Some know little of their past, a few not even their first language," Krell told the child survivors. Because of the early age at which they had experienced Nazi oppression, many people, including adult survivors, did not trust them as witnesses, and their stories of wartime were dismissed as unreliable.

Child survivors internalized this distrustful attitude. In his years of working with Holocaust survivors, Krell heard only child survivors "protest that their stories are not particularly important or that they have forgotten too much, or that their experience does not really compare with the 'real' survivors, namely those in concentration camps." Quiet, inconspicuous behavior is an old habit among child survivors, Krell said, since for many it was a survival tool, but it has also become a hindrance—as well as a possible reason for their reluctance to organize. Krell said child survivors have an obligation to share their stories. "We, the child survivors, must remember even the traces of our memories." To remain silent, he said, "is to collaborate in the erasure of our past."

Apparently Krell was persuasive. In time, the Child Holocaust Survivors Group of Los Angeles became a safe space for members to discuss their fragmentary childhood memories, their difficult experiences during and after the war, and their feelings of abandonment, guilt, and loneliness with others who understood what it is like to be, as Krell put it, "a survivor on the margin of survivorhood." They would not regard one another as pariahs and would commit to treating one another with the respect, acceptance, and understanding that spouses, children, and older survivors were unable to muster.

The child-survivor group was self-sustaining, led by an executive committee of six, although Moskovitz remained an adviser and godmother. Rap sessions were held in members' homes. The group threw parties on Jewish holidays. It published a newsletter with announcements and poems. They shared their sadness with one another, but there were also lighter moments, and new friendships blossomed. Many of the child survivors had no living parents or relatives, so they became like family to each other, referring to themselves as "phantom siblings." One of them told the *Los Angeles Times* that joining the child-survivor group "was like finding a bunch of brothers and sisters I should always have had." Their familial behavior also meant some bickering, but if anything this was seen as further evidence of their intimacy.

The Child Holocaust Survivors Group of Los Angeles was the first group of its kind, the beginning of the worldwide support network mentioned at the end of *Fragments*. It became a model for support groups in other North American cities and in Israel, Australia, and Western Europe. (Polish, Czech, and Slovak groups would follow after the fall of the Berlin Wall.) In June 1988 the American groups held their first national child-survivor conference in Lancaster, Pennsylvania. The Los Angeles group had a hand in organizing the intense workshops and art-therapy sessions. There were playful moments, too: a detour for outlet shopping, and an impromptu pajama party. One woman said the coed slumber party was a way of reclaiming "some of the foolishness young teenagers sometimes act out." The hotel owner, himself a Holocaust survivor, didn't seem to mind their antics, and welcomed them back the next year. After that, the conferences moved to larger cities in the United States and abroad.

During the pajama party, several of the women from Los Angeles decided they wanted to organize a bat mitzvah ceremony for themselves. After studying Hebrew for eighteen months, seven child survivors read from the Torah at a North Hollywood synagogue, and their rite of passage into Jewish womanhood was covered by the *Los Angeles Times*. "We missed out on so much when we were children," one was quoted as saying. Becoming a bat mitzvah took on an additional meaning for two of the women, who lived as Catholics during the war. For Gitta Ginsberg, the bat mitzvah represented "a complete divorce from baptism." After the ceremony, Ginsberg threw a party for eighty in her backyard.

Over the years, the Child Holocaust Survivors Group of Los Angeles blossomed. Its mailing list had more than four hundred names. It provided speakers to Los Angeles schools. Members met to converse in their native European languages. The group held an annual "summer bash" and each Passover held a third seder for child survivors and their families.

EVEN AFTER A dozen years, word-of-mouth referrals and occasional press coverage brought new individuals to the group as they each reached a point in their lives where they wanted to talk about their memories or associate with others with similar experiences. Lauren Grabowski first approached the Child Holocaust Survivors Group of Los Angeles in the spring of 1997. At first she seemed extremely shy about joining. In the note she included with her check for the summer bash, she said she "may not have gotten up the courage to attend by the time it arrives."

When she did start showing up for meetings, Grabowski was guarded about revealing her background. Newcomers usually introduce themselves with a brief sketch of where they were born, how they survived the war, when they came to the States, and who in their family survived, but Grabowski didn't get into specifics the first time. She could talk about being in emotional pain, but that was all. Holocaust survivors tend to be cautious about revealing personal data to strangers, and the group allowed members to open up at their own pace. It took a couple of months before she let it be known that she was born around 1941 and came from Poland, had been at Auschwitz-Birkenau, lived in a Krakow orphanage afterward, was smuggled into America in 1950, when she was nine or ten years old, and adopted by a non-Jewish family.

Around the same time she joined the Los Angeles group, Grabowski also began to explore her past on the Internet, where it was easier to share her thoughts while protecting her anonymity. Using the handle "child survivor," Grabowski became a regular participant in the online Holocaust discussion forum run by the Mining Co. The forum was a virtual community open to survivors, students, and other interested parties; messages that referred to "revisionist" web pages or argued the cause of Holocaust denial would be deleted by Jen Rosenberg, who established and monitored the site.

Despite her initial trepidation, Grabowski had a gift for expressing her emotional pain and an optimistic sense of the potential of the child-survivor community. Around Chanukah, she wrote "We Are One," a poem proclaiming the unity and equality of child survivors. "Let us not build walls between each other," she wrote. "None of us are any less or more than our Holocaust siblings." With the help of the Mining Co.'s Jen Rosenberg, Grabowski published "We Are One" on the World Wide Web, summoning up the courage to identify herself as "Laura Grabowski, Child survivor of Auschwitz-Birkenau." Grabowski, who answered to both Lauren and Laura, shared the poem with friends in the Los Angeles support group.

Grabowski also wrote to Binjamin Wilkomirski as she was getting involved with the Los Angeles child-survivor group. She told him how moved she had been by *Fragments,* and that the story reminded her of her own childhood. It wasn't just the emotional content of the book; Grabowski remembered being in some of the very places Binjamin described. Binjamin wrote back. He told Grabowski that he remembered a girl named Laura from Auschwitz-Birkenau who had hair so blond it was almost white. Even though they had not seen each other in more than fifty years, since they were four or five, he seemed to remember her. They discovered that they shared memories of Laura holding hands with a young girl named Ana, who was later killed. All three of them, they said, had been in a small group of young blond children at Auschwitz who were experimented on in the camp by Nazi doctors. Binjamin sent Grabowski several photographs of children at the orphanage on Augustianska Street in Krakow, one of which, he said, showed the two of them together. The more they revealed to each other, the more memories they found they had in common.

Grabowski told some of the Los Angeles child survivors about her connection with Binjamin, and when the group learned that he would be at Notre Dame in April, they invited him to stop in California to reunite with the little girl he remembered from Auschwitz. Since he had so eloquently expressed many of their own feelings and predicaments—the many unknowns of the past, their sense of loss, their anger at the world for disbelieving their stories and ignoring their pain—they asked him to speak to the entire group. He accepted their invitation.

Binjamin Wilkomirski's visit was among the more elaborate and expensive projects the group had ever taken on. The child survivors offered to pick up their share of the cost of Binjamin and Verena's airfare beyond Notre Dame, and though Binjamin at first said they would stay with family (I'm not sure who he meant, but my cousins in Los Angeles say he never asked them), in the end the group put him up for five nights in a hotel. The Los Angeles Museum of the Holocaust, a branch of the local Jewish Federation, signed on as a cosponsor, and its director, Marcia Josephy, helped find other sponsoring organizations. The Swiss consulate kicked in five hundred dollars for refreshments. The Polish consulate took care of the postage for mailing out invitations. Congregation Shaarei Tefila, an Orthodox synagogue on Beverly Boulevard, donated the use of a hall. The child-survivor group and the Federation found someone to lend a grand piano at no charge, but they had to pay a mover to cart it to the synagogue. Binjamin's presentation was to be part lecture and part recital, something he had done before in Europe. This time, however, the clarinetist would be accompanied on the piano by an old friend.

"I was in the Auschwitz-Birkenau barracks with him," Grabowski told the Mining Co. Holocaust forum. "He will be playing a short piece I have composed to remember the little ones we knew who didn't make it in the camps." Jen Rosenberg, who had struck up a friendship with Grabowski, made *Fragments* her site's book of the month, sparking an online conversation. One regular participant, Monika Muggli, described how deeply Binjamin Wilkomirski's story touched her when she read *Fragments* and later watched a television documentary about him. A government employee living outside Munich and born a decade after World War II, Muggli took part in the Mining Co. forum because she felt Germans had a responsibility to acknowledge their forefathers' wrongs. Grabowski wrote privately to Muggli to thank her for sharing her sentiments about Binjamin. "He is like family to me even though I haven't met him yet—at least again," she told Muggli.

Grabowski quickly warmed to Muggli, and soon she was telling her German pen pal about her dead friend Ana, the medical experiments, and their long-term consequences. "We who were young children of the experiments suffer from similar rare blood disorders,"

Grabowski wrote. "Doctors are baffled, for the most part, in know-ing how to treat us." She told Muggli she needed daily injections to stabilize her condition and they did not always help. "So many needles in the camp. And now I give four injections a day for the rest of my life." Binjamin Wilkomirski, who suffered from a similar hematological condition, was trying to get German officials to open the Nazi medical files concerning experiments on children; if they could determine the exact cause of their ailment, perhaps a treatment could be found. Muggli offered to help, supplying Grabowski with the names and addresses of institutions she and Binjamin might want to contact.

Grabowski told Muggli she was pleased to find a German she could trust. "I find it very hard to trust people," she admitted. It was not just Germans; interviewers for the Survivors of the Shoah Visual History Foundation, the video-testimony project funded by Steven Spielberg and based in Los Angeles, approached Grabowski for an oral history, but she was hesitant. "I would freak out," she said. "Maybe sometime. I am so new to all of this that it is still quite overwhelming. And I am anticipating learning so much more from Binjamin when he is here. So I want to wait."

Grabowski felt she had good reason to be cautious, since, even in the communities where she began to feel at home, there were hostile elements. Someone in the Mining Co. Holocaust forum—none other than Australian Michael Mills, who wrote the skeptical review of *Fragments* on Amazon—said that Binjamin Wilkomirski's memoir might be a concoction because of its author's consultation with a psy-chiatrist. Grabowski felt Mills's doubts about Binjamin cast asper-sions on her. She wanted to upbraid Mills but feared it would mean violating Binjamin's privacy, so she asked Muggli to do it.

Grabowski was "exhausted, still a little frightened and very, very angry" at Mills, but his comments struck closer to home. "You see," she told Muggli, "I have met the same kind of questioning by a few of my own child survivor group here in LA."

ABOUT A MONTH before Binjamin Wilkomirski's visit, members of the Child Holocaust Survivors Group of Los Angeles congregated at a member's house to watch a home video of a recent summer bash. The doctor husband of one of the survivors struck up a conversation with the cochairman of the group, Leon Stabinsky. A retired mechanical engineer who as a child was hidden in a Catholic orphanage in Belgium, Stabinsky had been sharing the helm since 1996. He saw the group's potential as an advocacy organization for child survivors, lobbying to get its name added to the Holocaust memorial in Pan Pacific Park, agitating for a congressional bill to reform the Claims Conference, and keeping members informed of the ongoing negotiations with Swiss banks over the withheld assets of Holocaust victims. While he enjoyed the social and political aspects of the Child Holocaust Survivors Group, Stabinsky was less than comfortable with the frequent discussions of members' past victimization and its lingering effects.

At the gathering, Stabinsky listened as the doctor, who was not a survivor, told him he'd heard about *Fragments* and didn't believe Binjamin Wilkomirski could remember his early childhood so vividly. Stabinsky found himself agreeing more or less with the doctor. *Fragments* reminded Stabinsky of an article he had read in *Scientific American*, "Creating False Memories" by Elizabeth Loftus, who had successfully planted childhood memories—pleasant ones of a birthday party with a clown, as well as potentially more traumatic ones, such as those of an overnight stay in a hospital or of getting lost in a shopping mall—in her experiment subjects. "Memories are more easily modified," Loftus wrote, "when the passage of time allows the original memory to fade."

As Stabinsky and the doctor discussed *Fragments* and false memories, Grabowski was nearby with group member John Gordon, who was making many of the arrangements for Binjamin's visit. To hear another child survivor, let alone the group's cochairman, violate the ethos of acceptance that was the foundation of their association was an outrage. It wasn't the first time Stabinsky and Gordon had clashed over Binjamin Wilkomirski. As cochairman, Stabinsky had been in on the planning of the reunion. When Binjamin asked for an honorarium for his presentation, Stabinsky objected to the idea of paying another child survivor to tell the group how children had suffered during the Holocaust. The *Los Angeles Jewish Journal*, the local Federation-sponsored newspaper, was planning a cover story on Binjamin's visit, but Stabinsky didn't want the group to be identified in print with Binjamin, or, for that matter, with Lauren Grabowski, who had made him uneasy ever since Stabinsky's wife first encountered her at a regional meeting. Dorothy Stabinsky had reported back that Grabowski was both extremely secretive and very emotional, and it made her suspicious.

"My heart is already bumping very strongly!" Binjamin wrote to Lauren Grabowski two weeks before his visit. He told her he looks at her picture often. "You still remind me of the little girl I have in my mind since 1944/45!" Then Binjamin told Lauren he had a last-minute illness, and he was worried he wouldn't be able to come to America, but in the end he and Verena got on the plane. "I think God had something to do with Binjamin and me reuniting after 53 years," Grabowski told her friend Monika Muggli. "It is too much of a MIRACLE to think my dream is coming true only by chance."

Binjamin arrived a few days before his presentation. He and Lauren Grabowski rehearsed for their joint performance, and they also spent their time remembering their shared past. He showed her a map of Auschwitz-Birkenau and pointed out the exact location of their barracks and the medical laboratories. He told her which Nazi doctor had "worked" on her, and showed her the doctor's photograph. He told her about the bonfires outside their barracks where children were burned. He told her he had found her name on the list of one of the orphanages. "We spent the afternoon falling apart and crying and holding each other," Grabowski told Muggli. "He keeps talking about how Ana and I never ever let go holding hands."

The reunited pair gave a joint interview to the *Los Angeles Jewish Journal,* although she insisted that she be identified only as Laura, no last name. Laura told the reporter how her adoptive parents in America forbade her to mention Poland or refer to anything Jewish. "Meeting Binjamin has been the dream of my life," she said. "It has been very healing just finding someone who can say, 'I know.'"

Leon Stabinsky was dismayed when he arrived on April 19, 1998, at Congregation Shaarei Tefila. Although he didn't exactly go out of his way to meet Binjamin Wilkomirski, Stabinsky nonetheless felt snubbed when Gordon didn't introduce him to the guest of honor.

Stabinsky was bothered that child survivors had to pay a five-dollar admission fee and that the front row was reserved for "sponsors" who had paid fifty dollars. He didn't know what to say when members of the group complained about the BBC camera crew that was following Binjamin and had shown up at the synagogue.

Some child survivors didn't want to be caught on videotape, and at first Grabowski had not wanted to be filmed either. "I do not trust the media," she said. "They have not proven themselves to be trustworthy to me. They usually are just out for the ratings and that means making everything as sensational as they can. I cannot tolerate my life in the Holocaust being sensationalized." But she had a change of heart. The day before the event, she told Muggli, "I feel as if the BBC is intruding on our special occasion. But Binjie thinks all of this needs to be documented for future instruction. And so we said it was okay." As the event began, organizer John Gordon told the audience that if they didn't want to be filmed, they shouldn't sit in the first few rows.

"I have spent five incredible days with Binjamin and his wife, Verena, and also with Laura," Gordon told the audience. He noted that Binjamin's visit came between Passover, which celebrates the liberation of the Jews from their Egyptian enslavers, and Yom Hashoah, which commemorates Jewish suffering during the Holocaust.

Binjamin, dressed in a white shirt and a black scarf draped like a prayer shawl over his shoulders, helped Grabowski, who walks with a cane, to the piano. They played an arrangement of the Kol Nidre, a prayer not usually heard on Passover or Yom Hashoah but in early fall, at the beginning of the Yom Kippur evening service. As Jews atone for their sins, they ask God to nullify any unfulfilled vows made in the previous year. The Kol Nidre is a formula for releasing individuals from the promises they have made to God; it cannot dissolve the promises they make to one another. Leon Stabinsky was put off by the choice of the Kol Nidre, and he wasn't impressed with the musicianship.

Later the two played Grabowski's composition, "Ode to the Little Ones," which she dedicated to the children who survived the Holocaust and also to the one and a half million who didn't. It was a pastiche of "*Oyfn Pripetshok,*" other tunes with an Eastern European Jewish inflection, and the standard "Try to Remember."

Then Binjamin spoke about his wartime experiences. "These last three or four weeks in Auschwitz-Birkenau," he said, "were for us the most difficult, the most painful of the whole period of the Shoah." They may also be the least well documented. Toward the end of the war, Binjamin says, some children at Auschwitz were not tattooed. "I remember that children had quarreled, and some said it's much better to get a number, and others said it's much better not to have a number," he said. And the handiwork of doctors not under Mengele's supervision—Wehrmacht doctors, for example, and private doctors who had short-term access to the camps—might be written down somewhere, but the records are inaccessible.

In the end, Binjamin said, having records wasn't so important, because traumatized children have an extraordinary ability to remember trauma. He gave a historical example. "In the Middle Ages, in little towns when people wanted to make a contract and nobody in the town could read or write, so it was no possibility to make a written contract, it was the custom in the country to take from both parties the small children—one, two, three, four years old—and they were terribly beaten, beaten almost to death. So they were artificially traumatized, and then they had to learn by heart the text of the contract. And in the documents we have about that custom, it says these children will never forget one single word of the contract, these children are the true witnesses of the contract. And such contracts in medieval Europe had the same weight as a written contract."

Leon Stabinsky kept quiet during the question-and-answer period. After the final musical number he approached Binjamin Wilkomirski and asked where he could find a written reference to this medieval curiosity.

CHARACTER
ASSASSINATION

In the year following his visit to New York, I keep in touch with Binjamin as I do with most of my cousins, which is to say indirectly, through my mother. She sends him our family's good wishes at Chanukah and Passover; he drops her a postcard while on vacation in the mountains. She makes note of advances in leukemia research in case Binjamin's illness should become dangerous again. She talks to Lester, the man whose childhood photograph Binjamin said resembled his son. Lester is happy to hear from her after all these years, but he can't say whether he's a relative or whether his mother was just a good friend of my great-grandmother Anna. With the data she collects from various Wilburs, Mom creates a big family tree on her computer, though she still doesn't know where to put Binjamin.

I think often of Binjamin, whoever he is and wherever he comes from. Invariably, thoughts of Binjamin lead me to another mystery: that of the Wilkomirski relatives who remained in Riga. Most of their names and faces are unknown to me, so I return again and again to the picture of Avram's son, Sima, the long-haired little boy in knee-socks and short pants. He must have been about ten or eleven when the Nazis reached Riga, and by now he'd be old enough to collect Social Security, but I can not see him any bigger or older than he is in the photograph. In my mind he remains a toddling innocent, a boy like Binjamin at the beginning of *Fragments* when he crawls down the stairs and sees his father die. I have no idea what Sima's experience with the Nazis was, though odds are it ended quickly.

For almost three years, doubt was Binjamin's ally. He thrived on doubt; it made his story true and meaningful. With each new translation, speech, article, and documentary, Binjamin Wilkomirski forged new connections with potential relatives, old friends, child survivors, scholars, psychologists, and thousands of readers. The doubts of those who knew Bruno Doessekker from the cafés and concert halls of Zurich remained separate from the doubts of those who couldn't believe the Binjamin Wilkomirski they encountered on the page. Nobody deciphered the well-camouflaged explanation in the afterword, and the suspicions of genealogist Gary Mokotoff, revisionist Michael Mills, concocted-memory opponent Mark Pendergrast, historian Raul Hilberg, and critic Lawrence Langer never came to anything. Nor did mine. As Binjamin's reputation grew, however, it was inevitable that the two kinds of doubt, local and literary, would combine. These vapors synthesized into a volatile substance in the mind of writer Daniel Ganzfried.

Born in Israel to a Swiss Zionist mother and a Hungarian father who survived Auschwitz, Ganzfried grew up with his grandmother in Bern. He moved to Zurich in the early 1980s and lives in the gritty but increasingly gentrified neighborhood behind the main train station, on the other side of the tracks from the tony neighborhood where Binjamin was raised. Before becoming a writer, Ganzfried was an active member of a Trotskyist political party and made his living among the proletariat. He drove taxis and trucks and worked as a printer. After leaving the party behind, he remained a leftist, campaigning for the rights of Kurds, Tamils, and other refugees fleeing their war-torn countries for Switzerland.

Ganzfried did not know the author of *Fragments*, but he read the book when it first came out and found it facile, sentimental, and generally unworthy of attention. At the time it was published, Ganzfried had just published his own book about the Holocaust. *Der Absender* (*The Sender*), a first novel that was based on Ganzfried's father's story but not intended as straight testimony, is in some ways the antithesis of *Fragments*. Where Binjamin Wilkomirski describes a partly successful journey of self-discovery, Ganzfried dramatizes the idea that a survivor's experience of the Holocaust is ultimately unknowable and inexplicable.

Georg, the protagonist of *Der Absender*, works in a Holocaust museum transcribing oral histories. One day he comes across a recording made by a survivor identified only by his tattoo number. As Georg listens to the survivor's story—childhood in Hungary, imprisonment in Auschwitz, refuge in Palestine—it sounds a lot like the life of his estranged father. By studying the sender's recordings and by interviewing his father's relatives and friends, Georg begins to envisage what his father might have lived through, though he can never be sure how closely this image corresponds to his father's experiences. When he next sees his father—a distant, philandering, working-class guy, nothing like the innocent hero of *Fragments*— Georg tries to see whether this father's tattoo matches the number belonging to the audiotaped survivor. He never manages to glimpse the tattoo, so he can know his father's experiences only indirectly, through what he has gleaned from other sources.

In *Der Absender*, which is several times longer than *Fragments*, Ganzfried juggles several narrative threads, jumping back and forth between Georg's investigations of his father, their face-to-face meeting, and the first-person account of someone who may or may not be Georg's father. Ganzfried drew critical praise for his independent and unsentimental style, but readers differed on whether the difficult novel had fulfilled all of his aesthetic goals. *Der Absender* sold respectably enough for a literary debut, but neither critical reception nor commercial interest marked it as a breakout success. Ganzfried thought American publishers might be interested since the climactic father-son scene unfolds atop the Empire State Building, but nobody offered to bring out a translation.

On his book tour, Daniel Ganzfried traveled some of the same circuit as Binjamin Wilkomirski, but they never met. Their orbits did not collide until Pro Helvetia, the government-funded Arts Council of Switzerland, tried to do both men a good turn. Pro Helvetia puts out a semiannual journal called *Passages,* and the theme of their autumn 1998 issue was multitalented Swiss artists. Interview subjects included Franco Ambrosetti, an industrialist who moonlights as a flügelhorn-playing jazzman; Ulrich Müller, a gynecologist who creates computer-generated poetry; Stefan Hübscher, a farmer and chainsaw-wielding sculptor; and Binjamin Wilkomirski, clarinetist turned Holocaust author. *Passages* asked critic Klara Obermüller, who had championed *Fragments* in the *Weltwoche* and for the Zurich literary prize, to write about Binjamin. When she declined, she recommended Ganzfried.

In addition to passing along the assignment, Ganzfried says, Obermüller was the first to share with him the rumors that Binjamin Wilkomirski had invented his Holocaust experiences. Ganzfried's editor, Michael Guggenheimer, also had his doubts about Binjamin. When Guggenheimer, the son of German Jews, attended a lecture in Amlikon, the farmhouse was filled with Judaica, more than you would find in most synagogues. At the lecture, Guggenheimer asked Elitsur Bernstein, whom he knew from Jewish circles, whether Binjamin spoke Hebrew. "Not at all," Bernstein told him.

The *Passages* assignment seemed to pay well, and Ganzfried accepted it with the understanding that he could look into the rumors about Binjamin's authenticity. For *Passages*, however, that was never the point. "We asked Ganzfried to write about the musician writing books," Guggenheimer said. "We told him, if you discover that he's more of a novelist, we'll mention it. But we don't want it at the center of the article."

As Ganzfried delved further, he found documentation of Binjamin's legal identity and talked to people who remembered him from early childhood, and Ganzfried couldn't see putting his findings anywhere but at the center. This wasn't a case of self-aggrandizing embellishment here and there; Binjamin's entire Holocaust past seemed to be a fantasy. *Fragments* never says exactly when Binjamin arrived in Switzerland, but it implies that he lived in Krakow for some time; the Swiss documentary *The Good Life Is Only a Trap* (1997), with which Binjamin cooperated, says he arrived in 1948. School records, however, show a Bruno Doessekker enrolled in the spring of 1947, and a photograph from the summer of 1946 has young Bruno standing before the Doessekker home in Zürichberg. Old friends and lovers told Ganzfried that Bruno spoke perfect Swiss German when he arrived at the Doessekker home; that he was uncircumcised; that, contrary to Binjamin's phobic reaction to the Alpine lift in *Fragments,* Bruno was an accomplished skier. Even in his school years, Ganzfried heard, he had a penchant for tall tales.

Binjamin and several of his friends begged Ganzfried to abandon his journalistic investigation because it was endangering the memoirist's already poor health. Binjamin's lawyer also tried to block Ganzfried, but he persisted in his investigation, which was becoming more time-consuming than anyone anticipated, not to mention more newsworthy. Since *Passages* is more a forum for international public relations than for breaking stories, the *Weltwoche,* the newspaper that had run Obermüller's rave review, signed on to help fund Ganzfried and run its own version of his piece. *Passages* accepted and edited Ganzfried's report, but at the last moment the journal informed Ganzfried they had decided against running his article. As he later told a reporter, Michael Guggenheimer felt Ganzfried's work was "a character assassination."

"The Borrowed Holocaust Biography" ran in the August 27, 1998, number of the *Weltwoche.* "Almost no one grows up in a country like Switzerland," Ganzfried writes, "without leaving a trail along the way from which one can, more or less conclusively, reconstruct his life," Ganzfried wrote. He provided a thumbnail sketch of the biography of the author of *Fragments,* one totally at odds with Binjamin's testimony:

On February 12, 1941, Yvonne Berthe Grosjean gave birth to an illegitimate child in Biel. Name: Bruno Grosjean. Hometown: Saules bei Tavannes, Canton Bern. Yvonne Grosjean's brother wanted to take care of the child, but could not prevent Bruno from being placed temporarily in a children's home in Adelboden or from being given up in 1945 for adoption.

Dr. and Mrs. Doessekker, a childless couple from Zurich Fluntern, took him in, at first as a foster child. Before his enrollment in the Fluntern elementary school on April 22, 1947, an application for a name change was submitted to the Bern cantonal authorities. After its approval, Bruno was no longer called Grosjean but rather Doessekker, like his foster parents. Bruno Doessekker's biological father, who later had other children, paid child support until the adoption was finalized in 1957. Yvonne Grosjean later married Walter Max Rohr, resident of Hunzenschwil, Aargau, and died in Bern in 1981, shortly after her husband. Her ashes were buried in the Bremgarten cemetery there.

Bruno Doessekker completed his secondary school education at the Zurich Free Gymnasium, became a musician and instrument maker and the father of three children. His biological mother had no other children, so her estate went to him, and he seems to have accepted the small inheritance. In 1985 his adoptive parents died. Since then, Bruno Doessekker has lived in comfort.

Though Binjamin was by all accounts an avid archivist, he was not interested in the names and dates and photographs Ganzfried uncovered. During an interview at Amlikon, Binjamin gave an elaborate explanation of the whole Grosjean story, which Ganzfried saw as a far-fetched conspiracy theory: "In a plot concocted by anti-Semitic small-town magistrates, cold-hearted foster parents and corrupt authorities, the child's Jewish origins were supposedly erased and replaced with a false identity, while the growing boy's mouth and soul were shut with the threat of punishment."

Ganzfried was not only the first to explicate the afterword of *Fragments* and identify its author as Bruno Doessekker, but he was also the first critic to pan the book. "Wilkomirski-alias-Doessekker is no writer. His dispatch has no place in the realm of literature," he wrote. Ganzfried is critical of "the bad taste that sets in somewhere between the coarseness of the accounts and the greeting-card pathos of the language," of a book written "as though someone sat down and tried to describe things he saw in a poorly captioned, horrifying book of pictures with which he had no personal connection."

"A witness bears a social responsibility," Ganzfried wrote, particularly in connection with the concentration camps, "which the Nazis constructed in such a way that kept people from believing in their existence." In playing Binjamin Wilkomirski for school groups, Ganzfried argues, the author of *Fragments* made those children more susceptible to the arguments of Holocaust deniers.

Some of Ganzfried's harshest words, however, were reserved not for Wilkomirski-alias-Doessekker but for his editors at Suhrkamp, his literary agent, the reviewers who ushered *Fragments* into the realm of literature, the psychoanalysts who "reverted to blind faith rather than asking hard questions" about his cockamamy therapies, and the two taxpayer-funded Swiss documentaries "which take Binjamin Wilkomirski as their subject without mentioning a single fact about the life of Bruno Doessekker." These people should have known better. The Holocaust may be unknowable, but that doesn't mean one shouldn't demand all information available in the pursuit of knowledge. But, faced with the story of Binjamin Wilkomirski, "they would lose not only the freedom to ask questions but the courage of their convictions. When we are no longer able to make judgments, we can no longer insist on quality, as is shown by the unanimous excessive praise for Wilkomirski's work and for other simply bad products of what passes for current literature and art."

IN MID-SEPTEMBER, about two weeks after Ganzfried's tirade appeared in the *Weltwoche* and almost a year after Binjamin's visit with the Wilburs, Seth Lipsky, the founder and editor of the English-language *Forward*, calls me into his office. A few months earlier, I had taken a job as arts editor of the *Forward*, a weekly newspaper spun off from the legendary Yiddish daily. Lipsky passes along a rumor he'd heard about Binjamin only pretending to be a Holocaust survivor. The story hadn't yet surfaced in the American press.

If I hadn't known Binjamin, it would have been a good scoop, but this was something more. I had never expected a definitive answer to the identity of the author of *Fragments*; that Binjamin might be a non-Jew untouched by the Holocaust floored me. I feel a surge of emotion as I assimilate the idea. I don't know what to think, and I feel many things at once. I would feel proud of myself if the rumor turns out to be true, since it would confirm my suspicions that the author of *Fragments* was probably not Binjamin Wilkomirski, but this is outweighed by my distress. I had never imagined the degree to which our visitor might *not* be Binjamin Wilkomirski, that the story which was the fruit of his archival and psychological probing might not have had any seed of truth at its center, that he had successfully grafted such a horrible past onto a life that had nothing to do with it. I feel terrible for Binjamin and what he must be going through, especially if he is a Holocaust survivor—it is a cruel historical irony that deniers would single out someone like him, someone unable to document his origins—and yet I already feel betrayed by him for misleading me. I regret that I held back from probing his story in more depth when we met face-to-face, resisted out of respect for his privacy asking him everything I wanted to know when I had the chance, but I still feel bound by my decision a year earlier to regard the author of *Fragments*, whoever he may be, as family.

Mostly, however, I am confused, since what I ought to be feeling depends on the truth. The easiest way to dispel my confusion would seem to be to ask Binjamin what's going on. So, before looking for the article or finding out what's in it, I call the farmhouse in Amlikon.

Verena answers the phone. Her voice sounds heavy and wary, but this dissipates a little when she learns it is someone who knows Binjamin.

I tell Verena I heard someone attacked Binjamin in the press, and that I want to speak to him.

Binjamin's not up to taking calls. "He's in a very, very bad condition," she says. "They are saying that it's all fiction." It started with the *Weltwoche*, but now it is spreading through the German-language press. "One reporter came here and he was very, very unfriendly. Binjamin didn't speak to him too much."

Cushioning my inquiry with a layer of cousinly concern, I press Verena for details, but she does not want to get too specific about the case being made against him. I ask Verena to send Binjamin my best wishes. I tell her I will call again soon, and that I hope he will feel well enough by then to talk to me.

If neither Binjamin nor Verena can tell me what is going on, perhaps the man accusing him of inventing his story can. When I reach

Daniel Ganzfried at his apartment in Zurich, he is friendly and calm as he tells me a little about his background and his novel. Then he begins to talk about the author of *Fragments*.

"I really have no pity for him. In the early stages, he could have admitted he had written a novel, but he went on with this lying. It's really disgusting." The book also disgusted Ganzfried. "It dealt with cruelty on an almost pornographic level." It is a story, he says, "on the level of *Heidi*."

I have always found it difficult when speaking a foreign language to be subtle, and perhaps it was this way for Ganzfried, too. But as he explains how he got the assignment from *Passages*, about the photographs from 1946, about the women who slept with the uncircumcised Bruno Doessekker, about the lecture at which Binjamin claimed he wasn't adopted, about the large inheritance he received from the Doessekkers and the smaller one from Yvonne Grosjean, about the threatening letters from Binjamin's lawyer, I realize Ganzfried is quite capable of expressing himself.

"When I met him personally, I was pretty damn sure something was wrong," says Ganzfried, who spent seven hours with the author of *Fragments* at Amlikon. "He cried a lot, but a lot of artificial tears. He didn't move his belly."

I find this observation much less persuasive than the rest of what Ganzfried has told me. Who is to say how someone should cry? Is Ganzfried, despite all his talk of research, simply trusting his own gut and distrusting Binjamin's? Instead of asking these questions, I press Ganzfried for more details, and he is cooperative, to a point. He withholds the name of the man he says is Bruno's biological father—"I'm not allowed to say, because there are other children alive," he says—and can't show me parts of the paper trail because maybe he wasn't supposed to see them. "There are ways to find out officially and openly," Ganzfried says. "They just take a little time."

I ask Ganzfried if he has considered he might be wrong. Holocaust denial is a crime in some countries, and under Swiss law he could conceivably be subject to a fine or even jail time if he is mistaken about Binjamin.

Ganzfried insists that he's right, but for the sake of argument, he is willing to entertain the possibility. "Even if I am a real criminal and a real asshole—maybe the publisher is paying me to stir up a scandal—even if it would be so, all of the questions are really legitimate," he says.

I ask Ganzfried whether Binjamin has responded to his article; I explain that I had spoken to his wife, who said Binjamin was not up to coming to the telephone.

First of all, Ganzfried says, Verena is not his wife.

This is too much. Does Ganzfried hate Binjamin so much that he thinks everything is a lie? Or is Ganzfried telling the truth, and if so, why would Binjamin deceive people about something that had nothing to do with his childhood?

Next Ganzfried explains that Binjamin did answer his charges. "He responded in another newspaper, the *Tages-Anzeiger*. This was on the Monday after my article came out. He said, 'You don't have to believe anything.'"

AT LEAST ON this last count, Ganzfried was telling the truth. On Monday, August 31, 1998, the Zurich *Tages-Anzeiger* ran an interview with Binjamin. The headline was a quote from the interview: "NIEMAND MUSS MIR GLAUBEN SCHENKEN"—"NOBODY HAS TO BELIEVE ME." Binjamin takes the attitude that Ganzfried's findings are old news, just another stumbling block in his ongoing struggle to escape the identity imposed upon him. "As any reader can gather from the afterword to my book," he tells the *Tages-Anzeiger,* "my papers do not agree with my memories. And so I have to rely on these memories to counter a seamless Swiss identity. That was clear from the beginning. These accusations are nothing new." They were "fully explored," he says, by Klara Obermüller in the *Weltwoche* (which mentioned neither the Doessekkers nor Yvonne Grosjean by name) as well as at public receptions for the book.

Binjamin denies being Bruno Grosjean, Yvonne's illegitimate son. "I know, however, that the piece of paper with the legal seal on it says otherwise. And nothing can shake this off." When asked to explain the discrepancy between his legal identity and his remembered past, Binjamin says, "For that I have no really good answer. Naturally I have strong hypotheses as to how it all could have happened. But I don't want to just toss those off, because they don't amount to a certainty." All the same, he goes on to describe cases during the postwar child-refugee crisis in Europe in which children were given false papers. They had documents contradicting their memories, and so does he.

Binjamin doesn't bother to rebut the other foundations of Ganzfried's case, the photographs he found or the old friends who remember things very differently. Apparently none of this can convince him that he is Bruno Grosjean. "I am not prepared to deny my memories because of external pressure," he says. And just as he doesn't have to listen to anyone else, nobody has to believe him either. "The reader was always free to conceive of my book either as literature or as a personal document," he says.

WITH THESE words, the disconsolate Binjamin Wilkomirski stopped giving interviews and retreated from public view. He was wounded, but very much alive, much to the chagrin of Daniel Ganzfried. It wasn't that Ganzfried meant any harm to Bruno Doessekker. In fact, Ganzfried worried as he was working that Doessekker might kill himself over the *Weltwoche* article. Ganzfried asked a psychiatrist friend whether Bruno could kill himself if his true identity were made public, and the psychiatrist said the possibility couldn't be ruled out. However, Ganzfried thought that deflating Doessekker's delusion could only help him. The sooner he faced his real past, the better.

Ganzfried did intend to take out Binjamin Wilkomirski, however. His article was meant as a character assassination, although perhaps not in the reputation-destroying sense Michael Guggenheimer of *Passages* had in mind. Ganzfried's intent was to kill off a fictional personage, to banish Binjamin from serious history and relegate him to cheap fantasy. It wasn't just Binjamin Wilkomirski Ganzfried wanted to destroy with his polemic, it was the idea Binjamin seemed to represent, the one-dimensional notion of the Holocaust survivor as victim. Binjamin Wilkomirski "spares us the task of thinking and the frightening experience of the failure of our human comprehension when it faces the fact of Auschwitz," Ganzfried wrote. Doessekker was not the only one to borrow Binjamin Wilkomirski's story; readers did, too: "Sympathizing without thinking, we find in a victim the hero with whom we can stand shoulder to shoulder on the side of morality."

Had his attempted character assassination been successful, Ganzfried might have started a cultural conversation about the image of survivors, but he didn't even meet his primary objective. Ganzfried's acerbic tone certainly didn't help, but I don't know that being less contentious would have made him any more persuasive. It may just be that Binjamin Wilkomirski could not be felled with one shot. Ganzfried took aim at an apparition, but he also hit the man who called himself Binjamin Wilkomirski, the man known only as Wilkomirski, not Grosjean or Doessekker, to a sympathetic public that, whether out of generosity or pity or the thoughtlessness Ganzfried accused them of, had wholeheartedly embraced his uncertain, undocumentable identity. For those who had accepted Binjamin without any documentation affirming his existence, their attachment could not be so easily undone by documents contradicting it. The author of *Fragments* remained tethered to his Holocaust memories, and many of the people who witnessed him bearing witness would not let Binjamin Wilkomirski go easily.

Nevertheless, Ganzfried tried to put Binjamin to rest again a week later. His follow-up article of September 3 restated the case against Binjamin in more detail. This time the *Weltwoche* printed the photograph of Bruno at the Doessekker home in 1946—if people see it, maybe they will no longer believe him—and a copy of the threatening letter from Binjamin's lawyer ("I hereby inform you my client does not permit the use of the name of Ms. Grosjean and/or Mr. and Mrs. Doessekker in connection with his name and/or his book and/or his work . . ."). Ganzfried named the archives and child-welfare offices in Biel and Zurich which held information on Bruno's past. He said the account of Bruno's early childhood had been corroborated by Yvonne Grosjean's brother, who was still alive and whose name and address were on file with his editor at the *Weltwoche*.

"No one has explicitly cast doubt on our review's factual findings, least of all Wilkomirski himself," Ganzfried wrote. Binjamin's

BRUNO (CENTER) WITH MARTHA DOESSEKKER (RIGHT) AT THE
DOESSEKKER HOME, ZURICH, 1946.

response—that nobody had to believe him—deviated from his earlier line; before, he "never allowed the slightest doubt as to whether
he experienced what he described."

Again, Ganzfried blamed "the almost total lack of civil courage
in the culture industry, which has contributed to a situation in which
Auschwitz has once again degenerated into a question of faith. . . .
There are those who doubt the book's authenticity when speaking
off the record, but they are all afraid of doing the dirty work and
having their reputations besmirched," said Ganzfried. "And so the
book remains a masterpiece."

AT THE VERY least, the book remains in circulation. Suhrkamp press
director Heide Grasnick tells me that if *Fragments* turned out to be
a fiction, "for the respect of the Jewish people we would have to
withdraw the book. Or to make a foreword or afterword explaining

it correctly." However, Grasnick says, "There are no documents at the moment that can prove that Wilkomirski is mistaken. Suhrkamp will never believe that he is a person who fooled the world."

Anyway, Suhrkamp knew about the document problem all along, says Grasnick. She faxes me a statement publisher Siegfried Unseld released on September 7. Before publishing *Fragments,* Suhrkamp asked Yad Vashem, the Holocaust memorial and research center in Jerusalem, to confirm that they had "accepted Binjamin Wilkomirski's life story and his application for a search for his parents without objection." Unseld cited various experts, including Lea Balint, "who analyzed and evaluated Binjamin Wilkomirski's story at Yad Vashem. Frau Dr. Balint regarded the life story of Binjamin Wilkomirski and his remembered identity as credible. She confirmed this explicitly on March 12, 1995, and once again a few days ago."

The contradiction between the author's documents and his memories, Unseld said in his statement, "is obvious and unarguable, but for 'children without identity' after the Shoah, it is hardly unique." Suhrkamp felt a responsibility to call the reader's attention to the discrepancy between the author's papers and his memories, which they did in the afterword, but "it is not the task of the publishing house to resolve this contradiction."

Nevertheless, someone at Suhrkamp got in touch with Holocaust historian Raul Hilberg in Vermont to ask him to read *Fragments* and tell them whether it could be a true story.

So did I. "The only problem I had is that there are scenes that could not have happened," Hilberg tells me. To begin with, he says, it is improbable that Binjamin escaped from the Riga ghetto as he describes. Binjamin remembers being invited to rejoin his brothers at Majdanek, yet Hilberg says German authorities referred to the camp as "Lublin." Like Gary Mokotoff, Hilberg points out that Binjamin would never have been sent from Majdanek to Auschwitz. The only documented transports from Majdanek to Auschwitz he knows of carried people "more in the age group twenty to thirty-five; mostly men, a few women. That was a time—August 1943—when there was a shortage of labor in Auschwitz. There were no little kids in that transfer." Like Michael Mills, Hilberg wonders about the tank near the Polish farmhouse. "There was no battle on Polish soil in 1943," he says. And, in an echo of Mark Pendergrast's letter, Hilberg says, "If some guy grabbed him by the feet and banged him against the wall, he'd be dead."

"To disprove something is very difficult," Hilberg says. "As always, you cannot step forward and say it definitely did not happen. It's highly unlikely, but conceivable." Had Ganzfried not found information placing the author of *Fragments* in Switzerland during the war, Hilberg would never have said anything.

Hilberg has little use for Holocaust novels—for him, they are nothing more than the price our society pays for freedom of expression—but *Fragments* crossed a line. "There are all kinds of people in the world, they'll do anything to sell a book. I'm not tearing my hair out because there are such people. I'm tearing my hair out because there are editors that take these things."

Hilberg's disdain for *Fragments* was not shared by all Holocaust scholars, least of all his onetime seatmate, literary critic Lawrence Langer. "I still think that the book is a very compelling work of literature," Langer tells me a few hours after I speak to Hilberg. "The book is outstanding anyway. One has to separate the quality of the work from the intentions of the author. What puzzles me is why he didn't call it fiction. Secondly, whoever wrote this is a talented writer. Why haven't we heard of him before?"

Another voice in favor of the book's literary merits was that of Deborah Lipstadt, a professor of Jewish studies and Holocaust studies at Emory University. Lipstadt is the author of *Denying the Holocaust* (1993), which catalogs and debunks the campaign to discredit Anne Frank's diary and other fringe efforts to diminish the historical record of the Nazi destruction of European Jewry. She also knew the author of *Fragments,* having spent a day with him when he came to Atlanta on his Holocaust Museum speaking tour.

"I think it's a very powerful work of literature," says Lipstadt, who assigned *Fragments* in one of her classes. "Nobody is saying the Nazis did this to little children based on Binjamin's story." The memories of survivors should not be the only source of information about the Holocaust; one has to "triangulate," to rely on external documentation to support them. Nevertheless, memoirs—and *Fragments* in particular—are useful because they personalize the story of the Holocaust for students.

If *Fragments* turns out to be a counterfeit memoir, adds Lipstadt, it "might complicate matters somewhat, but it's still powerful. If he had told the same story in terrible prose, it wouldn't have been mesmerizing."

I call Amlikon once more, hoping that Binjamin is up to talking this time. Verena answers the phone. I tell her I need to speak to Binjamin, since I am publishing an article and my deadline is fast approaching.

"He's absolutely down, he's absolutely pushed back to the time from in the camps," Verena tells me. He didn't want to defend himself in the *Tages-Anzeiger*, and they took his words out of context, so for now Binjamin isn't giving any more interviews. She then outlines a defense echoing Binjamin's afterword and his statements to the *Tages-Anzeiger*. "He found out about these papers thirty years ago, but they have nothing to do with him," she tells me. When I ask about the photograph of Binjamin with the Doessekkers from 1946, she tells me that he has never been sure of his exact arrival in Switzerland, that "he has said it can be at the end of '46, '47, or '48."

I asked Verena whether Binjamin had really accepted an inheritance from Yvonne Grosjean, but she would not address any more specific points. Lea Balint was on her way to Switzerland; she would clear up everything. And when he is ready, Binjamin will respond to the charges himself. "He has to come up again and then he will say many things," she said. "We will overcome."

"You have to know that the publisher is standing behind him," Verena tells me. "All the music school teachers stand absolutely behind him." There have been many telephone calls offering Binjamin support. "The only ugly ones have been the journalists. It's not possible to speak to them."

I am tempted to remind her she is speaking to one, but I stifle the impulse.

"Don't write anything now," Verena begs me. "You know nothing up to now."

I wish I could wait until Binjamin is better. I tell her it might be different if this were just between us, but the question of his identity is already a public matter. I ask Verena to tell Binjamin that I hope he recovers quickly and will talk to me soon.

"NOBODY HAS TO BELIEVE ME." I can see why, after Ganzfried's challenge, Binjamin might step back from his place at the vanguard of the children without identity into the sanctuary of his individual consciousness, but it is another thing entirely for him to say that others don't have to believe him, that *Fragments* could be fiction or autobiography, whichever you prefer. I never felt I had a choice when I read it—and certainly not when I heard him bear witness to his Holocaust experiences. His very presence as a Holocaust sur-vivor was supposed to offer living proof of what he had seen and suffered during the war.

It is as if there are two conversations going on. Those who insist on the documentary evidence and draw on their knowledge of Euro-pean history cannot believe Binjamin's story. Everyone who accepts him at his word, on the other hand, acts as if this is no big deal. "In my wider knowledge, this kind of dispute is not at all unusual in these traumatic personal histories," the translator and editor of the American edition of *Fragments*, Carol Janeway, tells me. "This seems to me to be another round in another argument that we're quite familiar with." If Janeway isn't putting Binjamin's case in the general context of Holocaust denial and instead means the argument specif-ically over Binjamin's identity, it is new to me. Binjamin's publishers may have known all about the Grosjeans and the Doessekkers and the adoption and the inheritance, but his readers did not.

I am still trying to give Binjamin the benefit of the doubt, though his quixotic interview with the *Tages-Anzeiger* makes it harder. Be-cause of his silence, I again try to fill in whatever blanks he has left, to put myself in his shoes and puzzle it through, to try and complete his story. When Philip Roth alerted Primo Levi to a contradiction in his description of his emotional state in Auschwitz, the Italian writer said, "Please grant me the right of inconsistency." Binjamin's incon-sistencies have to do with remembered facts, not emotions, but if I am at all still willing to believe him, he seems entitled to an extralarge helping of inconsistency. Some of his memories may be unreliable— after all, he's human—but his story must have some kernel of truth to it; even a confirmed masochist would never invent such a life for himself. I am able to invent plausible explanations for some of the discrepancies between his version of history and Ganzfried's. As to why he might be uncircumcised, for example, I can imagine that a European Jewish family on the eve of World War II might decide not to circumcise their son in an attempt to save him. It still seems possible to me that he is somehow a Jewish child survivor, though not a Wilkomirski from Riga. Who knows, maybe something did happen to this Bruno Grosjean and Binjamin—or whatever his original name is—was given his papers and then handed over to the Doessekkers, and everyone who knew maintained a conspiracy of silence.

Yet there were some questions I could not answer. How could other people remember the beginning of his life in Switzerland so differently? Were they breaking from the conspiracy that saved him, or were they part of a conspiracy against him? Hardest of all to resolve was the matter of how he could have accepted an inheritance from Yvonne Grosjean in 1981. If he knew he was not her biological son, if he was so keen on discovering his real identity, what was he doing accepting her estate? Especially if he came from such a well-off adoptive family, what could it mean that he took the comparatively small sum Yvonne Grosjean left behind, if not that he was claiming his birthright? Then again, I could see how a child survivor deprived of his birthright might feel justified in laying claim to an inheritance that was his only technically.

In short, I didn't know what to think, or whom to trust: the sequestered Binjamin, who in releasing me from having to believe him made me want to protect him, or the seemingly invidious Daniel Ganzfried, whose outlandish assertions had all checked out so far. But if I had been too quick to believe Binjamin, I didn't want to be too quick to believe Ganzfried.

In the end, I left my story on Binjamin's identity crisis open-ended. "If Mr. Ganzfried's allegations fall apart, this may be the story of a Salieri trying to sabotage a Mozart," I wrote at the conclusion of my report in the *Forward*. "If not, Mr. Wilkomirski's greatest work

of fiction may not be *Fragments* but his own construction of himself." This was not just a journalistic feint; I didn't have enough information to know who was right.

As I WAS reporting the story, I did not tell my family what
was going on. While I was looking into the question of Binjamin's
authenticity, I wondered how my cousins who had never been skeptical of Binjamin would take the news that he might be an impostor.
I hadn't put my full confidence in him as many other Wilburs had.
I hadn't kept in touch as my mother had since he went home to
Switzerland. They were far more invested in his story, or so it
seemed at the time.

Finally, after filing my story, I called my mother to fill her in on
Ganzfried's charges and Binjamin's anguish. A few hours later, she
sent a fax to Amlikon.

> Dear Binjamin and Verena,
>
>   Blake mentioned that he spoke to you today, and I felt guilty
> because I had been meaning to write to you for some time, but
> laziness prevailed. He said you sent your regards to me, and
> Robert and I send our warm regards to you.
>
>   We hope you are both in good health. I know that Binjamin
> has been having some health problems, and I hope they are
> under control. (If not, some new treatments have emerged in
> the last six months, and you may want to inquire more about
> them. I know of several people who are undergoing treatments
> that were not available in past years.) . . .

In her note, she treats his current crisis as a medical emergency
related to his leukemia. She asks no questions about Daniel Ganzfried or Bruno Grosjean. There are no demands that Cousin Binjamin explain himself.

AUSCHWITZ, SWITZERLAND

On September 16, two weeks after his interview with the *Tages-Anzeiger*, the author of *Fragments* broke his public silence. In a statement released on Suhrkamp letterhead, Binjamin stood by his story. This time, instead of repeating his invitation to interpret his memoir as fiction, he appealed for help in affirming its authenticity to a panel of Holocaust historians. "I ask the Bergier commission, which is investigating the relationship of Switzerland to the Jews in the 1940s, to explore my early years in the overall context of the history of refugee children and the Gypsies in Switzerland," Binjamin said. To help the commission members find the truth, he offered them exclusive and unfettered access to his own files and those of the Bureau of Children Without Identity in Lea Balint's Jerusalem basement.

At first glance, his plea for the Bergier commission to step into the dispute over his origins just as the Netherlands State Institute for War Documentation authenticated Anne Frank's diary might seem presumptuous. After all, the commission, headed by Swiss historian Jean-François Bergier and known formally as the Independent Commission of Experts: Switzerland–Second World War, was in the middle of a five-year audit of the nation's diplomatic, financial, commercial, and cultural relationships with the Nazi regime. The nine supervising historians included leading Swiss scholars like Jacques Picard, author of *Switzerland and the Jews: 1933–1945* (1994), and foreign Holocaust specialists Sybil Milton, Wladyslaw Bartoszewski, and Saul Friedländer. The Swiss parliament earmarked 22 million francs ($15 million) to support the commission's research and guaranteed them unprecedented access to primary sources, enjoining government offices, banks, insurance companies, and other institutions from destroying any documents that could possibly shed light on the war years.

However, just as Binjamin Wilkomirski's fragmentary account of the Holocaust seemed to typify the remembered experience of the young child survivor, his postwar struggles with a society in deep historical denial stood for the troubled history of Swiss national attitudes toward World War II. Half a century later, the prevailing myth of Switzerland as an impregnable oasis of benign impartiality and humanitarianism was challenged by an uglier picture of a pragmatic, selfish enclave eager to appease the Axis powers that surrounded it, of a nation less contemptuous of the Nazis than of the people the Nazis were hunting. Swiss Jews and left-leaning intellectuals have long held a cynical view of their country's wartime activities, but the proud, conservative establishment held fast to the idea that the Swiss did as much as they could for refugees and that their military might kept the Nazis at bay. Since the government established the Bergier commission to steer Switzerland through an identity crisis that was proving as difficult for the country to weather as Ganzfried's challenge was for the author of *Fragments,* it may have been the perfect place for him to turn.

THE THREE YEARS during which *Fragments* enjoyed unquestioned success coincided with a prolonged and wrenching debate over the Swiss national image. On May 7, 1995, a few months before the book's release, Swiss president Kaspar Villiger apologized for his country's complicity in the Nazi campaign against Jews. "It is for me beyond doubt that we burdened ourselves with guilt with our policies against the persecuted Jews," Villiger said in a speech marking the fiftieth anniversary of V-E Day. "The fear of Germany, the anxiety over foreign inundation through mass immigration, and the concern over providing political momentum to the anti-Semitism already existing in this country outweighed our tradition of asylum and our humanitarian ideals." Never before had a member of the Federal Council, the seven-member executive authority of Switzerland, expressed regret for his predecessors' decisions during the war.

In particular, Villiger apologized for the Federal Council's part in bringing about the J stamp. In the fall of 1938, after months of diplomatic negotiations, Nazi Germany and Switzerland signed an accord requiring all non-Aryans holding German or Austrian passports to have a red J stamped in their passports. Individuals with J-stamped passports would receive Swiss visas only if they could prove they would be returning to Germany or if they were already carrying an entry visa to a third country. The J stamp meant that, like Nazi Germany, Switzerland recognized the racial categories established by the Nuremberg Laws and regarded non-Aryans as different from other German citizens.

Swiss adoption of the J stamp reflected a xenophobia that had been brewing at least since the end of World War I. Despite its reputation as a haven for political refugees and a popular destination for foreign guest workers, Switzerland began to express a concern that *Überfremdung,* or an excessive foreign presence, would undermine the unique character of Swiss society. This fear increased even as the proportion of the Swiss population holding foreign citizenship declined from 16 percent in 1914 to 5.2 percent in 1941. *Überfremdung* manifested itself less when it came to Western Europeans, who were thought to be easily assimilable. It largely took the form of an antipathy toward Bolsheviks, intellectuals, Gypsies, and Jews, particularly those from Eastern Europe. Swiss leaders spoke of the creeping danger of the *Verjudung,* or "Jewification," of their country.

If Swiss xenophobia in the interwar period did not correspond to the size of its foreign population, the anti-Semitic fear was even more out of proportion. Fewer than 5 percent of resident aliens were Jews, and Jews had never made up more 0.6 percent of the overall population of the Swiss confederation. Then again, for a liberal democracy designed to protect minority rights, Switzerland had never been particularly welcoming to Jews. Well into the nineteenth century, twenty-one of twenty-two Swiss cantons barred Jewish inhabitants. Only two towns, Endigen and Lengnau in the north-central canton of Aargau, welcomed Jews, and those towns imposed personal and professional restrictions on their Jewish citizens. Jews were excluded from certain commercial transactions, their marriages had to be approved by civil authorities, and Jewish paupers were considered to be the financial responsibility of the Jewish community and not of the local government. By the 1848 revolution, enforcement of the ban against Jewish settlement had weakened, and Jews could be found in Basel and other cities. In 1866, economic pressure from the United States and European governments protesting the treatment of their Jewish citizens who visited Switzerland led to its repeal.

Once Jews won the right to settle where they wished within Swiss borders, most of those who came did their best to integrate themselves into the economic and social fabric of the country. Nevertheless, they were sometimes viewed as un-Swiss, and the public was wary of certain Jewish customs. A national referendum in 1893 banned the slaughter of four-legged animals according to Jewish law on the pretext that the practice was cruel to animals. The ban, which was intended to discourage Jewish immigration, has never been overturned. To this day, a kosher brisket of beef must be imported into Switzerland.

The escalation of organized anti-Jewish violence in Nazi Germany that followed the J stamp did not soften Swiss policy directives. "We haven't spent twenty years fighting excessive foreign influence and especially *Verjudung* with everything the Police for Foreigners has at its disposal just to have emigrants forced on us today," Heinrich Rothmund, who supervised the border police, said in January 1939, two months after Kristallnacht. From his appointment as director of the Federal Police for Foreigners in 1919 to his retirement in 1954, Rothmund embodied the government's policies on immigration and refugees. During his tenure, Switzerland stiffened requirements for naturalization such that it was impossible for recent Jewish immigrants to become citizens. Swiss Jewish women who married foreign Jews were treated as aliens, and refugees could not work without police permission. He spoke of Switzerland as a sanctuary, but only as a "country of transit," not a permanent destination. (To be sure, Switzerland wasn't the only nation concerned about *Überfremdung* and *Verjudung*. At the July 1938 conference on refugees at Evian, none of the participating countries indicated a willingness to take in a large number of Jews. The Australian delegate said, "As we have no real racial problem, we are not desirous of importing one.")

Rothmund presented himself as the protector of all Swiss, including assimilated Swiss Jews. Swiss Jewish communal leaders disagreed with his border policies, but they avoided speaking out against government policy, fearing that any public disagreement would invite questions about their loyalty and exacerbate anti-Semitism at home.

The J stamp could not prevent Jews from trying to enter Switzerland illegally and networks of smugglers, some humanitarian, others mercenary, sprung up to help them try. Hundreds of Jewish children were brought from France and Belgium and hidden in Swiss orphanages, sometimes under false identities, but most refugees were adults or children accompanied by family members. Those not caught at the border surrendered to the authorities in the hope that they could stay. Though illegal Jewish refugees were supposed to be returned to the country from which they had come, enforcement varied from canton to canton and their fate often depended on the whims, sympathies, and values of individual border guards. Among the more refugee-friendly Swiss officials was Paul Grüninger, the police commander of St. Gallen, a canton on the Austrian border. Grüninger, an outspoken supporter of opening Switzerland to refugees, helped 2,000 to 3,000 illegally arrived Jews gain asylum. In the spring of 1939, Grüninger was dismissed from his post and convicted of dereliction of duty. Toward the end of his life, he appealed the ruling, but it was not until 1995 that the district court of St. Gallen posthumously overturned his conviction.

All in all, Switzerland accepted some 28,000 Jewish refugees. They were housed in dormitories, hotels, and labor camps. The Swiss camps were not on the order of Nazi forced-labor camps—individuals incapable of physical labor still received food and shelter, refugee workers earned small stipends and took scheduled furloughs—but life was not exactly easy for refugees who found them-

selves hungry, isolated, and unwanted. Families were separated and
children fostered out to Swiss homes. What assets Jewish refugees
did have were held in trust by the Police for Foreigners; wealthier
emigrants and refugees had to pay a "solidarity tax" to subsidize
relief efforts. Following the Aargau precedent, the government held
the 18,000-member Swiss Jewish community financially responsible
for the new arrivals. "The burden of supporting the newly impover-
ished refugees," said Rothmund, "must be imposed on the people
who brought them here." The Jewish community accepted the
burden, but was able to shoulder it only with substantial assistance
from the American Jewish Joint Distribution Committee and other
humanitarian organizations.

Most Jewish refugees were not lucky enough to enter Switzerland on the watch of someone as sympathetic as Paul Grüniger. Swiss
authorities documented the expulsion of about 22,500 Jews who tried
to cross the border. The exact number is unknown; estimates rise as
high as 100,000.

One rationale for the reluctance to accept refugees was that, even
though Switzerland was neither a belligerent nor an occupied country, it suffered economically as a result of the war. An industrial and
financial center, Switzerland relied on Germany and other trading
partners for food, fuel, and raw minerals, and goods arriving by road
or rail had to cross through Axis territory. Many products were
rationed; the government declared two meatless days a week, and
soccer fields were plowed to free up land for raising crops. Switzerland feared that an increase in the flow of refugees would threaten its
scarce resources. Eduard von Steiger, a member of the Federal
Council, compared Switzerland to a lifeboat, and declared that "the
boat is full."

As the war progressed, stories of the mass extermination of Jews
filtered into Switzerland. The first reports of Nazi atrocities could
not be corroborated and, as elsewhere, were dismissed as rumors, but
Swiss citizens and refugees kept arriving with bits and pieces of news.
By August 8, 1942, Gerhart Riegner, the Geneva representative of the
World Jewish Congress, had gathered enough information to send a
telegram warning his colleagues in America and England of the Final
Solution. The International Red Cross, based in Switzerland

and run by Swiss, also knew about the concentration camps, although they considered Jewish civilian prisoners to be an internal matter and therefore outside the organization's international mandate.

On August 13, 1942, at the apex of Nazi expansion and five days after Riegner sent his telegram, Rothmund's Police for Foreigners ordered a tight seal of the Swiss borders: no more judgment calls, no more bleeding-heart exceptions. Political refugees would be accepted, but "those who took flight only because of their race—Jews, for example—should not be considered political refugees," the directive read. Public protests briefly delayed the implementation of Rothmund's order, but restrictions were not relaxed until July 1944, when the Allies were beginning to beat back the Nazi armies.

Despite its tough border policies, Switzerland did not wholly abandon its mission of providing asylum, particularly when it came to children. Beginning in 1940, groups of foreign children from war-torn areas entered Switzerland for visits lasting three months, during which time they were fed well, received medical care, and recuperated from the stresses of life in wartime. Swiss families clamored to play host to foreign children, and individuals donated their own rations to feed young visitors. Swiss doctors noticed how quickly the visiting children shed their anxieties and became playful again, as the Joint's Paul Friedman would later observe with respect to Jewish child survivors. The largest number of short-term visitors came from France, but children arrived from Eastern and Western Europe, Allied and Axis territory. In May 1941 Rothmund asked Swiss relief agencies to stop accepting Jewish children, and as a result quotas for French Jewish children were imposed. The Swiss Federal Council rejected proposals to welcome Jewish children abandoned in France after their parents had been deported.

With the Nazis in retreat, the number of restorative visits increased, and after the war a contingent of Jewish children from Buchenwald was brought to Switzerland. Seven hotels in Adelboden, the village where records say Bruno Grosjean lived in a children's home before the Doessekkers claimed him, were temporarily converted into sanatoriums for foreign children at risk of contracting tuberculosis. The Swiss Red Cross counted 67,337 children who came to Switzerland for temporary relief by March of 1946. News-reels captured the refugee children disembarking at Swiss train stations and being fed and groomed in typical Swiss homes. Although *Fragments* does not explain how, when, or where Binjamin entered Switzerland, documentary films about him, including those made after Ganzfried questioned Binjamin's authenticity, use footage of little children with large Red Cross tags around their necks to illustrate his arrival in Switzerland. In his interview with the *Tages-Anzeiger*, the author of *Fragments* makes the same association, raising the possibility that young Jews, himself included, had been smuggled in under false identities among the child visitors, "perhaps without the knowledge, perhaps with the winking acquiescence, of the authorities." He talked about an unnamed humanitarian doctor who thought the only chance for Jews to survive was to disappear into the rest of the population. "And this person was also responsible, as a consultant, for the decision as to which adoptive children went to which adoptive families," he said.

While the movements of Jewish refugees were circumscribed and their assets immobilized, Nazis were free to cross Swiss borders, and so was their money. With the United States entering the war, the Swiss franc became the only currency that could be used universally for international purchases. The Swiss National Bank and, to a lesser extent, commercial banks in Switzerland bought gold from the Nazis in exchange for francs, which the Germans used to purchase raw materials. Some of the gold reserves sold to Switzerland came from pre-1933 German reserves, but much of it had been acquired by force. Some had been stolen from the central banks of countries the Germans invaded, like Austria and Belgium. Some had been collected from the Nazis' victims—jewelry confiscated from the living, dental fillings extracted from the mouths of the gassed—and resmelted into coins or bars. Swiss central bankers were aware that the gold they purchased included ill-gotten loot, yet they did not insist on knowing the provenance of the gold until the Allies prodded them to do so toward the end of the war. In 1945 the Federal Council ordered a freeze of all German assets held by Swiss institutions. The financial freeze, which lasted into the early 1950s, made no distinction between the monies of Aryans and the property of those with J-stamped passports.

PRESIDENT VILLIGER'S 1995 apology reads like a speech marking the end of a long quarrel, but the fracas over wartime Switzerland was just beginning. The golden anniversary of the war meant a worldwide surge of interest in the Holocaust, of which the popularity of *Fragments* was but one result. Another dimension was the revival of efforts to restore Jewish property, namely the assets of Holocaust victims who held numbered Swiss bank accounts. In 1995 the Swiss Federation of Jewish Communities, the World Jewish Congress (WJC), and the Israeli government urged Swiss banks to look again for Holocaust-era assets, and a Swiss government commission asked financial institutions to examine their files for dormant Jewish accounts.

These accounts had been a point of contention since war's end. The secrecy that had made Swiss accounts so attractive to European Jews in the 1930s became an insurmountable obstacle for many survivors and their heirs attempting to reclaim deposits. Swiss requests for death certificates and proof of inheritance were often impossible to satisfy, and the banks insisted on maintaining their secrecy, in part, they said, to protect Jewish customers now living in Communist Eastern Europe from having their assets nationalized. In 1962, after years of lobbying by the Swiss Jewish community, the government ordered a search for the accounts of victims of racial or religious persecution. Financial institutions reported finding fewer than a thousand accounts, which led individual claimants and organizations to suspect that the search was not nearly as thorough as it ought to have been.

Swiss law permitted financial institutions to destroy account records once they had been inactive for a decade, but in September of 1995 the Swiss banks announced a preliminary discovery of at least $34 million in dormant accounts that could have belonged to Holocaust victims. This number seemed far too low to Jewish organizations, which expected dormant accounts to contain as much as

$7 billion. When the banks reported back in February with a final figure that was slightly lower than the preliminary $34 million, the WJC asked Senator Alfonse D'Amato, the New York Republican in charge of the Senate Banking Committee, to initiate hearings.

The call for congressional hearings came during a tense period in relations between the international advocates, the Swiss banking establishment, and the Swiss Jewish community. The advocates, mostly American and mostly Jewish, took an aggressive tack. D'Amato and the WJC made regular press announcements about Swiss wartime policy to shame the Swiss banks into acting responsibly. Some news flashes involved fresh discoveries; others recycled long-known facts. The conservative, press-shy bankers took the public campaign as an affront, and it only made them more reluctant to cooperate. Caught in the middle were the Swiss Jews, even though the accounts in question were not theirs. Although Swiss Jewish communal leaders had long wanted an honest audit by the banks, they were not much more comfortable with publicly confronting Swiss institutions in the 1990s than their predecessors had been during World War II.

In May 1996 an agreement between the advocates and the banks established an Independent Committee of Eminent Persons (not to be confused with Bergier's Independent Commission of Experts), headed by former United States Federal Reserve Bank chairman Paul Volcker, to audit all Swiss banks that had been open for business during the Third Reich and search for dormant Holocaust-era accounts. That October, before the Volcker commission was fully under way, the banks released a list of more dormant accounts, but D'Amato and the WJC considered this latest update to be incomplete. More than four million Swiss bank accounts were opened between 1933 and 1945, and the Volcker commission would identify 46,000 of them as the most likely to have belonged to victims of Nazi persecution.

The dormant-accounts dispute led to a diplomatic rift between Switzerland and the United States. The Swiss ambassador to Washington, Carlo Jagmetti, wrote in a memo to his colleagues back home that the dormant-accounts issue was "a war which Switzerland must conduct on the foreign and domestic front, and must win." According to Jagmetti's memo, the American and Jewish advocates were threatening the Swiss with sanctions and boycotts unless the banks quickly established a substantial restitution fund to support needy Holocaust survivors, many of whom might well die of old age by the time Volcker and Bergier finished their careful research. The advocates denied making any threats.

Jagmetti's briefing, drafted in December 1996 and sent the same week the Swiss government approved the establishment of the Bergier commission, made its way to Jean-Pascal Delamuraz, who was Switzerland's economics minister and Villiger's successor as president. The Swiss presidency is a mostly honorary position that rotates annually among the seven ministers on the Federal Council. Like Villiger, Delamuraz represented the centrist Free Democratic Party, one of the four parties that have shared power since 1959 in a left-center-right unity coalition. Delamuraz was coming to the end of his own presidential term, and on December 31 he gave a perfunctory exit interview to two Swiss-French newspapers. When asked what had been the most difficult issue of his tenure as president, he said it was the dormant bank accounts. Establishing a restitution fund before the historians finished their work was tantamount to Switzerland admitting its guilt, said Delamuraz, and the tactics of the American Jewish advocates were "nothing less than extortion and blackmail." Delamuraz sensed something sinister beneath their aims. "Apart from dogged research into historical truth, there is also a strong political desire to destabilize and compromise Switzerland," he said, expressing a sentiment akin to the fear of *Überfremdung* his predecessors on the Federal Council felt. "Sometimes, listening to some people, I wonder whether Auschwitz is in Switzerland." Delamuraz tried to retract this last comment, but one of the two newspapers published it anyway.

The next day Delamuraz said his talk of blackmail had been "misunderstood" and that he was sorry for causing anyone grief, but his comments prompted the American Jewish groups to withdraw from the negotiations. Then, two weeks later, just as Delamuraz yielded to pressure and issued a carefully worded, still-less-than-full apology, a security guard at the Union Bank of Switzerland (UBS) noticed a batch of decades-old ledgers being sent to the shredder. The guard, Christoph Meili, had no personal interest in the dormant-account scandal, but he was aware of the new federal law forbidding banks from destroying documents predating the end of the war. Meili intercepted the ledgers and delivered them to the head of the Zurich Jewish community; together they went to the police. UBS suspended Meili for making the documents public, and eventually he was fired.

Meili's action showed UBS to be breaking Swiss law and acting in bad faith at a critical juncture in the negotiations. Switzerland took steps to recover from what became an international public relations disaster. By February UBS and the two other major Swiss banks agreed in principle to establish a charitable fund of 100 million francs ($70 million) for the benefit of needy Holocaust survivors. The first payments of $400 per person, made that fall, went to poor Jewish survivors in Riga. The Swiss government proposed using its gold reserves to create a multibillion-dollar humanitarian fund, part of which would support needy Holocaust survivors. Swissair stopped handing out chocolates packaged as ingots, so passengers craving sweets would not be reminded of the gold fillings extracted from dead concentration-camp victims.

In his exit interview, Delamuraz warned that the tactics of the American government and Jewish groups would stir up anti-Semitism in Switzerland, and soon enough the presidential admonition (some saw it as an invitation) became a reality. A 1997 survey of young adults in Zurich found that 31 percent agreed with the statement "The Jews have too much influence in the world," a marked increase from 1995, when only 14 percent of those polled concurred. A torrent of angry letters landed on the desks of newspaper editors and Swiss Jewish communal leaders. Some of the letters shared Delamuraz's concerns about blackmail and conspiracy, while others fell back on old stereotypes about greed, underhandedness, and world domination. "I am neither a racist nor a xenophobe, but one can't help but gradually feel that the entire campaign against Switzerland is only a beginning," read one letter printed by the *Zofinger Tagblatt*. A letter writer in a Lausanne newspaper called Senator D'Amato "the ideal attorney for the American Jews, whose omnipotence in the USA is well known." A note to a leader of the Zurich Jewish community said

that if the "smear campaign" of the "Jewish World Dominance Congress" were to go on much longer, "the Swiss Jews will definitely be
the ones to suffer."

In response to the Delamuraz speech, the Meili incident, and the
eruption of latent anti-Jewish sentiment, a group of psychoanalysts,
journalists, and liberal members of Parliament drafted a petition
proclaiming a lack of confidence in the Swiss Federal Council. The
manifesto of January 21, 1997, rejected the equation of the commercial interests of the banks with Swiss national interest and supported
a reckoning with the wartime past as a path toward a more democratic and just society. "Political pressure, whether from Switzerland
or from abroad, is valid if it serves the finding of truth," said the
petition, which was eventually signed by some 3,700 Swiss citizens,
including Gerhart Riegner, the World Jewish Congress official who
had warned of the Final Solution fifty-five years earlier.

One left-wing intellectual who refused to sign the manifesto
"neither as a Jew nor as a Swiss citizen" was Daniel Ganzfried. In
Ganzfried's view, Delamuraz wasn't an anti-Semite or a mouthpiece
for national anti-Jewish feeling; the Swiss president was merely ful-
filling his official duty by defending his besieged nation. If Jewish
organizations "that take it upon themselves to represent the entire
Jewish people, including the dead," were going to assail Switzerland
for its past wrongs, they should not be above listening to views other
than their own. Anyway, Ganzfried said, the members of the Swiss
Federal Council weren't the only ones with dirty hands; the Swiss
Jewish community made its own moral compromises during the war.
No real understanding of Switzerland's responsibility, Ganzfried
said, could come from herd action; it would require an open and
ongoing national conversation that allowed people to express their
sometimes hateful opinions and experience their own breakthroughs.

Ganzfried had little company in Swiss intellectual circles. Swiss
writer Adolf Muschg, one of the signers of the anti-anti-Semitism
manifesto, wrote that Auschwitz may be 897 kilometers from Bern,
the Swiss capital, but "the silence that answered Delamuraz's willful
little phrase has, in its abominable innocence, at once collapsed the
distance between the two places." To the Swiss who argue that
World War II may have happened all around them but had nothing

to do with them, Muschg replies that Auschwitz transcends its geo-graphical location. Muschg wrote, "Auschwitz is not only every-where, but also in Switzerland."

This tectonic shift recalls the Swiss episodes in *Fragments*. When Binjamin starts telling stories about his wartime experiences, guardians and teachers demand that he stop; his stories are inexplic-able, alien fantasies to them, and they dismiss them as nightmares. When Binjamin first enters his foster parents' basement and sees the "oven doors for children," he feels tricked: "That's why they want me to forget what I know. The camp's still here. Everything's still here." Auschwitz followed Binjamin to Switzerland—and not just anywhere in Switzerland, but to the private home of a wealthy doc-tor in Zürichberg, at the heart of the insulated Swiss upper class. Nobody around him could see the concentration camp, or at least none of them would acknowledge it was there. Finally, with his testimony, he can force them to view the symbols of his nation through the eyes of a refugee orphan. At the Swiss orphanage, he sees the cheese rinds left behind by other children and assumes they are for him. On the ski slopes, he fears the lift will carry him to his death. When his teacher points to a picture of an armed William Tell, the symbol of Swiss liberty, Binjamin is alone in perceiving him as dangerous. The rest of his class is inexplicably "all full of awe and admiration when they talk about this hero and SS man Tell, who shoots children."

If the author of *Fragments* has invented his story, he would not be the first writer from the upper strata of Swiss society to adopt the Holocaust as a metaphor for his personal torment. In 1976 Adolf Muschg received an unpublished manuscript, the psychoanalytically informed, emotionally raw autobiography of a thirty-two-year-old Swiss schoolteacher who discovers the essence of life only after dis-covering he has a terminal cancer. With Muschg's help, *Mars* was published posthumously the next year under the pseudonym Fritz Zorn. Zorn (or whoever he was) believed that his cancer was caused by an "anonymous hostile principle" arising from the repressed, bourgeois Swiss Protestant society in which his wealthy parents raised him, a milieu similar to Bruno Doessekker's. "My life is hell," Zorn writes before switching to a modern metaphor for his wilting existence. "I'm in a concentration camp now, and I am being gassed to death by the 'parental' legacy inside me. But I am *in* the concentration camp, and the people who are gassing me are *outside* it."

If the author of *Fragments* is a child survivor of the Holocaust, however, the questioning of his authenticity could be a further sign of Swiss denial concerning its own ugly wartime past. For Binjamin and his supporters, it seemed that the government-funded arts council went out of its way to commission an investigation that would embarrass the country's best-known Holocaust survivor. Pro Helvetia's decision not to publish Ganzfried's results was nothing more than a way to cover its tracks. "Pro Helvetia is a nationalistic organization," John Gordon of the Los Angeles child-survivor group would tell me. "If I wrote a book, nobody would have ever said anything," another child survivor from Los Angeles would say, "but this guy lives in Switzerland." *Passages* editor Michael Guggenheimer dismisses this scenario as a conspiratorial fantasy, and likewise dispatches Ganzfried's claim that the arts council's magazine backed off after well-placed officials said that exposing Bruno Grosjean would threaten its funding.

ONE DAY AFTER the author of *Fragments* made his public appeal to the Bergier commission, one of its nine members addressed Binjamin's request in an interview with the *Frankfurter Allgemeine Zeitung*. It would be hard to think of a first-rank Holocaust historian more likely to be sympathetic to a plea from the author of *Fragments* than Saul Friedländer, a professor with chairs at the University of California at Los Angeles and Tel Aviv University. Unlike Raul Hilberg, Friedländer does not think Nazi documents are the only materials of historical value; in the introduction to his projected two-volume history of Nazi Germany, Friedländer says that "the victims' attitudes, reactions, and fate are no less an integral part of this unfolding history" than Nazi records of their own policies.

Friedländer is himself a child survivor, and his 1978 memoir, *When Memory Comes,* is among the earliest and most eloquent of child-survivor accounts. Born in Prague into an assimilated family, Friedländer fled with his parents to a resort town in France. In 1942, as the threat of deportation increased, his parents sent him to a Catholic institution and asked that their son be baptized. His parents tried to cross the French border into Switzerland, but border authorities returned them to France. They were sent to the Rivesaltes transit camp and put on a transport eastward from which they never returned. Meanwhile their son, twelve and a half years old at the end of the war, nearly became a priest but ended up a Zionist and moved to Israel, where he changed his name from Paul to Saul.

Friedländer has long been curious about history's relationship to memory and psychology. The title of his memoir is taken from a quote by novelist Gustav Meyrink, author of *The Golem*. A longer citation serves as Friedländer's epigraph: "When knowledge comes, memory comes too, little by little. Knowledge and memory are one and the same thing."

However, Friedländer told the *Frankfurter Allgemeine Zeitung* that the questions about Binjamin Wilkomirski's authenticity did not fall within the Bergier commission's purview, and therefore the historians would not be taking on his case.

THE
SECOND
HOLOCAUST

A couple of weeks after the Bergier commission turned down his request, the author of *Fragments* was scheduled to travel from Zurich to Nashville to take part in Vanderbilt University's annual Holocaust commemoration. In addition to lecturing on the "shattered generations" of the Holocaust, he was to present his approach to treating children without identity at a psychiatry department seminar. His friend Lauren Grabowski was flying in from Los Angeles; a musical performance was in the works. The university promised to cover plane fare and accommodations for Binjamin and Verena plus an honorarium of $1,000.

Jay Geller, a lecturer in Vanderbilt's religious studies department, initially tried to bring Binjamin to Tennessee in April after the Notre Dame conference so he could speak at the university's Yom Hashoah event, but the author of *Fragments* was too busy. Geller assigned *Fragments* to his classes on the Holocaust and autobiography, and he also shared it with the university's Methodist reading group. "It always had an incredible effect," said Geller, who found that the book worked particularly well late in the semester, when his students were becoming inured to the brutality of Holocaust stories. "They would read this, and all of a sudden it was fresh again." Geller assumed that meeting the author in the flesh would make that much more of an impact. "For my students, the most significant part is to hear from a survivor that they were there. That has more reality than anything they read."

When Binjamin sent Vanderbilt a message saying he was too weak to make the trip, Geller already knew about the talk of imposture; a friend at another university e-mailed him after reading about Ganzfried's article on the Internet. Geller and his colleagues weren't sure what to do or how to respond. Geller wondered whether accepting Ganzfried's accusations would lead to what he called a "double dying." Geller chose the same metaphor to describe the assault on Binjamin Wilkomirski's authenticity as did Michael Guggenheimer of *Passages* and one supporter of Wilkomirski who, in a heated letter to the *Weltwoche,* wrote, "Daniel Ganzfried is hunting a human being!" To refuse to believe Binjamin—or, for that matter, any Holocaust survivor—was construed as a lethal gesture. As Geller put it, "To question their memory is to commit another murder."

Vanderbilt did not want to kill anyone. "We still gave him the benefit of the doubt," says Geller. In Vanderbilt's response to Binjamin, delivered via Verena, the professors said they understood his decision to withdraw given the circumstances, but told him that should he by any chance change his mind, the invitation to Vanderbilt was still open. In the end, Geller ended up addressing the psychiatrists himself, laying out Binjamin's therapeutic strategies within the context of the controversy over his authenticity. And Geller found a pair of replacement speakers from Los Angeles: psychologist Sarah Moskovitz, who stepped into the breach with a talk on child survivors and restitution, and Daisy Miller, a founding member and former chairman of the child-survivor group.

"IF THIS vicious attack on Binjie had not happened, I would be at Vanderbilt University with him this evening. We would be giving each other a big hug," Lauren Grabowski wrote to her friend Monika Muggli on October 6, 1998. "The most meaningful experience of my life has been thrown in the gutter."

The experience of getting acquainted with the adult Binjamin had not been easy for either of them. Grabowski reported loneliness and nightmares brought on by Binjamin's visit. More feelings were stirred up when Binjamin told her about yet another girl from their barracks who survived and was living in Berlin. "She was experimented on, also," Grabowski told Muggli. "Electric shocks, blood tests, etc. Too much to describe right now." Grabowski also felt her privacy slip away after she agreed to let the BBC film her. She complained that, against her wishes, one child survivor shared private details about Grabowski's childhood with the BBC.

The reunion continued to disrupt the Child Holocaust Survivors Group of Los Angeles even after Binjamin returned home to Switzerland. Binjamin never provided cochairman Leon Stabinsky with a reference about the role of child abuse in medieval contract law, and Stabinsky became more outspoken in his skepticism. Stabinsky still associated Binjamin's story with the false-memory syndrome he had read about in *Scientific American*. "He does not believe in therapy nor does he believe in early childhood memories," Grabowski complained of Stabinsky. "So he does not believe Binjie's and my stories. And he is telling everyone this."

Stabinsky may have thought he was protecting the integrity of the group, but his statements disturbed many members. "The original idea behind the formation of this group, *to provide emotional help and support to child survivors, to be there for each other, and the unquestioned acceptance of each other,* has taken a back seat and is often ignored," read the text of an open letter signed by Grabowski and sixty-six other members of the Child Holocaust Survivors Group of Los Angeles. The letter called for new elections. Stabinsky's cochairman, Lya Frank, submitted her resignation, saying that "the total atmosphere of our 'Group' has changed." Grabowski admitted to Muggli that she thought of leaving, too, "but there are so many precious child survivors in the group who have become almost like family."

The group's June board meeting was held in a room at the Simon Wiesenthal Center's Museum of Tolerance. "The fur will be sure to fly," Grabowski predicted beforehand. Stabinsky began by talking about how Binjamin's visit was the reason for the rift, but it soon became clear that was not the only source of bad feeling. Among the complaints aired at the board meeting were that Stabinsky made too many decisions unilaterally and that the group had become colder and less social during his tenure. From other quarters, Stabinsky received compliments on his efficient leadership. One man said that, judging from the other survivor organizations he knew of in Southern California, the child survivors could do much worse than have Stabinsky at the helm.

The phantom siblings had never before had such a bitter dispute. Former president Daisy Miller told members they were acting like children. Moskovitz offered to call in a consultant to troubled organizations so the leadership could work out their disagreements. Stabinsky felt betrayed and insulted, however; for him, it was too late for mediation. "Leon the Terrible resigned at the board meeting last night," Grabowski told Muggli. "We are free!"

In an open letter to group members explaining his resignation, Stabinsky gave as good as he felt he had gotten from some of the other child survivors. "I wish you all good health and happiness, and I hope that you skip adolescence and grow up fast to take your place among the adults," he wrote. "Remember: the past is history." Between pettier sentiments, Stabinsky regretted that some of the child-survivor group's big dreams—group-owned burial plots for members who couldn't afford a proper funeral; a retirement community for child survivors—would never be realized.

Stabinsky also defended his questioning of Binjamin's story, fending off allegations that he was an unscrupulous Holocaust revisionist. "It is a fundamental right I have as an American citizen," Stabinsky wrote. "If Wilkomirski cannot tolerate criticism, which indeed can be painful at times, he should not have published the book. Many survivors could and perhaps should have written books about their experiences and recollections, but chose not to expose themselves to public scrutiny or commercialize on the Holocaust."

When the Child Holocaust Survivors Group of Los Angeles held new elections, Stabinsky was returned to its board of directors, but he decided not to serve. Instead he banded together with other disgruntled members to form the California Association of Holocaust Child Survivors, and Stabinsky became chairman of the new, smaller group.

"At least our child survivor group is standing behind Binje and myself," Grabowski said. The Los Angeles Museum of the Holocaust, one of the partners in Binjamin's April visit, sponsored a screening of Esther van Messel's *Born a Stranger,* a 1997 Swiss documentary about the author of *Fragments.* An announcement of the screening of the film (one of two government-funded movies that Ganzfried criticized for not mentioning anything about Bruno Doessekker) acknowledged the reported controversy, but museum director Marcia Josephy said that "the only truth we know for sure is that people who were children during the Holocaust have memories that must be acknowledged."

As for Grabowski, she had many people standing behind her. Child survivors and psychologists affiliated with the group offered her emotional support, and after Grabowski indicated she was in tight financial straits, they helped her apply to the Swiss humanitarian fund for needy Holocaust survivors. Over a twelve-month period, Grabowski received more than $2,000 in disbursements from Jewish Family Services to cover food, medicine, and automotive repairs.

Her online friends also pitched in. "What is decisive for me are your memories and experiences," Monika Muggli reassured Grabowski. When Grabowski described her precarious finances, Muggli sent off a $1,000 check so her friend could visit Binjamin again. Grabowski said her medical condition necessitated a first-class seat, and her doctors said she couldn't carry heavy luggage, so she'd need a suitcase with wheels. Muggli sent another check for $150.

Jen Rosenberg of the Mining Co. buoyed Grabowski's spirits by giving her a teddy bear with a scarf wrapped around its neck to resemble the author of *Fragments.* Grabowski referred to it as her "Binjie Bear." When Rosenberg left on a tour of Poland, Grabowski gave her a pair of pink plastic sandals in memory of her and Binjamin's friend Ana. Rosenberg left the sandals at one of the Auschwitz crematoria. "Dear Ana, I wish you had had these in the winter of 1944. I will love you forever," Grabowski wrote in an accompanying Anne Geddes greeting card showing two babies dressed up as sunflowers. Rosenberg shared Grabowski's story with her tour group, and together they said kaddish for Ana and for the children who died at Auschwitz. When she returned, Rosenberg posted a report on her trip on the Mining Co. Holocaust web site.

Ganzfried's articles had not mentioned Grabowski, but she nevertheless felt that the cloud over Binjamin's life story cast shadows upon hers. She denounced the *Weltwoche* as a "trashy rag of the first class" and dismissed the interest in the Wilkomirski story as "yellow journalism." Online, she kept a low profile, curtailing her regular participation in the Mining Co. discussion forum.

Grabowski's supporters, however, came to the defense of Binjamin and of child survivors in general as discussion spread on the Mining Co. forum and on other online Holocaust forums. When someone commented on the academic bulletin board H-Holocaust that Binjamin's memories were unreliable because he was a child, one child survivor from the Los Angeles group responded. "I have— unfortunately perhaps—an excellent memory, as do many, many other Child Survivors whom I know," she wrote. "Among them are several Child Survivors who were Wilkomirski's age—about 3 years old or 4 years old when the war ended. Like mine, their memories are also fragmentary, but THEY DO REMEMBER."

"The discounting of Benjamin [*sic*] Wilkomirski's book is consistent with a continuing history of discounting the memories of child survivors," psychologist Sarah Moskovitz wrote on H-Holocaust. "I have been listening to child survivors [*sic*] memories for over 21 years and have heard close to 300 individual accounts. Benjamin Wilkomirski's book is consistent with the way young children's memories for traumatic events are sensed, stored, and related; consistent with the struggle to make sense of a chaotic, horrific world during the Holocaust and in the aftermath." Ultimately, only Binjamin Wilkomirski could say what he remembered and what, if anything, he imagined, but for Moskovitz this distinction was not paramount. "The important question is this; is *Fragments* a worthwhile book that adds to our understanding of young child survivors, even if it were a work of fiction by a gifted, empathic writer? To that I will answer, and many with me, a resounding YES."

"It seems to me that asking Wilkomirski to *prove* that he is a survivor is very similar to asking someone to *prove* that the Holocaust did occur," Jen Rosenberg wrote on H-Holocaust. Rosenberg explained that she had met Binjamin at dinner in Los Angeles. "He is a very timid man who is just now opening up to share just a sliver of what he has gone through," she wrote. Not only was he too ill to defend himself—ill "from life-long illnesses stemming from his time in the camps"—but witnesses could corroborate his story. "I know of two other survivors who remember him from Auschwitz."

To LEARN more about Binjamin and the two survivors who remember him, I telephoned Lea Balint, who, as Verena said, was vouching for Binjamin. From her home in Jerusalem, Balint told me she would talk to me, but only with Binjamin's permission, and that I should call again a couple of days later.

In the meantime, I studied the statement she had circulated in Binjamin's defense. It came on the letterhead of the Ghetto Fighters' House, a Holocaust museum on a kibbutz in northern Israel founded by survivors of the Warsaw ghetto uprising, which supported Balint's children-without-identity research. She was not "Frau Dr. Balint," as Suhrkamp publisher Siegfried Unseld had described her, but an amateur historian like the author of *Fragments*. In the statement, Balint explained how, when she first met Binjamin in 1993, he remembered a few bits and pieces: the parallel bars at the orphanage, a Purim party there, an anti-Semitic riot in Krakow. After their trip to Warsaw, she left documents she had amassed concerning the Krakow orphanage with Binjamin for the day. "When I met him that evening to collect the documents, he fell into my arms crying," Balint said, because he'd found the name of a girl he remembered listed therein. The name Binjamin Wilkomirski did not appear in any document Balint had found, but to her this proved nothing; many documents were destroyed during the war, and afterward the Communists had burned files about Jewish orphanages. To show that his story could be plausible, she cited cases of children with false papers, a chart showing that the liberators of Auschwitz found more than two hundred living Jewish children there, stories of children taken from Auschwitz to Krakow and from Poland to Switzerland after the war. Balint's implicit message was that Binjamin's story was true if only you trust his memory. And why shouldn't you trust it when none of the other children without identity are treated with such suspicion? "Is it because one person who dared put the fragments of his memory on paper with talent, sensitivity and [the] gentleness of a young child," asks Balint, "that would lead us to doubt the authenticity of his experience?"

When I called Balint again a couple of days later, I didn't know whether she would talk to me, since I wasn't certain Binjamin would give her the go-ahead. In the weeks following my brief conversations with Verena, I left messages for Binjamin on his answering machines in Amlikon and at the Zurich apartment, and I sent faxes and e-mails, but I never had any response, not even a request to stop bothering him. Other people told me he was still too ill to talk. I was willing to believe this, since he hadn't responded to my mother either, although I'd also heard he was considering giving an interview to *60 Minutes*.

"When child survivors refuse to interview, somebody thinks they are hiding something," Balint told me. "They are not like everybody. Some of them, because they can't prove who they are, they didn't get any restitution, they are poor, they are living without any help, they are ill, they are hurt. They have no ability to help themselves. They are children." When Binjamin is vindicated, she adds, "all the others will come out. One of them called me. She is writing a book, and she will leave it until later because she is afraid the same thing will happen to her."

I explain to Balint that my great-grandmother was a Wilkomirski from Riga, and ask her what she has learned about Binjamin's connection to my family. "I am not sure that he is a Wilkomirski, but I am sure he is not a Swiss child," she tells me. She admits that she cannot prove who he is. "I never said I can prove he was in Auschwitz," she says. "I can prove that he was in Krakow and that the children in Krakow were in Auschwitz." At the same time, she cannot fathom how Binjamin, with his many aptitudes, could be the offspring of Yvonne Grosjean, an unmarried, uneducated, low-class shikse. "Do you believe that Wilkomirski—a gifted writer, a talented musician, a painter who is very good—could be her child?" she asks.

Balint complained that Daniel Ganzfried never called her while researching his article, and she couldn't understand why he had pursued Binjamin. That Ganzfried's father was a survivor of Auschwitz "doesn't give him any privilege," she said. "My father was in Auschwitz. All my family was killed in Auschwitz. All the time I am thinking about them. I don't blame them. I am doing my duty."

Balint may have been willing to talk to me on Binjamin's behalf, but she was not about to broker a conversation between me and him. "I'm happy that I don't have to call him," she said. "He can't sleep afterward."

As for Binjamin's friends who remember him from the camps, Balint says they are "very fragile people." I had gotten similar warnings about Lauren Grabowski before, that she was too weak or troubled to speak about Binjamin. Nobody would tell me how to find her, and her telephone number was not listed. When Balint asked Grabowski to go public, Grabowski replied that she would maintain her privacy. "I feel as if I have failed you & Binjamin," Grabowski wrote. "I don't know if I know the things you need to help him fact wise. He & I corroborate each other more with memories of the heart. And I know this would not help him in the Swiss Embassy or in a court of law. We were simply too young to have the documents and names, etc. If you read the corroborations we gave to each other when we were together, you would see what I mean."

ANOTHER POTENTIAL intermediary was Harvey Peskin. A clinical psychologist and the onetime president of the Psychoanalytic Institute of Northern California, Peskin met Binjamin in the spring of 1998, when he gave a speech in San Francisco on his way to meet Grabowski and the child survivors in Los Angeles. Before that, Peskin reviewed *Fragments* along with two other child-survivor memoirs for a journal published by the American Orthopsychiatric Association, an interdisciplinary mental-health professional organization with a strong interest in children's welfare. Peskin's essay was rooted in the writings on child survivors by the likes of Moskovitz and Judith Kestenberg. Peskin was particularly interested in the resistance young survivors faced when they gave testimony. "Children lack the insistent subjectivity of adolescence or resolute will of the adult to bear witness," he wrote. "They are more apt to comply with grownups' overprotectiveness against, or mistrust of, children, believing or prolonging the testimony of their horrified senses." Binjamin Wilkomirski's story was not only a rarity but "a masterpiece of emergent healing that commands our respect for the disparate tides of traumatic memory."

The review appeared at the end of 1997, months before Ganzfried began his research, but Peskin unwittingly anticipated what would befall the author of *Fragments*. He began his review of *Fragments* and the two other books with a general statement about the precariousness of testimony. "When telling meets with disbelief, indifference, or retaliation, hate crimes live on in their victims as congealed trauma or stigma—suspended between remembering and repeating, between total concealment and unending disclosure," he wrote.

Binjamin was suspended between concealment and disclosure when Harvey Peskin got involved, taking on the sort of role discussed in another paper he published that year called "The Second Holocaust: Therapeutic Rescue When Life Threatens," which appeared in the *Journal of Personal and Interpersonal Loss*. "We have found in our psychotherapeutic work with survivors and their children," Peskin and his coauthors wrote, "that often it is only the intervention of a helping other, a therapist or rescuer who brings the survivors and their children back to life." This resurrection is not a literal raising of the dead but a metaphor for the resuscitation of their patients' spirits, one "that can allow them to reverse what they believe is their fated course."

Similarly, a second Holocaust is not literally a new genocidal attack on the Jews of Europe. It is an individual event, a cataclysm that symbolically replays some trauma that occurred during the Nazi attempt to rid Europe of Jews. To clarify the concept, Peskin et al. cite the example of a Jewish man who survived a concentration camp but lost his wife and children. He remarried after the war and had more children, but a fire destroyed the family home and killed everyone but the Holocaust survivor, who, Peskin wrote, "linked the new cruel events to the earlier ones via the recurrence of a sense of total devastation." As the survivor himself put it, "Their death has reopened all the graves. In those graves, my people, my parents, my siblings, my friends were coming back to life; my people, my family, died in them a second death." The author of these words was Martin Gray, who wrote *For Those I Loved*.

The term "second Holocaust" originated with one of Peskin's coauthors, Dori Laub, a professor of psychiatry at Yale Medical School, who uses the phrase in *Testimony* (1992), a book about the collection of videotaped Holocaust testimonies he helped establish. In the book, Laub explores the relationship between testimony and historical truth, and ends up arguing that inaccurate testimony can nonetheless represent the truth. He tells the story of a woman who was at Auschwitz when inmates rose up and attacked a crematorium. She remembered seeing four chimneys on fire, even though only one of the four crematoria was attacked. While historians thought the woman's error rendered her entire eyewitness account suspect, Laub believed that "she was testifying not simply to empirical historical facts, but to the very secret of survival and resistance to extermination." The inaccuracy of her memory, in other words, mirrored the unbelievable nature of the event.

In Harvey Peskin's view, the challenge to Binjamin's authenticity had put the author of *Fragments* in the grip of a second Holocaust. (Peskin believed Binjamin had lived through it the first time, but, as he and Laub argued in "Therapeutic Rescue," one need not be an actual survivor to suffer a second Holocaust; the phenomenon can also trickle down to the children of survivors.) Since the initial trauma described in *Fragments* was the abandonment and loss of identity during the war, the suppression and negation of Binjamin's wartime past by his adoptive parents, teachers, and schoolmates in Switzerland reinforced that trauma, the effects of which lessened only when Binjamin reclaimed his history and wrote his memoir. The assault on his identity led by Ganzfried and the resultant potential for abandonment triggered a recurrence of his childhood fears. This was another way of expressing what Verena meant when she said "He's absolutely pushed back to the time from in the camps."

"Not being believed has a quality almost equal to the trauma itself," Peskin told me when we first spoke on the phone. He had written an impassioned defense of Binjamin, which relied on psy-

choanalytic research and the corroborating materials assembled by
Lea Balint. He was hoping to publish his apologia in an attempt to
stem the tide of media hostility toward Binjamin, and asked whether
the *Forward* would consider publishing it. If the swirling scandal
were to abate, Peskin argued, perhaps Binjamin would get a fair
hearing, one divorced from all the sensation and the emotions stirred
up in those who felt duped.

"We're all so quick to believe; we're all so quick to disbelieve,"
Peskin told me. "What is very, very sad to me is that the media will
lose interest in Wilkomirski and leave the impression to the world
that the book and his person is a hoax. It may be well that he is who
he says," Peskin said. "I'm just afraid he's going to be lost and forgotten after he's been defamed."

"In many ways, he's not very smart," Peskin said. "He spoke to
Ganzfried for six or seven hours anyway; he's got to be pretty dense.
To submit to that kind of an interview, it's not safe." Peskin was an
advocate, however, for the author of *Fragments* in his dealings with
60 Minutes. Peskin urged the producers to interview Balint and psychologist Elitsur Bernstein, Binjamin's coauthor and friend. When
word got around that the television program was planning to interview Leon Stabinsky, the skeptical child survivor in the Los Angeles
support group, Binjamin almost pulled out of the story, but in the
end Peskin believed that *60 Minutes* would give him a fair shake, and
he urged Binjamin to sit for an interview.

THE *60 Minutes* segment that aired on February 7, 1999, presented
the Binjamin Wilkomirski story as a hoax, plain and simple. It was a
classic debunking job of the type *60 Minutes* is famous for. I had
suspected it would be, since, weeks before the broadcast, two producers paid a visit to my office. I don't know whether they were
looking for information or for a character they could put on television, but in any case they seemed to have the gist of their story
pretty much figured out. Bruno Doessekker, they said, fit the classic
profile of a fraud.

In its signature gotcha style, *60 Minutes* allowed the author of
Fragments to hang himself, so to speak. After pointing out that Bin-

jamin said he witnessed the 1947 anti-Semitic riots in Krakow, Ed Bradley confronted the author of *Fragments* with evidence placing him in Switzerland in 1946. Binjamin countered by saying he had since learned that "the first riots against the orphanage was on the fifteenth of August 1945." Bradley then countered with a record indicating that the author of *Fragments* first visited the Doessekkers in June 1945, when he was four. When Bradley asked him to explain what had happened to the real Bruno Grosjean, his simple reply of "I don't know" lingered in still air.

Besides being able to document the memoirist's presence in Switzerland even earlier than Ganzfried had, *60 Minutes* added several other damning tidbits to the Doessekker dossier. They unearthed a film script titled *Binjamin* he had helped draft in early 1980s; it described some of the same episodes that later appeared in *Fragments*. "Years before the book is written," Bradley says, "he's treating this all as a commercial venture." Another old friend produced letters in which the author of *Fragments* boasted of flying airplanes at an Israeli military base; *60 Minutes* found out he had no pilot's license. Annie Singer, an ex-girlfriend, described Bruno Doessekker as someone who lied habitually because "he wanted to be noticed."

To provide historical perspective, *60 Minutes* trotted out Raul Hilberg, who made many of the same points he shared with me. A four- or five-year-old boy would not have been transported from Majdanek to Auschwitz, he said.

"YOU WANT TO KNOW what the second Holocaust looks like?" Peskin asked me when I called him to find out his reaction to the *60 Minutes* piece. "When Wilkomirski gets into situations with journalists—that's what it looks like."

Peskin was angered by the way they had employed Hilberg to denigrate testimony in general. "There is an effort to elicit the story from every single survivor able to talk," Hilberg said. "Everybody who says 'I'm a survivor and I have a story' will be told, 'Come on in.' And if he's capable of writing something very interesting, he'll be celebrated." Hilberg is not the only one to blame, Peskin said; behind him are the reporters and producers who rely on him as an expert.

Even taking into account the new information *60 Minutes* turned up, the case against Binjamin is, Peskin said, "at best ambiguous. What's happening now is that a man is slowly dying, and he is dying because of what the media has done to him. You have a responsibility to write about what's being done to him." Peskin told me he had no intention of brokering a conversation between me and Binjamin. He tried to explain "how much of the journalistic enterprise is itself a derivative of a Holocaust experience. That's not easy to take in. The investigative journalist has to be aware of this."

The author of *Fragments,* Peskin said, "feels from you collectively an attack, where, for him to stand up—and I use his words—is that he runs the risk of being killed. When Binjamin is investigated around this issue now, under these conditions, he looks guilty because he's shaking. You become a derivative of an SS man. Now that is part of his craziness, but it's part of how he sees the world, feeling like someone is out to get him—and let me tell you, you are." It didn't matter, Peskin said, whether the avalanche of hostility that started with Ganzfried's tirade was a coordinated effort or not.

"It doesn't take much for him to get into a Holocaust situation," Peskin said. "It's not a theoretical or psychological notion. He feels you are responsible."

Again Peskin pleaded with me to publish a defense of Binjamin—if I wouldn't run Peskin's article, then at least I could lay out the evidence collected by Lea Balint. I told him that Balint's corroborating materials proved nothing, but that as soon as I found some hard facts I would be happy to put them in print.

"Not publishing right now, it's like the bystander phenomenon during the Nazi era," Peskin said. "I think you have to understand that very metaphorically."

I told him I would try. It was a step up from the SS.

Harvey Peskin finally found a sympathetic editor at the *Nation,* the publication in which the initial reviewer of *Fragments* had wondered whether he "even had the right to try to offer praise." Peskin's essay, "Holocaust Denial: A Sequel," offered an impassioned defense on behalf of Binjamin in the name of all child survivors. He compared Binjamin to Richard Jewell, the security guard who was hounded by news organizations after being publicly identified as the target of the FBI investigation of the bombing at the 1996 Atlanta Olympics. Like Binjamin, Jewell had originally been treated as a hero, in his case because he spotted the bomb and helped evacuate people before the explosion. Both men had been set upon by a mob of vigilante journalists who had no respect for the principle of presumption of innocence. Peskin also compared the rejection of Binjamin to the hostility many survivors faced from Swiss authorities: "To put on a child survivor the onus of disproving Swiss birth documentation is darkly parallel to the disingenuous insistence by Swiss banks that Holocaust survivors unearth the death certificates of victims for whom they are claiming reparations." Finally, he criticized Hilberg for both his facts and his methods. Hilberg said several times that children as a rule were not transported from Majdanek to Auschwitz, while Peskin cites "evidence in published German or Poland documents that several trains carried nearly 400 children either from Majdanek to Auschwitz directly or via the transit camp of Plaszow (the site depicted in the book and film *Schindler's List*) or the children's camp of Konstantinov Lodzi." For example, the *Auschwitz Chronicle* notes that on April 15, 1944, a few months before the Red Army captured Majdanek, thirty-eight children were transferred to Auschwitz from Majdanek; two nursing infants arrived the next day. Hilberg's disdain for testimony, Peskin wrote, "gives comfort to a new revisionism that no longer attacks the truth of the Holocaust itself but only individual claims of survival."

Peskin equated disbelieving Binjamin Wilkomirski and denying the Holocaust, and he also condemned more broadly the public's lack of faith in the capacity of adults to retain reliable childhood memories. "The attraction of believing in Wilkomirski's Swiss birth may go hand in hand with recoiling from the reality of the child survivor's deep traumatic memory," he wrote. "Nowhere else has Hitler's plan to leave no witnesses of the Holocaust come closer to being realized than in separating the young from their own experience."

OTHER
PEOPLE'S
SHOES

"Can you tell me your name, please?"

As the interview begins, his face fills with dread. A gold Magen David hangs on a chain around his neck, but he seems unsure whether the amulet will protect him this time.

As I wait for him to answer, it occurs to me that his answer should be "No," or, more properly, "Well, not exactly, but . . ."—that's the whole point of his book, right?—but there is no quaver in his voice when he says, "My name is Binjamin Wilkomirski."

I am staring at the author of *Fragments* on a small monitor in the fifth-floor library of the United States Holocaust Memorial Museum. Since he has not responded to any of my requests for an interview or an informal chat, the only way I can make him explain himself to me is to view the testimony he recorded for the benefit of future generations of researchers two days before meeting the Wilburs in New York. The recording is six hours long. I am hoping that Joan Ringelheim, the museum official who conducted it, pressed Binjamin for concrete details about his papers, his life in Switzerland, and his process of self-realization. I am hoping to find something in these tapes that will restore my confidence in Binjamin. Knowing that it's a serious possibility that he's an impostor, I am equally wary of having my trust abused any more than it may already have been. I do not assume he will be lying, but it no longer seems possible to suspend my disbelief altogether.

Ringelheim asks Binjamin when he first discovered that his childhood memories had to do with the Holocaust. He talks about a teacher, a mathematician and psychoanalyst, whom he told about his memories when he was about seventeen. "He looked very Jewish, and I thought, Oh, that's one of us," Binjamin says. The teacher, now deceased, was the first person who made him feel comfortable enough to discuss his past openly, he says. His foster parents shushed him, other children taunted him.

As a child, however, Binjamin would bear witness at the Doessekker house when there was nobody around to listen. "When it was nice weather and I had a free afternoon, I went into the garden. My foster family had a beautiful garden with wonderful old trees—pines—and I climbed up," he says. "I was alone, I was in security, nobody could reach me, and then—really, I do not exaggerate—but for hours I repeated loudly every detail of my memory, everything I could remember."

"Out loud?" Ringelheim asks.

"Yeah. Again and again and again, with really every detail. I remembered that I even repeated how we locked the door of the barrack in Majdanek, because that was not the normal locking mechanism on something, no, it went something like this"—he pantomimes a wooden bar pivoting into a latch—"all kinds of little such things. And again and again and again, until I was maybe fourteen, fifteen years old."

It sounds like the beginning of a fable, both enchanting and slightly unreal. Now that I am attuned to how unreal his story might actually be, I find myself far less enchanted than I once was, far less able to take him at his word. I wish he had kept this garden scene to himself, that the entire story of Binjamin Wilkomirski had remained a secret between him and the pine trees.

This wish only becomes stronger as he goes on to describe the first time he realized he might not have been born in Switzerland. It happened, he tells Ringelheim, even before he began to testify from his perch in the garden. One afternoon at the Doessekker home, just after he'd gotten his first schoolbook with a map of Europe in it, he took a big blue pencil and, without fully understanding what his hand was doing, drew a circle around Riga. "And then I thought: direction Dvinsk"—now the city of Daugavpils, in the Latvian interior—"and then somewhere down, direction Bialystok." The blue pencil goes further south into Poland, takes a westward arc toward Lodz, and then dips south again, to a point near Krakow. "Then again I made like this," he says, drawing a circle in the air with his invisible stylus, "and then I flash down to Switzerland."

It is possible that had I come across this story when I first read *Fragments*, when I assumed Binjamin was a Holocaust survivor, I might have believed it referred to an authentic moment of discovery. Today, however, I cannot fathom how Binjamin's geographical trajectory could have been mapped onto his consciousness in a form that somehow corresponds to a Mercator projection of Europe. More than ever before, I want the author of *Fragments* to produce a fact, a document, a tangible certainty. Without corroborating evidence, this episode sounds less like a real memory from childhood than a just-so story plotted out in retrospect, a representation of his primal fears or perverse wishes traced with a planchette on a Ouija board. If Binjamin could show me the map he scribbled on and if the graphite in his pencil markings could be analyzed as the ink from Anne Frank's pens was, I would accept this story as credible, but any evidence of his cartographic epiphany is gone. "Unfortunately, they took away this book from me," he says. "But I remember the movement." All the author of *Fragments* can offer is a bodily memory of a decades-old gesture.

Sitting before the video console, I feel the ground shift under me. In any confidence game, there comes a moment when it dawns on the mark that he has been had. Sometimes it takes a lead weight to rouse him from his trust, but in other situations all it takes is a feather to nudge him into disbelief. The story of the map may not be weighty, but it has just this disillusioning effect on me. Momentarily I am tempted to forget about the five other hour-long videotapes, switch off the VCR, and catch the next train back to New York.

And yet, though the scales have fallen from my eyes, I stay. My anger and disappointment notwithstanding, I feel a professional obligation to keep watching and hear him out. Implausible as the story of the map sounds, it does not amount to proof that Ganzfried is right. It's one thing to acknowledge that the author of *Fragments* is an unreliable narrator, quite another to conclude definitively that he is Bruno Grosjean. The rest of his testimony might offer further clues to his identity as well as to the new round of questions rushing in as my confidence in Binjamin hits bottom. Why would he take on such a history if it wasn't his? How could someone so seemingly sensitive to the delicacy of memory offer up his fantasies for the historical record? Can he believe everything he has said? Does he know he's putting one over on us? How did he weave this story together? Is he merely making all this up as he goes along? And what made me believe him in the first place? Was it his writing voice? The reputations of the publishers and museum that brought us together? My own feeling that I had to believe him, that to do otherwise would be to deny the Holocaust?

Unfortunately, Joan Ringelheim was not posing these questions back in September of 1997 when she conducted the interview. Mostly he reprises the stories he told in *Fragments* or in other interviews; here too he says he arrived in Switzerland in early 1948. There are also occasional hints at his method. At one point he says that the most stressful moments in his adult life come when he wonders whether a terrible event actually lies behind one of his memories. "For me," he says, "it's better to know a terrible truth than to live constantly in this uncertain feeling."

With the spell broken, his stories have lost much of their power to scare me, to sadden me, to inspire me, to teach me lessons about the heights and depths of human nature. Even when he touches on the medical experiments—experiments he says he feels too ashamed to describe in detail—it is not as upsetting to absorb as it first was, because after all none of it may ever have happened to him. His talk of cruel Polish block wardens and oozing skulls and William Tell, which once seemed poignant, has now become an exercise in tedium. He weeps often and breaks down crying several times, yet I cannot summon up the compassion I felt for him just a few hours before.

Again and again, my eyes wander from the screen. Through a skylight I can see part of the Washington Monument covered by scaffolding. I glance at the archivists toiling at the reference desk and at the eight other researchers in the room. I hope they don't look back; I worry that they could detect some callousness in me, so out of place here, if they studied my face. I wonder what brought each of them to the Holocaust Museum library today, what real person, place, or event each of them is studying in the high-ceilinged reading room, a room filled with volumes cataloging and analyzing every aspect of the tremendous atrocity that was the Holocaust. Any book chosen at random, it would seem, would be more deserving of my attention than these six one-hour videotapes.

At the end of the interview, the camera zooms in on a photograph of dozens of children, a group portrait from the Krakow orphanage. It has been labeled 1946, but Binjamin thinks it could have been taken in 1947.

"And this is you?" Ringelheim asks. There is a small boy toward the front of the photograph. He has a round face. His hair is parted to one side, and he is wearing a white shirt and overalls.

"In the second row, yes," he says.

"I DON'T THINK I've ever interviewed someone who's lying," Joan Ringelheim tells me when I go to speak to her after watching Binjamin's videotaped testimony. We are sitting in a large, austere conference room near the archives. Most of the videotapes in the Washington museum's collection have come from Yale and other oral history projects, but Ringelheim has conducted many of the original interviews in the collection herself.

Just because she thinks she never interviewed a liar does not mean that everyone told her stories that are one hundred percent accurate. "Most people in an oral history don't tell you facts. They tell you what life felt like," she says. "Most people didn't understand what was happening to them while it was happening. Nobody experienced 'the Holocaust,' they experienced what was happening to them—and only afterwards did they wonder what was going on."

Sometimes survivors make mistakes when, in hindsight, they interpolate historical data into their own lived experience, she says. For example, survivors of Auschwitz tend to say that the selection made upon their arrival was conducted by Josef Mengele himself. "Sometimes I know that Mengele wasn't there when they were. They don't know there were twenty-two or twenty-three doctors there. But I don't say to them, 'You know, it couldn't have been Mengele, because he wasn't there that day.' I ask them, 'How did you know it was Mengele?' and they say, 'I found out afterwards.' It's clear what's going on."

The museum's policy, she says, is not to edit interviews, even when someone has obviously misspoken. "There's one person who says she was liberated by the Germans. Nobody heard her say it when they did the interview, but the interviewer heard it when she played it back." The interviewer wanted that sentence erased from the tape, but Ringelheim wouldn't because the interview was part of the historical record. "Initially when we were doing transcripts we would put footnotes to correct them, but it is so time-consuming. We have to leave it to scholars to do that."

Binjamin Wilkomirski's situation has little to do with the normal hazards of oral history, where decades later Mengele can be mistaken for another doctor or one exploding chimney can seem like four. "The question for him is not, Does he misremember here or there? but, Is the whole situation true or not?" Still, she would like to think that Binjamin is telling the truth. "I'd rather his story not be discredited," she says. "Even if his story is a total construction, he says something about the perception of children that I don't know that anyone else has said. How does a child take in language they didn't understand? I don't remember anyone writing about it so constructively. It's given me another insight into the Holocaust, or when I think about Mozambique or Bosnia. Adults, they at least know what war *isn't*."

On the other hand, if Binjamin's whole situation is false, the author of *Fragments* would be an example of a larger phenomenon of overidentification with the Holocaust. "I don't think we should be taking on other people's lives," she says. Ringelheim tells me about a woman born long after the war who hired a tattooist to burn a number into her arm, and about twinning—"that's when kids who are getting bar or bat mitzvahed find the name of a child who died in the Holocaust before they could get bar mitzvahed, and they mention their name. Twinning is kitsch." Ringelheim says she has seen a lot of kitschy responses to the Holocaust. "The more survivors die, the more you're going to get—and it's going to get stranger."

I ask what the Holocaust Museum will do with Binjamin's testimony if his identity cannot be authenticated, or if he is proven to be an impostor. I admit I'm a little surprised that his testimony is still available in the archive, since *Fragments* has been withdrawn from the gift shop on the ground floor.

"I wouldn't have taken it off the shelf," says Ringelheim. "We don't know." Besides, she says, "there are so many books down there that are terrible. They may be true, but they are boring."

AFTER WATCHING Binjamin's videotaped testimony and talking to Joan Ringelheim, I make my way through the museum's permanent exhibition. Although I'd passed by the museum a few times since it opened in 1993, I've managed to avoid going in until now. Many Americans—not only survivors and their families, and not just Jews— have made a point of stopping at the museum when they come to the nation's capital, and some have even made a special trip there just to see the museum. Not me. Though I felt the tug of duty, I felt ambivalent about visiting the museum, confused about the extent to which it would represent, as Ringelheim put it, my experience. I was aware that I would have been targeted by the Nazis if I'd lived in a country under their control, but until recently I had also thought that my whole family settled in America decades before the war began. In that sense the Holocaust didn't quite seem like my history. And I had read enough about the Holocaust to know I'd much rather spend an afternoon looking at Sargent portraits or lunar landing modules than spend the time thinking about myself as a potential victim just because I happen to be Jewish. It wasn't the discovery that Avram, Sima, and other family members remained in Riga which led me inside, but my doubts about a man who I feared was a gentile orphan from Switzerland. After spending so many hours listening to the author of *Fragments,* I figured a tour of the museum would be a worthwhile corrective, a way to ground myself again in the reality of this enormous tragedy.

To an extent, the museum does its best to make the Holocaust everyone's experience. At the start of the permanent exhibition, you get a booklet in the shape of a passport with the picture of a real person caught in the Nazi snare. As you advance through the dark exhibition halls, you are supposed to page through the passport to learn what happened to the person it portrays. The passport was not the bar-mitzvah twinning mentioned by Ringelheim, but in light of our conversation the pairing of visitor and victim made me slightly uneasy.

Architecturally, the galleries close in gradually as the exhibit progresses, as if to parallel the tightening constraints on German Jews in the 1930s and the confinement, impoverishment, deportation, and extermination of the Jews of Europe. The various documents, photographs, and artifacts of the Nazi years help dispel the callous feeling that had haunted me earlier in the library. At one point the exhibit passes through a boxcar once used by the Nazis for transporting people to camps. The wall text explains that one hundred people were crammed into the car, and as I stand inside it I picture how ninety-nine other people would have fit around me. I can only fill the space as if it were a grid—four columns by twenty-five? five by twenty? Inevitably it would have been a disorderly jumble, with fearful people staking out their own turf.

Again and again, I feel as if I am being asked to use my imagination to enter other people's shoes—at one point, almost literally. Toward the end of the exhibit, there is a room filled with thousands of shoes. The museum tells nothing about the particular person who wore any one shoe, for nobody has any idea who did, only that they arrived on the feet of people brought to Majdanek. They are also explained by a poem by Moishe Shulstein. "We are the shoes, we are the last witnesses," it reads. "And because we are only made of fabric and leather / And not of blood and flesh, each one of us survived the hellfire." In the dim light, the shoes, flattened by fifty-five years of disuse, dissolve into a somber brownish-black mass. After a few minutes, my pupils adjust and I can make out a variety of styles and occasional glimmers of individuation, a white lacy pattern or a red strap.

Like other objects displayed in bulk in the museum—a pile of empty suitcases chalked with their owners' names, a glass case filled with rusted scissors—the shoes conjure the specific and the massive at once. From the shoe with the red strap and the pictures of prewar Jewish life that came in earlier galleries, I begin to trace the seam of its former occupant's stockings and see her pleated dress, her rosy-cheeked face, her jealous boyfriend, her parents' hopes for their grandchildren. By multiplying that vision of human life by the thousands of shoes here or the millions of people murdered in concentration camps one might begin to approach the total of the destruction wrought by the Nazis, yet tabulating the result is overwhelming.

Joining me in the room with the shoes are two young women with two young boys in tow. A toddler, by the looks of him about eighteen months old, reclines in a stroller while an energetic tyke bounds around the room in a pair of blue and white Reeboks. Occasionally he rests his weight on the concrete-and-steel barrier that separates the shoes from the visitors. He is about a foot shorter than the fence, which comes up to my chest; I'd guess he is about five. His face betrays no understanding of what he is seeing, only that there are lots of shoes.

I take visual measurements of his sneakers and of the toddler's rubber-soled felt slippers, and then look back into the pile, casting about for something their size, a shoe that could have been stolen in Majdanek from a three- or four-year-old boy who wandered around the concentration camp with rags on his feet. Finding a pair of children's shoes would prove nothing about the authenticity of the author of *Fragments*, but I spend several minutes searching anyway. However pointless this exercise may be in my search for the truth about him, Binjamin still seems very real to me, and I am looking against all logic for a way to hold on to him.

AFTER A LONG day at the museum, I take the Metro out to Silver Spring, to have dinner with one of my Wilbur cousins. I have never met Ronald before—I know only the photograph of his father in Palestine in 1929, shirtless with a giant scar on his back—but he and his wife, Natalie, are nice enough to invite me over. Ronald is a tall, thin man in a blue tracksuit and a leather yarmulke. In the dark, he

points out the various synagogues along the road between the station and his home.

Dinner begins with a tasty chicken consommé and a lot of explanations of how we are related, what we do, why I am in Washington.
Ronald and Natalie met Binjamin when he came to the museum to
record his oral history, and they are not sure what they think of him
anymore. Ronald tells me that when he last saw Miriam, she told
him, "He's not one of us." Natalie tells me she sees the book not as
fact but rather as one man's personal memories, and that she doesn't
understand why people are so upset about the whole thing.

Both Ronald and Natalie say they were affected by Binjamin's
story, though not as much as their son Jonathan, who developed a
fascination with the Holocaust after visiting Auschwitz as part of the
March of the Living, an educational tour of Poland and Israel for
Jewish high school students. The centerpiece of the trip is a two-mile
walk from Auschwitz to Birkenau along the very path that an earlier
generation of Jews once followed to the gas chamber. Natalie told
me her son went mostly because it was "the in thing to do" for
seniors at his day school, but he returned transformed. That summer
Jonathan worked with the Holocaust Museum as a volunteer. The
building on the Mall hadn't opened yet, so he was helping to ready
the collection at a Maryland warehouse, where he got to see all of the
artifacts before they were put on display. For two months Jonathan
was part of a three-person team that cleaned and disinfected, one by
one, the thousands of shoes sent over from the museum at Majdanek. After that protracted opportunity to contemplate the massive
through the specific, he went on to take Holocaust studies courses in
college, and later became involved with the Spielberg-funded Shoah
Foundation's oral history project. In law school, Jonathan had written a paper on *Fragments,* considering Binjamin's questionable memories and his "interdisciplinary therapy" in the context of American
legal attitudes toward recovered-memory therapy, a process that is
controversial but "has been well received by the legal community,"
Jonathan said. He argued that criticism of such therapy on grounds
that it can plant false memories in patients would not be applicable
to the author of *Fragments,* since he reports having similar memories
before he went into therapy. "It may seem unnatural that Wilkomir-

ski buried memories of his childhood, but it was necessary as a protective measure to insure his psychological survival," Jonathan wrote.

On a gray afternoon back in New York, I meet Jonathan for
lunch at a kosher Italian restaurant on West Seventy-second Street.
He is tall like his father, and a few years younger than me. He is wearing a plaid flannel shirt, khakis, and a black suede yarmulke. Before,
when we spoke on the phone, Jonathan said it was "very apparent"
that *Fragments* was not a fabrication and "pretty evident" that Binjamin was a Holocaust survivor. He wasn't sure Binjamin was a relative, but if he were it might explain Jonathan's intense curiosity
about the Holocaust. Since then Jonathan had seen Binjamin on *60
Minutes,* which made him a bit more dubious, but Jonathan still
thought Binjamin might be our cousin.

A COUPLE OF months later, I return to Washington to see Binjamin
again. This time he is there in the flesh, though not to see me. The
American Orthopsychiatric Association has flown him in from
Zurich to accept the Max A. Hayman Award, given to recognize
"work done to increase our understanding of genocide and the
Holocaust." The Hayman award comes with a $500 cash prize. This
was the first speaking engagement he'd accepted since Ganzfried's
article in the *Weltwoche.* It was in a publication of the American
Orthopsychiatric Association (Ortho for short) that Harvey Peskin
reviewed *Fragments* in 1997; Tsipora Peskin, a doctor of social work
and Harvey's wife, sat on the Ortho board of directors.

Binjamin was a late entry at the Ortho conference, and when
Ortho sent out a letter announcing he would be getting the Hayman
award, some members objected to the decision. One lifetime member of Ortho, a psychologist who had seen Binjamin on *60 Minutes,*
complained that the award "dishonours the memory of legitimate
survivors of the Holocaust." The United States Holocaust Memorial
Museum, which was the previous recipient of the Hayman award,
was also dismayed by Ortho's choice of nominee. A spokeswoman
for the museum said that "very serious issues" about Binjamin
Wilkomirski remained unresolved, yet the Hayman award was tantamount to an endorsement of his authenticity. "There is a sufficient

range of materials, programs and activities that further understanding of the Holocaust that could be recognized that don't come with that sort of baggage," she said.

In light of these objections, the leadership of Ortho reexamined its decision, and the executive director called Holocaust literature specialist Lawrence Langer to ask him whether giving Binjamin an award at this juncture would be a good idea. Langer said no, not while his authenticity remained in doubt, but Ortho went ahead with their plans. Ortho president Ira Lourie, a child psychiatrist, told me, "We are not particularly taking a stand on the controversy—we don't have the information to make that judgment—but we decided that, regardless, he had made an important contribution."

Binjamin's speech is scheduled for early evening, but I arrive at the Crystal Gateway Marriott several hours early to collect my credentials. In the lobby I meet a television producer who has come all the way from Germany to cover Binjamin's first public appearance since Daniel Ganzfried's challenge. The Ortho conference turns out not to be as public as the German producer anticipated; her crew is denied permission to film Binjamin's presentation, as is a team from the BBC. Rather than asking to be admitted as a member of the press, I present myself as an interested civilian and buy a day pass.

The German television crew asks to interview me. I'm not sure why I'm worthy of their attention, other than that they won't get any fresh footage of Binjamin and need something new for their viewers, but I consent. It is an unseasonably warm spring day, and we drive around the city to find a scenic location. In the van the producer, a young German woman born after the war, tells me she cannot understand why Suhrkamp has kept *Fragments* in stores. Of all people, she says, her countrymen should feel compelled to distinguish between testimony and fantasy when it comes to the Holocaust.

The van parks, and the crew and I file out onto an open square around a large rectangular fountain. It is a popular location for skateboarders and, since the Capitol dome is visible in the distance, television production teams. The camera starts rolling, and I respond to the producer's questions about Binjamin, explaining to her how I was skeptical of his being a cousin. I talk about my great-grandmother Anna, her brother Avram, and his son Sima. I show the producer their photographs. The cameraman zooms in and scans the faces.

After the interview, the producer asks me to walk the perimeter of the large rectangular fountain so the cameraman can take an establishing shot. I walk to the corner where they suggest I begin. I go forward, turn left, and move unhurriedly toward the rolling camera. As I walk, I sense that the interview may not have been such a good idea. I know what journalists are capable of, and yet my caution disappeared on the other side of the questions. I realize I have been parading my own authenticity so they can undercut Binjamin's. Much as I disapprove of his appropriating the Wilburs' family history as his own, I feel rotten about betraying him, on German television of all places.

I also wonder how the author of *Fragments* felt when the lens, the microphone, the flattering attention was pointed in his direction. How did the ingratiating, reverent attitude of the journalists he encountered affect his sense of himself? Did their faith in him encourage him to embellish? Did their probing for telling details, precise wheres and whens and whats, put him under so much stress that he presented more of his uncertain memories as terrible truths?

I walk past the camera, as I was told. The cameraman murmurs something to the producer. She tells me the first take wasn't quite right, and asks if I would please walk around the fountain again.

ABOUT FIFTY people are in the Marriott ballroom at 7 P.M. for the presentation of the Hayman award and Binjamin's speech. He is sitting in front, along with Verena, psychologist Elitsur Bernstein, and, from the Child Holocaust Survivors Group of Los Angeles, Lauren Grabowski and John Gordon. I settle in on the end of an empty row of chairs in the back half of the room. I'd written ahead to let Binjamin know I would be here, but I will wait until after his speech to say hello.

A tweedy, clean-shaven man drifts back and introduces himself as Harvey Peskin. We pick up our ongoing conversation about Binjamin and the media. As long as reporters keep consulting documents and historians, Peskin tells me, they are missing the point of Binjamin's story entirely. Why should historians be the only experts?

Reporters will not understand Binjamin until they start listening to psychologists and accord as much respect to the validity of human memory as they do to documentation. After all, the documents are man-made, and they are as liable to carry the errors and biases of their creators as individual testimony. Then a hush comes over the room, and Peskin returns to his seat.

A bald, bearded psychologist from Maryland named Richard Ruth introduces Binjamin. Ruth explains that the Hayman award is being given for *Fragments* and for the therapeutic concepts its author developed with Elitsur Bernstein. "The method that Wilkomirski and Bernstein have elaborated is important not only to survivors of the genocide of the Holocaust, but to survivors of genocide around the world and currently in our own time," Ruth says. He refers to wars under way in Eritrea and Kosovo, and ties in *Fragments* with the struggle for black liberation in America. "Wilkomirski's book brings to mind memories of the slave narratives of an earlier time, the truth they revealed and the controversies and criticisms they evoked," he says. Several "autobiographies" of ex-slaves, published to bring attention to the abolitionist cause, turned out to be the fictive creations by whites or black freemen.

"Controversy cannot be allowed to kill ideas," says Ruth. "We are honoring Mr. Wilkomirski not as historians or as politicians, but as mental health professionals. What he has written is important clinically. For far too long the experiences of children under conditions of genocide have been seen as too complicated, too threatening, too ambiguous, or too marginal to command attention."

Binjamin comes to the microphone in a white shirt and black jacket to accept his award. It is the first time I have seen him without a scarf. He nibbles on his lower lip as he begins, but he gets comfortable quickly. If the Ortho audience knows about Daniel Ganzfried's findings, they seem not to take them seriously. They accept their guest as Binjamin Wilkomirski, or at least give him the benefit of the doubt.

"Just to give you one example of my work," he says, "I would like to tell you a story which has many parallels to my personal case. It's the story of a woman in Switzerland, a child survivor, with whom I worked during the past year trying to find historical evidence backing up her early childhood memories so she could feel more secure in her identity."

With that, Binjamin launches into a clinical presentation. Sabina—he does not say whether it is a pseudonym—is a woman around his age. After the war, she took over the identity of a Swiss girl who died in a sanitarium, and until she went to see a psychologist decades later, nobody would take her childhood memories seriously. Sabina did not remember her family name, or where she was from, or what language she spoke, only that she had been called Zizi as a child, and that she had an older sister. She also remembered the word Terezin.

Binjamin describes one of Sabina's recurring nightmares. "She was standing in the middle of a street in a camp and saw many children coming towards her. The children walking in front were holding up a kind of banner on which the initials 'E.E.M.' were written." The initials on the banner, which always made Sabina cry, seemed to stand for *Elle est morte* (She is dead); the woman in question was Sabina's mother. Binjamin asked Sabina to listen to the phrase "She is dead" in various European languages. "This sentence spoken in every Eastern European language had not the slightest effect on her, but whenever it was said in French, her pulse went up and she started perspiring," reported Binjamin, who concluded that Sabina lived in a French-speaking country.

There is an overhead projector by the podium, and Binjamin turns it on. On the first transparency is a map of Terezin. Sabina remembered a series of letters and numbers on a sign in a stone fortress; Binjamin has found a building matching the coordinates at the concentration camp. Sabina remembers a shoemaker, a Mr. Klein, from Terezin; Binjamin projects a crude sketch of a mustachioed cobbler, drawn by Sabina from memory. Then he puts up a postwar studio portrait of a dapper and bewhiskered man who, Binjamin says, was named Mr. Klein and made shoes at the camp.

Sabina produces a sketch of another place, one much hotter and drier than Terezin, full of white buildings with narrow doors and high windows. "After about half a year of looking through all available photographs of concentration camp buildings, by chance we found this." Binjamin projects a photograph of Rivesaltes, in southern France.

The last clue to Sabina's identity falls into place by chance, when she is telling Binjamin about her school days in Switzerland. " 'When I had trouble in school or with my teacher—I wasn't so good in school, you know—I had something that always helped me a lot. I had a magic word,' she said. 'I still remember it,' and she laughed."

Binjamin performs his rendition of the magic word for the clinicians at Ortho. It is a rapid drumroll, in three-four time, repeated again and again: *rom-pom-pom rom-pom-pom rom-pom-pom*. He tells Sabina, "If this word gave you a good feeling, even a feeling of security, it might be your real name." To him, it sounds like "Rappaport." Sure enough, Binjamin finds a Sabina Rappaport, born 1938, on a 1944 transport list of French Jews.

"It took nearly fifty years until Sabina could accept Rappaport not only as her magic word but as her, and her family's, true name," Binjamin concludes. "Today, Susan"—he pauses; it is the second time Binjamin has stumbled and called her Susan—"Sabina is a very balanced, realistically thinking and speaking person."

Binjamin receives a small but fervid standing ovation. The Hayman award, Binjamin says, "is encouraging me to continue collaborating with therapists to help people like Sabina despite all the obstacles I have met in the last few months." He thanks the audience, reads aloud from a message of congratulation sent by Lea Balint of the Bureau of Children Without Identity, and begins to answer questions from the audience. No, his memories are not recovered memories; yes, adults don't believe children's crystalline memories because they feel threatened by them. What advice would you give to guardians of a Kosovar Albanian or a member of an endangered Native American tribe? Make a record of everything they say, especially those words you can't understand.

There is no open microphone; the questions have been submitted by audience members on index cards that were distributed at the beginning of Binjamin's lecture. I consider my card carefully. I could ask whether Sabina (or is it Susan?) is a real case history or a character invented for the purposes of this evening's presentation. I could ask about the map of Europe he marked up as a child. I could ask him why he hasn't made public the documents he controls pertaining to Bruno Grosjean. I could ask him whether he still believes, as he said back in New York, that the Wilkomirskis are all somehow related. In truth, I cannot possibly fit all the questions I have about Binjamin on one index card, and I would not know what to make of his answer if it demanded that I trust his memory. My mother has asked me to send Binjamin her regards, and I think about writing that down on my card, but I leave it blank.

The talk ends, and as the room empties I approach him. "Hello, Binjamin," I say.

He looks up. I say my name and remind him of who I am. I do not know what to expect: an angry outburst, a flood of tears, a look of terror, perhaps an outburst of rage. In the Holocaust Museum testimony, he told a story about throwing a schoolmate down several flights of stairs because the boy sneered at him the same way the Nazis' Ukrainian henchmen had.

His reaction is none of the above. His expression is blank, as if we had never met, as if there were never a connection between us, as if I were not standing three feet away from him. He walks away, and retreats to Verena's side. A severe woman in a textured black dress approaches. It is Tsipora Peskin. "This is a mental health conference," she tells me, and asks me not to talk to Binjamin for the sake of his mental health. I agree to abide by her wishes, but I try to reopen the lines of communication by asking Tsipora Peskin to convey to Binjamin and Verena my mother's regards.

She walks over to them, and returns a minute later with a message. "They say thank you, and they love your mother very much."

THE
WILKOMIRSKIS
OF RIGA

"When my grandmother spoke of Riga," my mother tells me, "it never struck me as a real place. It was more like something out of a fairy tale. Not necessarily a good or bad fairy tale, but some sort of mythical place." A place where Anna, her tomboy grandmother, clambered over the stepped roofs of the brightly painted houses; a gingerbread colony with a river view. My mother's other ancestors came from elsewhere in Eastern Europe, but Riga became the place she longed to visit. For whatever reason, it was Riga that had come to represent her past.

Thanks to my mother's stories, I too longed for Riga. The Eskins, to the best of my father's knowledge, came from the Belorussian hinterland, and I much preferred to think of my ancestors as coming from a metropolis known not only for its bustling commerce but for its diverse population and its intellectual life. Isaiah Berlin, the polymathic scholar who became perhaps the epitome of the Oxford don, grew up in Riga, as did cinema revolutionary Sergei Eisenstein, whose frequent youthful trips to the theater, opera, and circus emboldened him to stray from the engineering career his strict architect father intended for him. I knew little about how my ancestors lived in Riga, although I assumed that they would not have left for America at the beginning of the twentieth century in search of a better life had they been as well fixed as the Berlins or the Eisensteins.

My mother and I both felt a nostalgia for this city we had never seen, and it didn't seem right to go there without her. Using the Russian I learned in college, I could investigate the origins of the author of *Fragments* while helping her research family history. The research would likely take us to the same sources, and even if he was not a relative (and my mother's hopes that he was one had been tested, but not destroyed), an attempt to authenticate the memoirist's claims might lead us to more genealogical information about our Wilkomirski forebears.

When we first began discussing the trip, I had high hopes of resolving our questions about Binjamin and the Wilburs. Since we began planning it, however, I had been to Washington twice and the author of *Fragments* had let me down twice, first with his videotaped testimony and then with his stoic silence when I approached him after his speech at the Ortho conference. In addition, just before we left for Riga, two other journalists published articles that turned up nothing new substantiating Bruno Doessekker's claim that he is Binjamin Wilkomirski of Riga. What Elena Lappin, writing in *Granta,* and Philip Gourevitch of *The New Yorker* did find were details of how his identity was constructed: that his kinky mop of hair was professionally curled, that the Yiddish inflection in his German came and went depending on whether he was discussing the Holocaust. They also talked to people who remembered Doessekker telling them about his hidden past decades earlier. Annie Singer, the ex-girlfriend who appeared on *60 Minutes,* recalled that he told her he came from the Baltic when they were in high school together, in the late fifties. Zurich musician Gertrud Voegli said that in the sixties and seventies, the clarinetist had talked of being in the Warsaw ghetto and claimed kinship with a family of Polish musicians named Wilkomirski. Elitsur Bernstein said that when he first went to Does-sekker for music lessons in 1979, a portrait of the last rabbi of Wil-komir hung in his teacher's atelier.

Lappin's more thorough and more empathetic treatment of the case included an interview with the brother of Yvonne Grosjean, the woman listed as the memoirist's birth mother in official Swiss docu-

BRUNO GROSJEAN (B. 1941) IN SWITZERLAND WITH MOTHER
YVONNE AND UNCLE MAX.

ments. Max Grosjean had a family photo album with pictures of
Bruno as a baby; he told Lappin he had tried to adopt the boy himself.
Lappin also identified another person whose life had been folded
into Binjamin Wilkomirski's story. In the original German text of
Fragments, Binjamin describes an encounter with a slightly older girl
called Karola at the Krakow orphanage. (For the English edition, her

name was changed to Mila.) "We knew each other from somewhere, from one of the many barracks probably," he says. He meets Karola for a third time in Switzerland as an adult, and for a time they shared "a love fed by sadness." Lappin dug up records indicating that the first two meetings with Karola could not have happened; she was never in a concentration camp, and she arrived at the Krakow orphanage only after Binjamin says he left for Switzerland. The real Karola Fliegner might have shed more light on her portrait in *Fragments*, but she declined to be interviewed.

The reclusive author of *Fragments*, meanwhile, consented to full-day conversations with Lappin and Gourevitch, just as he had done with Daniel Ganzfried. His published comments revealed little more than his own confusion and moodiness. He did tell both reporters about meeting the real Bruno Grosjean when they were young. This Bruno had left Switzerland, he said, perhaps for the United States, and was living under an alias.

By the time we landed in Riga, I suspected that looking in Latvia for evidence of the author of *Fragments* might not be any more productive than dredging Loch Ness to find pieces of the eggshell from which the legendary monster was hatched. Moreover, the Nazis were famous for destroying Jewish communal records in the places they conquered, and I did not expect Riga to be any different. If anything gave me hope of finding evidence of a Binjamin Wilkomirski in Riga, it was, paradoxically, my distrust of the author of *Fragments*. Perhaps he hadn't told us everything he had found out about the family's presence in Riga. Conceivably there was a real Binjamin Wilkomirski, maybe a little cousin of mine and maybe a complete stranger, whose identity the author of *Fragments* had usurped.

Ironically, the best leads I had came from him; in his first letter to my mother, the author of *Fragments* mentioned two longtime residents of Riga whom he met on his own fact-finding tour. The first was a Mr. Vestermanis, the official historian of the Riga Jewish community, who supposedly told the author of *Fragments* that a few houses away from the spot where he remembered seeing his father killed, the engraver Avram Wilkomirski lived until 1926. The second source was another Avram; his last name was Lat. Avram Lat was one of a trio of old Jews at the synagogue who supposedly remembered a Wilkomirski boy from school seventy years earlier. If Vester-manis and Lat could not confirm Binjamin's account of events, per-haps they could lead me to information about my own relatives, or give me insight into how the author of *Fragments* became Binjamin Wilkomirski.

Even after I filled her in on my own research and shared with her the latest reports, my mother still spoke of Cousin Binjamin hope-fully. It wasn't her ongoing interaction with the author of *Fragments* that kept her loyal to him; he had never responded to her supportive fax or later attempts to reach him other than through the message relayed by Tsipora Peskin. I didn't quite know what to make of my mother's attachment to him. To see the woman who'd taught me about the importance of research let her desire to find living relatives blind her to information increasingly suggesting that the author of *Fragments* wasn't one of them was disheartening. I felt like the bet-ter reporter, yet her compassion for Binjamin made her the better human being.

Though I doubted that the author of *Fragments* was my relative or indeed a Holocaust survivor, his story had become part of the fab-ric of my thirdhand nostalgia. The compelling scene at the beginning of *Fragments* in which young Binjamin watches the death of his per-haps-father seemed more substantial than anything I knew about my own family's life or death there. His sketch of Riga, however frag-mentary, suggested a fuller narrative than the names and photographs preserved by Aunt Miriam and my mother.

Whatever we were to discover about Binjamin, the trip to Riga would be an opportunity for my mother and me to reconcile our image of this city of our origins with the people and places we found there. As we rode in from the airport along the pitted highway past billboards and Soviet-era housing blocks and approached the bridge crossing the Daugava, the city of my mother's imagination, the myth-ical place we had dreamed of, began to recede.

ALL THINGS considered, it was one of the better moments in history for my mother and me to go to Riga. Had we arrived two hundred years earlier, we would have been required by law to stay at the

Judenherberge, or Jewish inn. Local law required visiting Jews to sleep apart from other visitors. The *Judenherberge* was but one expression of an intermittent but long-standing discomfort with the presence of Jews in Riga. In 1561, when Sigismund II of Poland signed a treaty to annex Livonia, local potentates asked the usually tolerant king to exclude Jews from Riga "so that they may not besmirch or injure the citizens with their unchristian usury and business transactions." Edicts barring Jewish inhabitants or traders were also issued by the Swedes, who conquered Riga in the seventeenth century, and the Russians, who followed in the eighteenth century. These decrees were not always thoroughly enforced, and royal physicians and the occasional wealthy merchant received an exemption. In 1785 Catherine the Great allowed Jews to establish citizenship in the nearby town of Schlock, but it was not until 1841 that more than a handful of Jews obtained the right to reside in Riga indefinitely.

Had we visited Riga one hundred years ago, my mother and I might have stayed with our relatives in the Moscow Vorstadt, a working-class district southeast of the Old City that became a home to Jewish migrants. The Moscow Vorstadt had a Jewish cemetery, a Jewish hospital, Jewish schools, and several synagogues; the Great Choral Synagogue was built between 1868 and 1871. At the end of the nineteenth century, there were about 30,000 Jews in Riga, out of a population of 260,000. Yiddish was but one of the languages spoken in the city. Riga, part of the Russian Empire, had a sizable German aristocracy, and industrialization brought an influx of Latvian-speaking peasants from the countryside.

Had we arrived fifty-eight years earlier, my mother and I would have been wise to turn around immediately. Jews were well integrated into the independent Latvian republic established after World War I, but this came to an end in 1940. As a result of the Hitler-Stalin pact, the Red Army occupied Latvia and folded it into the Soviet Union. While some Jewish individuals found common cause with the Communist regime, observant Jews and Zionists suffered from its repressive policies. A year later, the treaty between Russia and Germany was about to fall apart. To many Latvians, this was cause for hope; the Nazis seemed like the lesser of two evils, and their arrival would reverse the Soviet Union's nationalization of the economy and suppression of religion.

On June 22, 1941, the Germans invaded Russia. Before the Nazis occupied Riga on July 1, several thousand Jews managed to flee eastward, but those who remained were arrested, beaten, tortured, and killed by the Nazis and by Latvian fascist volunteers who equated Jews with Communists. It was a Latvian commando that herded hundreds of Jews, locals along with refugees from Lithuania, into Riga's Great Choral Synagogue on July 4, locked them inside, and set it on fire. The Nazis established a ghetto in the Moscow Vorstadt, and nearly thirty thousand Jews were rounded up and sent there. At the end of November, about four thousand able-bodied men were selected; along with a few hundred women, they were moved to a small section of the ghetto which was then sealed off. The rest of the Riga Jews were forced to march out to the Rumbula forest, where they were stripped and shot. After the liquidation of the local Jews, the Riga ghetto became a holding pen for Jews deported from the German Reich.

The Red Army chased the Nazis out in 1944, and Latvia again became part of the Soviet Union. Had my mother and I visited Riga, say, twenty-five years ago, we would have been assigned to a hotel operated by Intourist, the state-run travel monopoly, and been watched by guides who would steer us away from unauthorized contact with Soviet citizens, particularly those subversives who clung to their Jewish identity.

Latvia is independent once again and showing signs of prosperity, and the approaching summer solstice makes it an auspicious time of year for a visit. Riga is situated at almost 57 degrees latitude north, and the sun hovers above the city twenty hours each day. On the streets, everyone seems aware of a brief window of opportunity; they know the cycle will repeat and the long winter will return. So the Old City—with its narrow winding alleys crowded with three- and four-story Hanseatic houses dating back to the thirteenth century, it is the only part of Riga that looks anything like my mother's fairy-tale image of the place—fills up with tourists lapping Pinguin ice cream cones and locals drinking pints of Aldaris beer at outdoor gardens. The poplar trees release downy white spores, and the wind whips up summertime flurries of weightless flakes in the dusty downtown streets.

DOWN THE street from our hotel is a white four-story building that opened in 1926 as the city's Jewish theater. After a half century of playing other roles—as a workers' playhouse, a Nazi storehouse for confiscated communal property, a Communist Party meeting hall, and a marionette theater—the building was returned to what remains of its original audience. It now contains a lending library, a Hebrew school for children, social welfare programs for the elderly, and a museum and archive called Jews in Latvia. The museum takes up a modest two-room suite on the third floor, with one room devoted to the years before 1939 and the other to the years since.

On the fourth floor, my mother and I find the office of the director of Jews in Latvia, Margers Vestermanis. The floor of his office is painted yellow, and rusty water stains snake down the peeling white walls. There is a personal computer, a fax machine, and a small copy machine, all donated by German foundations. High on one wall hangs a portrait of Vestermanis's hero, Simon Dubnow, the author of a ten-volume *World History of the Jewish People*. After fleeing the Bolshevik regime, Dubnow settled in Riga in 1933. According to Vestermanis's guidebook to Jewish Riga, which is sold downstairs in the museum, the last words Dubnow uttered at Rumbula were "*Shraybt, yidn, shraybt*"—Write, Jews, write.

Vestermanis, a short, stocky seventy-four-year-old man with white hair and thick plastic-rimmed glasses, founded Jews in Latvia in the waning days of the Soviet Union, and he runs it on a shoestring. He serves without salary, but perhaps the opportunity to do the work is sufficient compensation. Vestermanis explains that years ago he ran the archives at Riga's Museum of the Revolution while working on a book on the political, economic, and racial dimensions of Nazi terror in the Baltic. Vestermanis knew that Soviet historiography did not consider the racial dimensions of the war—the Holocaust, in other words—an acceptable topic of inquiry, so he submitted the manuscript under a non-Jewish pseudonym. However, no sooner did Vestermanis hand his book in than he was called urgently to Leningrad for military training, and when he returned he learned that his manuscript had been rejected and his job no longer existed. Vestermanis finished his career as a high school teacher. If he is bitter about his experiences, he hides it well beneath a robust geniality and gentle wit.

I show Vestermanis Binjamin's first letter to my mother, the one in which the author of *Fragments* mentions the local historian's name. English is the historian's fourth or fifth language and he reads it slowly. He grunts when he finishes, and in Russian he tells me his version of events. On a busy day about five years earlier, two men came to his office to ask if it was possible that a person could have escaped from a certain house on the edge of the Riga ghetto on the eve of the first mass murder at Rumbula. Vestermanis told the men that it was possible. He had no idea that one of his visitors was the potential escapee or that he was writing a book. Vestermanis forgot about the two men—the author of *Fragments* and his friend Elitsur Bernstein—until the investigations of Binjamin Wilkomirski's authenticity began.

Like other people whom the author of *Fragments* encountered on his quest, Vestermanis says his input was misrepresented. The local historian recites a long list of reasons why the Latvian part of Binjamin Wilkomirski's story is impossible. There was no way Binjamin could have seen the towers of Old Riga from within the ghetto, as he describes. The author remembered hearing a cry of warning— "Attention, Latvian militia"—but this made no sense to Vestermanis, as the Latvians didn't call police "militia" until they were subsumed into the Soviet Union after the wars. Then there was the matter of Binjamin's riverine escape, which Vestermanis thought had been adapted from the story of Janis Lipke, a longshoreman who helped more than fifty Jews flee the ghetto in 1942, but this was after the Nazis repopulated the Riga ghetto with Jews from Germany, and long after the local Jewish children were sent to Rumbula. There were no records of such an escape during the winter of 1941, however, and it was hard to imagine how it could have been done. If a boat made its way inland, it would have had to go against the current, and upriver the water had frozen solid. Had they sailed out into the port of Riga, a major Nazi marine base, their vessel would surely have been noticed by German boats. It's theoretically possible, Vestermanis says, but highly improbable. "Maybe on a little boat," he says weakly.

However unlikely Binjamin's story may be, Vestermanis will not say for certain that the author of *Fragments* is a liar. "Every person who survived, who was *a priori* condemned to death, his story is unbelievable," he says. At the end of the war, Vestermanis explains, Soviet soldiers found him hiding in the forest and asked for his documents.

"What documents? I ran away from such and such a camp," he remembers telling them. They hadn't heard of the small camp in northern Latvia where he'd been kept; nor did they know of Kaiserwald, the camp on the edge of Riga where Vestermanis worked as a carpenter; nor had they heard of the camp at Skrunda, where Jews were forced to dig peat.

" 'And before that?' they asked.

" 'I was in the ghetto.'

" 'How is that possible?' they said. 'We've been across all of Latvia and we haven't met one living Jew. And along comes a guy, he survived the ghetto, he survived a camp, he survived the next camp. And then he joined a group of partisans, we destroyed all of them, and again he survived. That cannot be.' " Vestermanis says they imprisoned him until he thought to drop his pants and show his captors that he was circumcised. "Life is full of miracles," he says.

He repeats the sentence in Yiddish and English for my mother's benefit. After an hour or so of listening to Vestermanis speak to me in Russian and waiting patiently for occasional rough translations, she takes her turn to talk to Vestermanis, to ask him about her relatives. She is not the only one relieved to move on; Vestermanis, overheated by the talk about Binjamin Wilkomirski, tells avuncular jokes once the topic shifts from *Fragments* to our own Wilkomirski ancestors from Riga. "This is a lot more meaningful to me," he says with a smile.

Conversation shifts into Yiddish, a language I have not heard my mother speak since I was a little boy. She unfurls a computer printout, several pages taped together showing the Wilkomirski family tree, and spreads out color copies of family photographs. The pictures, some of the same ones the author of *Fragments* flipped through at her home, are of relatives from Riga, from elsewhere in Latvia, from the Lithuanian town of Panavezys. In her excitement, my mother is not methodical. She jumps from node to node on the tree, offering Vestermanis details about people who have nothing to do with the Riga Wilkomirskis. *Dos iz mayn bobe,* she says. *Dos iz der bruder. Dos iz mayne groystante.* That's my grandmother, that one's her brother Avram, that's my great-aunt. As he peruses the materials before him, Vestermanis tells my mother she speaks Yiddish like a Courlander. She beams upon hearing that the fumbling, long-dormant language of her youth carries any residue of her heritage.

Vestermanis is particularly intrigued by a picture of the bar mitzvah of one of Miriam's brothers, and he asks my mother for a copy for his archive. "Without documents, there is no history. That's why I'm still collecting documents," he says. What happened in Riga is well enough known, but "nobody's written about how people in little villages died—here five families, there two families." Vestermanis wants to find out what happened to as many Jewish families as he can.

"Behind every Jewish family name, there is a story," he says, and uses his own name to illustrate his point. A Vestermanis is a man from the west, and in the course of a few sentences he paints half a millennium of Jewish migration, from the flight from Spain during the Inquisition up to Holland, across Germany and Poland to the east coast of the Baltic Sea. I am amazed and a bit jealous that he can see that far back; I had never even thought about where the Wilkomirskis lived at the end of the fifteenth century or what their name was then.

VESTERMANIS suggested a few places where we might pursue the story behind Wilkomirski, using the little information we have about our ancestors. We cross the river to the national archives, where, following Vestermanis's instructions, we ask for archivist Irina Veinberga. I am prepared for the worst of Soviet-style bureaucratic obfuscation, and at first it seems like I will not be disappointed. Veinberga is not in, we are told by an assistant. She'll be back next week; maybe you can come back then.

We cross back into Old Riga, and head to Richard Wagner Street and the municipal library. Up two flights of stairs and tucked away above the conservatory, the library is musty, informal, and computer free, what one might find in a neglected American public school. We ask for the annual city directories, beginning, for no particular reason, with 1896. My mother and I divide them up. No Wilkomirskis in the first volume I open, but in the 1900 edition I find:

> *Wilkomirsky, Anna, Schndrn, Dünaburgerstr. 42*
> *Wilkomirsky, Liebe, Schndrn, Dünaburgerstr. 42*

Anna is my great-grandmother's name; Liebe was Anna's mother. A *Schneiderin* is a seamstress, and the Dünaburgerstrasse, I see on the map, runs through the Moscow Vorstadt. So the Wilburs are not impostors after all; we come from Riga—and we can document it. It's not that I thought we weren't from Riga, but my experience with the inconsistent tales of Bruno Doessekker has led me to distrust family lore. I show my mother the listings, and she lets out a yip of delight, breaking the silence. The reading room is empty except for the librarian, who flashes a bemused smile.

This first discovery energizes us as we progress through the twentieth century. The type in the directories shifts from year to year, from German black letter to standard Cyrillic to the Latinate Latvian alphabet. Nor is anything consistent about the Wilkomirskis we find. One year they appear, the next year they are not mentioned. Their addresses change, as does the spelling of the family name. We find "Wolkomirski, M.," a tailor and perhaps Anna's brother Meir, in three consecutive books beginning with 1909. *Portnoy, Schneiderin, drebnieks;* the Wilkomirskis made their living with needle and thread.

Anna's brother Avram finally turns up in 1925, as "Vilkomirskij, Abr.," also a tailor. It is the first time we see his name, although several volumes from the previous decade are missing. In the 1926–27 directory, he is "Wilkomirsky, Abr.," an engraver. This must be the citation the author of *Fragments* stumbled upon; Rucha, Aunt Miriam's mother, is listed at the same address. "Vilkomirskis, Abrams," appears in 1928 as a tailor again. Each time he's listed at a different address, all of them in the Moscow Vorstadt. After 1928 and up until the war, he does not surface in the city directories. The books tell us something, but mostly they tell us there is much more we do not know. If he moved each year, who knows whether Avram stayed in Riga through 1941?

It is early evening by the time we finish up at the library, and the sun is still bright. This being a Friday, I suggest that we walk over to the Peitavas synagogue a few blocks away. Built in 1905, it is the only synagogue left in Riga, the only one that the Fascists did not burn. The front doors are unlabeled and locked, so we walk around back, through one alley and then a smaller alley that takes us into an unpaved courtyard. A slow-moving and unkempt old man limps along behind us. My mother stiffens, and I am not sure whether it's because we have been followed into the empty yard or because she has spent much of her life avoiding traditional Jewish settings where women are relegated to the balconies.

The old man, who wears a threadbare brown jacket and a blue cloth cap, catches up to us. He looks gentle and slow-witted. It is hard for me to understand him when he opens his mouth, since he is missing most of his teeth and has a speech impediment, but I finally make out that he is welcoming us to the synagogue. He is an army veteran, he says with pride, doffing his cap and revealing a scar where his head was split open during the war.

I ask him if he knows Avram Lat, the other man Binjamin mentioned in his first letter to my mother, the man who says he knew a Wilkomirski from the school he attended. He says that Lat might show up for services soon. He takes me inside, up to the second floor. Sitting behind a desk is a woman who looks old enough to be the limping veteran's mother. I explain to her I am looking for Avram Lat, and she calls around looking for his phone number. She calls his house for me. Lat says he won't be showing up for this evening's services, but he might be there tomorrow morning. She gives me Lat's number. She invites my mother and me to come to tonight's service, but we decline politely. We wish the woman a good shabbas and I promise to return for the morning service.

Mom decides to sleep in on Saturday, so I set out by myself in jacket and tie. I have a yarmulke in my pocket, which I put on my head once I am inside the synagogue courtyard. I feel a bit uneasy because I have come not to pray but to work, to ask around for Avram Lat or anyone else who might be able to tell me about the

Wilkomirskis of Riga or about the author of *Fragments,* who came
looking for them five years before I did.

I arrive early, and there are maybe fifteen people when I get
there. I sit down next to a rail-thin man in his seventies. He has a
gray mustache, eyeglasses, and a resigned elegance. I ask if he knows
Avram Lat, but he doesn't.

The service begins. My knowledge of Hebrew is poor, and the
man sitting next to me repeatedly helps me find my place in the
prayer book, which, like the rabbi, has been supplied by the Lubav-
itcher Hasidim. By the time the reading of the Torah commences an
hour later, the number of men in attendance has risen to thirty-five.
Most of them are elderly, but there is one young boy, perhaps six
years old, sitting with his father, and a pair of young Lubavitch emis-
saries from Brooklyn. When I look up to my left I see a few women,
their heads covered and peeking out over the balcony ledge. The
Jewish population of Riga was replenished after World War II, when
the Soviet authorities, wary of nationalism, moved hundreds of
thousands of Russian speakers to the Baltic states. Beginning in the
1970s, the Jews among them began leaving for Israel, America, Germany, and elsewhere. Riga now has 10,000 to 12,000 Jews, but most
people with a strong Jewish identity and the means to leave have
done so. The man next to me tells me he would like to emigrate to
Israel, but doesn't think he can afford it.

People mill about during the service, and those curious about my
presence come over to me. A small, barrel-chested man wearing a
Zionist lapel pin acts suspicious at first, but after I explain myself, he
keeps coming over to tell me that Avram Lat has not shown up yet.
The longtime Riga residents I meet are kind, but they have never
heard of my Wilkomirski ancestors and nobody remembers anything about the author of *Fragments.* As I do not understand most of
the service, I start to daydream about Avram Lat. Into my head pops
the fantasy that he is actually Avram Wilkomirski, my great-great-
uncle, but I try to banish the thought; it's only an expression of my
desire to find someone, anyone, to connect me to this place.

Toward the end of the service, the veteran with the scar on his
head grabs me by the arm. He takes me over to a pious old man with
the face of a salamander. "This is Avram Lat," the veteran says, but

the man he points to says he's not. "Lat isn't here today," he says.

Back at the hotel, I call the number I've been given for Avram Lat. I'm told he's out, and I leave a message.

WHEN THE national archive reopens on Monday, Mom and I ask for Irina Veinberga, who emerges after a long wait. Veinberga, a slight woman in a cardigan sweater, knows the Binjamin Wilkomirski case. She has searched the files for him before, to no avail. She seems exasperated by our inquiry until my mother shows her a copy of our family tree and asks Veinberga to look for Anna Wilkomirski and her brothers and sisters. She copies names and dates from my mother's genealogy and tells us to come back in a few days, just before our flight leaves. In the meantime, Veinberga directs us to the hall of records, where births, marriages, and deaths since 1920 are recorded.

At the hall of records, an ugly modern building near our hotel, I fill out two forms requesting birth information. One is for Sima Wilkomirski, the son of Avram; the second is for Binjamin Wilkomirski. I write down that Sima was born around 1930; Binjamin sometime between 1938 and 1941. After fifteen minutes, the tender of the ledgers, a surly woman with bleached hair, calls me into her office. She flips slowly through the 1930 ledger until she finds a Simanas Bers Volkomirskis, born on May 1, 1930; his father was Abrams Volkomirskis, a Jew. His mother's name is Baseva. I ask her whether there is a record of their marriage, and a few minutes later she produces a 1928 certificate.

The ledger clerk is confused by my other request until I tell her that I am trying to find out if Sima's father had any other children. She asks why I can't just ask Sima or his father, and I explain that they probably died in the ghetto. She looks through the ledgers from 1930 to 1941 but finds no Binjamin, and no other Wilkomirski child under any spelling of the name.

With the addresses we found and Vestermanis's map of Jewish Riga, Mom and I decide to walk through the Moscow Vorstadt. Up to this point, the Riga neighborhoods we have visited were full of scaffolding, noisy tools, and placards boasting of foreign investment, but on some blocks in the Moscow Vorstadt, which lies behind the main railway station, it seems as if the last construction project here was the dismantling of the ghetto wall. The quarter is poor, dusty, and deserted. We see few pedestrians and no other tourists.

At each address where the Wilkomirskis were listed in the city directory, we stop to look around and take snapshots. On the block where Anna lived in 1900, there is a row of two-story wooden houses, purplish brown with rotting beams, sagging roofs, and crumbling window sashes. Even one hundred years ago these could not have been choice accommodations, and we begin to see in three dimensions what life might have been like for Anna's widowed mother and her seven children. We also find the six-story building on Moskva Street where Avram lived with Aunt Miriam and her brothers a couple of years before they emigrated.

Along the way, we pass the corner where the author of *Fragments* says he saw his father die. I look around for some sign of what might have given him that impression, but nothing registers.

MEANWHILE I keep after Avram Lat. When I finally reach him at home, I ask whether I can come visit him, but he puts me off, telling me to call again the next day. We repeat this dance several times, and with each delay I grow more eager to see him, even though he says he can't tell me anything about either the author of *Fragments* or the Wilkomirskis. When he finally consents to meet me, he does not let me come to his home, insisting instead on traveling for an hour in the midday heat to meet me downtown.

We meet in a hotel lobby. At eighty-seven, Lat has a head of thinning white hair, a trim mustache, and an alert mind. We walk over to the Café Lolo, which is the closest thing to a Viennese coffeehouse in Riga. Although I have invited him, he asks me what I want—a chocolate sundae, perhaps?—and holds up two fingers as he orders. A minute later, he calls over our waitress and says a few words in Latvian. When she returns, she delivers two glasses of mineral water and one sundae. I ask Lat what happened to the other sundae, and he tells me he ate already today.

An uncomfortable silence descends on our table, but there is nothing for me to do but start in on the whipped cream as Lat launches into his war stories. He says that on June 29, 1941, two days before the Nazi invasion of Latvia, he took his wife and six-month-old daughter—she'll be fifty-nine in October; she's a school principal—and ran to Siberia. I remember that Avram Wilkomirski's marriage license identified him as a Russian citizen. Maybe he too fled east, just like Avram Lat, thus avoiding the fate of Lat's father, brother, sister-in-law, uncle, and aunt, and tens of thousands of Riga Jews.

From Siberia, the Red Army sent Lat to the front. In the effort to hold off the Germans, he was wounded three or four times. Reaching under the short sleeve of his collared shirt, Lat touches a spot on his left upper arm where there is still shrapnel inside. He was in the hospital when the war ended, so upon his release he went back to Riga. His family used to live in the center of town, not far from the café where we are sitting today, but they were assigned a two-room apartment on the outskirts of town, where he and his wife still reside.

Lat was a secular Jew who went to synagogue rarely before the war and even less often during the Soviet occupation, but in 1992 his son-in-law died. Lat went to say kaddish, the Jewish prayer for the dead, for him every morning. It took him forty-five minutes each way to get to the synagogue, but he was as dependable as a postman. Going every day to say kaddish reminded him, he said, of the values he learned as a boy in a Latvian scouting troop and what he learned in grammar school at the Cheder Metukan.

I show Avram Lat an old picture of Miriam's family, who also went to the Cheder Metukan, and ask him if he recognizes any of their faces or remembers their names. He doesn't, although he says of their mother, "There's something in the oval of her face that looks familiar. But that doesn't prove anything."

I ask him what he does remember about the Wilkomirski boy at school. He was shy and obedient, Lat says. He thinks he had rosy cheeks. That's all he can tell me.

"Lat doesn't sound like a Jewish name," I say.

He tells me that his family changed it at some point from something else, maybe Hirshson or Hirshman, he doesn't know exactly what.

I finish my sundae and the check arrives. Avram Lat fights me for it just long enough to be appalled that my trifle costs the equivalent of a few days' allotment of his pension.

"So you didn't get what you came looking for," he says as I count out coins to pay the bill.

"I didn't think I would," I told him. I told him it was like looking for a needle in a . . .—I couldn't remember the Russian word for haystack, but Lat understood. He asked how long I'd been in Riga. A week, I said.

"You'd have to be here a year or two," he said, to find what I was looking for. "You'd have to talk to old Riga Jews. Most of them aren't at the shul. To go around and talk to people and find them, you'd have to spend more than a week."

Of course, even after a year or two of knocking on the doors of suspicious octogenarians, I might not find any better source of information than Avram Lat. It would be much easier to integrate Avram Lat's story into my own, to extrapolate from his survival that Avram Wilkomirski and his wife and their son could have survived, too, and that the family could be alive somewhere, if not in Latvia, then in Russia or Israel or Brooklyn, but definitely somewhere we can't find them. Never mind that more than 90 percent of the Jews in Latvia were killed during the war, that Avram Wilkomirski's sister Anna looked for him afterward and found no trace, that Avram Wilkomirski is a distant relative I know only through a photograph and a couple of documents. Faced with this uncertain family history, I am tempted to resolve it by folding one Avram into the other, by seizing upon whatever information presents itself and making it part of my own legend. This is what our family had done with the author of *Fragments* when he came to visit—if he's not a cousin, we'll make him a cousin—and this is, I suspect, what the author of *Fragments* did in crafting his persona. It would be so easy to adopt Avram Lat's story—he lives thousands of miles away, he doesn't know English, and since he is eighty-seven, who knows if he will still be alive when I publish anything about my trip—and yet it wouldn't be the right thing to do, to him or to the Wilburs.

I thank Lat for helping me to find what I was looking for, and wish him well.

ON THE DAY before we leave Riga, we return once more to the national archives. Archivist Irina Veinberga greets us with a small packet of papers. It includes photocopies of the voided passports of Aunt Miriam and her brothers; they had to surrender them to the Latvian authorities when they left for America. The faces in the Latvian records match those in the photographs my mother has brought with her from New York. Veinberga has also drawn up her own version of the Wilkomirski family tree, with names and dates of birth for Anna, Avram, and their siblings. The information, which dates from the 1870s and 1880s, comes from the logbook of a local rabbi. How it ended up in the Latvian state archive I don't know, but it lists the names of Anna and her brothers and sisters, their dates of birth in the Jewish and Russian calendars, their father's occupation, and, for the boys, the name of the mohel who circumcised them. In addition to the tree, Veinberga gives us copies made from the logbook. We learn that Anna's father was a veteran, an ordinary soldier who came from a place called Utena. Veinberga has also photocopied a map of Lithuania; Utena is a few miles from Wilkomir.

"That's all I could find quickly," Veinberga says apologetically. There is probably more information in the files, she adds. If we give her a list of who and what else we want to know about, she'll mail the results to New York.

Back at the hotel, Mom and I talk about how our week in Riga has changed our ideas about Binjamin. When we arrived, she says, "I was believing him less and less, but I was still willing to accept any information that would rule him in." She had stuck with her theory that the author of *Fragments* was a child whose last name wasn't necessarily Wilkomirski, perhaps a maternal cousin or a neighbor's child who had been taken in by Avram's family at the beginning of the war. After a week in Riga, however, she says, "I don't see any evidence whatsoever that there was a child he could have been." It's true that we found no evidence of such a child, but then again, we found nothing to refute her idea that the author of *Fragments* had a different last name. I ask her whether she saw anything in Riga that made her disbelieve him.

"It's the documents I didn't see that make me believe him less," she says. On the other hand, we did find documentation corroborating Anna's stories. "Ever since my grandmother died, I hadn't thought about the people she talked about," she says. "The most amazing thing to me is that when I checked out details, they were basically correct. My grandmother also told me there was a sister still in Riga and a brother, and she gave me their names. These were very shadowy memories. I heard it all in the forties or fifties. The things I thought she told me were true, because I could have been elaborating on them, all these details I remembered turned out to be accurate, although I didn't have names." What we found didn't tell us that much, but the papers and the buildings were enough for her to let go of Binjamin.

"If I had to go into a court and swear it, I would have to swear I don't see how he could possibly be the person he says he is," Mom says. "But that's not because of the Swiss angle, that's because of the Riga part. And because we know the people. It's not as if this was a mythical family."

There is still plenty we do not know about our own relatives, however. "I hate to hold out hopeful thoughts," says Mom, "but you told me you met this man Avram Lat, and you told me he had managed to get out and go to Siberia the week before all this stuff happened. Who knows, it might be possible that people in our family did that, but I doubt it," she says.

"Why do you hate to hold out hopeful thoughts?" I ask her.

"Because when I first heard about Binjamin's book, I had been very hopeful that he was one of the lost relatives. And now that all this doubt has come up, I don't want to start hoping that there is a lost relative out there." A quizzical look comes over her face. "Avram Lat didn't say his name was Wilkomirski, did he?"

I tell her I was wondering the same thing myself, and we laugh.

ANNUAL
MEETING

"What are you doing here?"

The question comes from the woman in the red blazer sitting next to me. She is in her late fifties, maybe her early sixties. I know her age because the narrow white room in which we are sitting has been designated for a workshop for child survivors born between 1936 and 1940. We are in Prague, at the twelfth annual convention of Jewish child survivors of the Holocaust, and this morning's workshops are segregated by age, in keeping with the idea that individuals persecuted at a particular stage of childhood might have similar kinds of memories and might, as the research of Hans Keilson showed, exhibit similar psychological responses. In these workshops, according to the conference program, child survivors will talk about their past experiences of persecution and the emotions that remain.

The woman's question, neither hostile nor welcoming, is a good one, better than she knows. I have come to Prague looking for Binjamin, though what that means is not so simple anymore. Of course, I am hoping that the author of *Fragments* will turn up at this conference, and, since he says he was born around 1939, in this room. Not that he would be any more likely to speak to me here than in Washington, but I want to run into him, if only to see whether he still is welcome among child survivors. I also want to talk to the people he speaks for, and perhaps emulates, to find out what his self-presentation has in common with theirs. How many of them share Binjamin's emotional responses? How many embrace his methods of reclaiming the past? Do they regard him as an impostor in their midst, or do they see him as a child survivor who has been wronged?

This is too much to explain all at once to the woman in the red blazer, but I do tell her I am a journalist writing about a fellow called Binjamin Wilkomirski. His name rings no bell. I explain further that he wrote a memoir about being a child survivor, and before I can explain further, she cuts me off.

"So did everybody else," she says, uninterested and unimpressed. "I'm the only one who hasn't."

As the white room fills up with her peers (but not the author of *Fragments*), I get a few suspicious stares. Then a trim woman in a gray suit enters the room. She is the first person I have seen here with the bearing of a professional, and I would have guessed that she was the facilitator even if I hadn't seen her name tag. She is Daisy Miller, the former head of the Child Holocaust Survivors Group of Los Angeles. Miller had tried to be a voice of reconciliation as the fight in her support group began, and when Leon Stabinsky resigned to form his own child-survivor group, Miller stayed. "I realize that you feel 'vindicated,'" she wrote to Stabinsky after the questions about Binjamin's authenticity were raised in the press, "but frankly I only find this a terrible thing for the Child Survivor community."

I don't know whether Miller knows about my interest in Binjamin Wilkomirski, and I tell her that I am a reporter curious about young child survivors and ask whether it would be okay for me to stay. Polite but firm, Miller tells me that the workshop is only for child survivors and their children. "If it was up to me, I'd tell you to go away right now," she says, "but I'm going to ask the group." Only if everyone is comfortable can I stay. Miller introduces me to the workshop and asks whether anyone would mind if I stayed. About half the people do, and I leave the child survivors to themselves.

· · ·

Upstairs, in the grand ballroom of the opulent neo-Renaissance palace where the conference is being held, the chief rabbi of Prague, a former Czech dissident, is holding forth on the city's Jewish life, past and present. Prague was an important center of European Jewish life back to the Middle Ages, he says, and its Jewish quarter was filled with scholars and beautiful synagogues. The Jewish population of Prague was decimated by the Holocaust, but the neighborhood was spared because Hitler wanted to turn it into a museum of an extinct people. Today, one synagogue has become a Holocaust memorial, another a gallery of artifacts, and together with the old Jewish cemetery, they have become popular tourist destinations. It's not so different from what Hitler had in mind, the rabbi says. His high-minded lecture doesn't seem to reach his audience, and the question-and-answer period drifts away from Prague, turning into a loose forum, with speaker after speaker struggling to express their own ideas about the catastrophe that indelibly marked their lives.

In the foyer outside the ballroom, there is a bulletin board set up on an easel. It is only the first day of the conference, but the board is already covered with index cards and scraps of paper ripped from notebooks, with messages written in English, French, German, Dutch, Czech, Polish:

> We are seeking for relatives of Benjamin Abramovich Goldstein from Kharkov, Ukraine. He was born March 8th, 1907 and murdered in Kharkov 1941. His brothers left Kharkov in 1919/20 and moved 'to America.' Any message please to family Bednar, Prague.

> Eckstein: I too am a born Eckstein. I am staying at the Abri hotel. We may be related.

> Ich suche MARILLA SALA aus LVOV (vater Karl, mutter Rona) Mein name HENRYK LEWANDOWSKY.

> Stephen Kroh and/or Martin Goldberg were in the copper mines of Bor in southern Serbia during World War II. Please contact.

Looking for anyone who was in Dora (Mittlebau). Berna

Who knows these girls? There were in a convent in Lodève, France 1942–3.

Ruth Springer is looking for children from children's house in Otwock, Poland.

Lookin' for who knows this photo. Mr. Masek

I am looking for my brother, Israel Malinger, born in Poland, and 3 friends from Poland. Rala Malinger

More than half a century later, many of the six-hundred-plus child survivors here are still looking for their kin among the living, for their kin among the dead, for names they have never known, but their chances of finding what they are looking for are slimmer than winning the lottery. The bulletin board might have less to do with finding what they have lost than with seeing that they are surrounded by other people who are also searching.

When Daisy Miller's workshop ends, a few of the participants who wouldn't have minded my staying seek me out and brief me on what happened. One man, a balding London optometrist, says the child survivors in the workshop talked less about the details of their own disrupted childhoods than about their feelings. "I was born one month before the German invasion of Holland," says the optometrist. Other people who spoke in the workshop, he says, "they went through camps, and that is not my story. I didn't have all these horrible things happening." For a long time, he refused compensation, and avoided the first child-survivor conference he heard about. "After that, I got involved via an acquaintance with the child-survivor organization in London. I also got bothered about my work. I felt every morning as I walked to work as if someone was sitting on my chest. So I went back to the Dutch embassy and I said, 'I have some problems, and maybe it has something to do with it.'" After an evaluation, the Dutch government agreed to pay for psychotherapy once a week, without limits on time and money.

"For some time before she gave me away—I was two and a bit—my mother told me what she was going to do. 'You were too young, you don't remember,' my mother told me. However, when my mother came to collect me—and there were half a dozen witnesses there—I said to her, 'You stayed away for a very long time.'"

The optometrist had been to international child-survivor conferences before, and he was glad to be among those in his own age cohort. His support group in London, he says, is one "where people say, 'You were much too young, you can't remember.'"

OVER THE course of the four-day conference, I meet dozens of child survivors. Some people steer clear of me when they see my reporter's notebook, but for others it is like flypaper. I meet first-timers as well as regulars who come back year after year to reconnect with friends they made at previous meetings. "People come to feel normal," one woman tells me. They want to tell me their own childhood stories, or clue me in to the stories of others. More than one child survivor asks me, "Have you met the sisters?"

The sisters, Ewa Sonne and Tereza Kuzmicz, were given a rousing ovation at the opening session of the conference, and one afternoon I go over to meet them. Dark-haired Ewa spent the war in Poland in hiding with a family, and her mother reclaimed her after the fighting ended. Tereza, who was fair, had been left at a convent and was given to another family before her mother could return for her. Ewa, who left Poland for Denmark, tried tracing her sister through the Red Cross, but a few months before the conference a Polish television crew helped Ewa find Tereza. Tereza, who knew she was adopted, had no idea she was Jewish, but now felt she finally understood why her daughter's favorite movie is *Fiddler on the Roof*. Tereza, who wears a cross around her neck, drove in from Poland with her tall, mustachioed Catholic husband and their twenty-year-old son. Tereza, blond and pretty at fifty-eight, looks more than two years younger than sixty-year-old Ewa, who arrived alone. She has a thin, weathered face that, despite her frequent sisterly smiles, betrays a familiarity with solitude.

Ewa and Tereza make for a heartwarming human-interest story

if one does not probe too deeply, and conference organizers steer local television, radio, and newspaper reporters toward them. After all, their reunion can stand for the larger theme of the conference, which is building bridges between child survivors who stayed in Eastern Europe and their counterparts who made lives in the West. Ewa and Tereza are what passes for a happy ending here, but they are an exception, even among these survivors on the margins of survivorhood. Most of the stories here, like the ones hinted at on the bulletin board, have not come together so neatly.

When I steer the conversation toward Binjamin Wilkomirski, responses vary. One woman from the French-speaking part of Switzerland who read *Fragments* tells me, "It's a beautiful book, but I don't think it's important whether he's Jewish or not." On the other hand, Chaja Verveer, the leader of a support group in Houston, tells me she was troubled when she first read *Fragments*. As a child, Verveer was part of a group of fifty-two unidentified children who were sent from Westerbork to Bergen-Belsen in 1944. About half of them, Verveer included, were under five and did not know their own names. After reading the book, she asked a psychologist whether it was possible that Binjamin's memories could be that much more detailed than her own. She is angry about *Fragments,* and also about another child-survivor book she read. "Do you know about the woman who lived with the wolves?" Verveer asks.

Misha: A Mémoire of the Holocaust Years, by Monique (Misha) Defonseca, begins in Brussels in 1941, when the poor Belgian Jewish parents of seven-year-old Mishke put her in the care of a bourgeois Christian family. When Mishke hears that her parents have been taken away to the east, she runs after them, navigating with the help of a tiny compass and her memory of the map of Europe. Through the cold of winter, Mishke crosses Germany and enters Poland, sleeping outside, foraging for flora, and stealing food and clothing along the way. The French-speaking Mishke pretends to be mute, until one day, when she is alone in the woods, she lets out a howl of despair. Her cri de coeur is heard by a pair of wolves, and she lives with them in the forest. "Transformed by injustice, I was reborn in a form I understood and respected. No longer human, I became in my heart an animal, a wolf." When the wolves are killed by hunters, Mishke continues east, arriving in Warsaw in the summer of 1942. She slips into the ghetto to look for her parents, and she escapes by scaling a wall before the deportations to Treblinka begin. After witnessing a massacre of children in Otwock, Poland, she finds another pack of wolves in Ukraine who welcome and protect her for months. An encounter with Russian partisans toward the end of the war leads to her being called Misha. She returns to Belgium through Romania, Yugoslavia, and Italy, walking when she cannot hitch a ride. Misha hid her Jewish identity until the late 1980s, when she left Belgium and came to the Boston area.

In the course of her three-thousand-mile journey, young Misha walks right up to the fence of a concentration camp, sees a dead Jewish laborer in the forest, meets a group of Jewish partisans in the Polish countryside, and sees a Nazi rape and kill a naked Jewish woman, but through her brushes with so many facets of the Holocaust experience and hundreds of burglaries, she passes unnoticed. She describes two acts of violence in vengeful self-defense: knocking out the hunter who killed her wolf friends with a pipe, and stabbing the rapist to death with a dagger.

"None of the things in there can be checked," Verveer says. "It sent my BS meter through the roof." High meter readings also registered when the publisher of *Misha*, Jane Daniel of Mt. Ivy Press, solicited blurbs from historian Deborah Dwork and Lawrence Langer. Independently, Langer and Dwork concluded that *Misha* was a poorly constructed historical fantasy, and each asked Daniel how her small press could publish the story as nonfiction.

Nevertheless, *Misha*, which was written with help from Jane Daniel and ghostwriter Vera Lee, appeared with blurbs from Elie Wiesel ("very moving"), the Anti-Defamation League, and the North American Wolf Foundation. (Another endorser, *Summer of My German Soldier* author Bette Greene, demanded that the blurb attributed to her be removed because she found *Misha* unbelievable.) *Misha* was optioned by Disney and the book sold to publishers in Europe and Japan. Defonseca has spoken before synagogue groups and at Holocaust education conferences. She told *The Sunday Times* of London, "There are people who say, 'Unbelievable.' That is their problem, not mine."

Mt. Ivy has acknowledged that "no official records have surfaced to substantiate any portion of Misha's story," but Jane Daniel adds that "publishing a book is part of a larger process of truth-finding." In a public statement that refers to the controversy over *Fragments,* Daniel asked, "Is Misha's story fact or invention? Without hard evidence one way or the other, questions will always remain. . . . It is left to the reader to decide."

Verveer's anger over *Fragments* puts her in the minority. Most of the child survivors I talk to in Prague have no strong feelings about Binjamin either way, since, like the woman I met at the seminar, they've never heard of him. Just inside the entrance of the conference center, there is a long table with an array of child-survivor memoirs, along with videos, compact discs, and crafts. *Fragments* was not among the books on offer; most of them were published privately and in small editions.

"You're looking at a very difficult book to sell," says Murray Greenfield of Gefen Publishing House. The American-born Greenfield, who came to the conference with his child-survivor wife, publishes Holocaust memoirs, and as a rule survivors pay Gefen to see their memoirs in print. "People say you're taking money from people," he says. "It's not just a vanity press, we're preserving a piece of Jewish history. We do mailings to Holocaust museums if we think it's of special value." It costs $5,000 to $10,000 to produce a book, Greenfield says. At first Gefen prints one or two thousand copies. Even when the book doesn't break even, the author profits, says Greenfield. "He gets a great deal of attention paid to him and develops a confidence he may never have had."

"Most reviews of Holocaust books don't say whether the book is good or bad; I think they don't want to hurt the feelings of the narrator," says Greenfield. "The best-selling books are the ones with the big speakers. It can go to five thousand books. My wife's book sold over twenty thousand." He hands me a copy of a short paperback by Hana Greenfield, published in 1992. The title is *Fragments of Memory.*

. . .

ONE MORNING a convoy of buses leaves from the main conference hotel for the hour-long ride to Terezin, where some conferencegoers were once incarcerated as children. When we arrive, we file into a theater to watch a film about the history of the garrison town. In 1941 the Nazis began deporting Jews to Terezin and emptying out its Czech inhabitants. By July 1942 Terezin was wholly converted into a ghetto for Czech Jews and for special categories of German Jews: old people, artists, veterans of World War I. Food was scarce and disease rampant, but some cultural and religious activities were permitted, in part because the Nazis intended Terezin to serve as a showcase for their humane treatment of Jewish prisoners. To this end, Nazi officials orchestrated an elaborately staged and tightly scripted performance in July 1944 for a Swiss delegation from the International Red Cross. Of the 140,000 Jews brought to Terezin, 33,000 died there and another 88,000 were sent on to extermination camps.

On the way out of the theater, we pass a gift shop that sells books (including Hana Greenfield's *Fragments of Memory* in four languages) and assorted Judaica. A handful of child survivors stop to buy golden Magen David pendants and other trinkets before moving on to the graveyard for a memorial service. Sandwiches are distributed after the service, and we are given time to visit the museums and walk around the walled town, which is once again inhabited by Czech families.

On the bus back, I share a seat with a boisterous fair-haired man. A semiretired language teacher from Portland, Maine, he now gives talks about the Holocaust. He describes himself as the Elie Wiesel of Maine, even as he confides his resentment of the Nobel laureate for having the nerve to speak for all other survivors. When I ask the Elie Wiesel of Maine what he thinks of Binjamin Wilkomirski, he begins telling me his own story, which begins in Strasbourg in 1932 and takes up most of our ride back to Prague. I find him to be an exhausting storyteller, but it's more likely that my own capacity to listen to such stories has been exhausted—by the trip to Terezin, by the many child survivors I have encountered at the conference, by the skepticism aroused by the dispute over the authenticity of *Fragments*.

A petite woman sitting in front of the Elie Wiesel of Maine pulls out a tape recorder and leans over her chair to capture his story. Back at home in Colorado, she works as a storyteller, talking to school groups about the Holocaust. Many of the students, she says, have never met a Jewish person before.

"I'm on the speakers' bureau for the Holocaust Museum, and they don't like the idea of me getting paid," she says. "I'm a story-teller. I'm dramatizing it; I'm reliving it. I was born in Lithuania. They don't pay me anything."

"Elie Wiesel, do you think he speaks for free?" his counterpart from Maine asks.

"I've listened to other survivors speak. They drone on and on. They mean well, but I can't do that. I'm a professional storyteller," she says. The story she tells in schools is based on her own experi-ence as a hidden child in Lithuania, but it is a fictional one. She altered it, both for dramatic effect and out of necessity. "I'm still missing pieces," she says. "I'm writing a fictional autobiography because I don't have enough facts."

"I THINK THAT what happened to us is such an extraordinary piece of discontinuity—I don't know how to find the words for it, okay?—that anything we do to try and establish continuity for ourselves is a healthy exercise," psychiatrist Robert Krell tells me one morning in the lobby of his hotel. When Krell talks about "what happened to us," he is referring to child survivors like himself, people who were too young to remember life before wartime. He was born in 1940, and between the ages of two and five he lived in hiding with a fam-ily of Dutch Christians. Krell, a dark-haired, rumpled man who looks almost too young to be attending the conference, insists that his early-childhood memories are real, as are those of his patients. Months earlier, when we first spoke on the telephone, he told me, "When I see child survivors who are sixty-something, it doesn't take long to get them back to two or three. I'm not a hypnotherapist. At age two you're preverbal, but that doesn't mean you can't remem-ber." Memories emerge naturally, Krell says, when his patients start talking about a smell or a tactile sensation they associate with childhood.

Krell isn't referring only to young child survivors when he talks about those affected by the extraordinary discontinuity of the Holocaust. "How can American Jews think that scar has nothing to do with them? How is that possible? They came a generation earlier, after the second major pogrom. They left behind grandparents, aunts and uncles and brothers and sisters, and in one generation, those people disappeared in the Shoah. The Americans would have been in touch with them today if those families still existed. It's a peculiar pretense to say there's no connection. There's no one who's disconnected from the roots of their immigration. No one. I have found people in Vancouver who don't belong to the survivor community and live every day as a survivor, because they came in the late twenties and early thirties and they failed to bring their six or seven brothers and sisters over. There wasn't enough money to bring them over, so they sat in Canada with proper shelter and proper food and they suffered silently the losses of their entire families. They didn't go through the Shoah, so they don't call themselves survivors. They don't feel comfortable with a survivor group, they're not part of anything. And I see them as victims of those events.

"I'm not so concerned about the precise accuracies," he continues. "Someone once told me of a crematorium in an area where I knew from a historian it didn't exist. It was just an innocent misidentification, but something like that would arouse my suspicion. But if somebody makes a mistake about something that I wouldn't even know it was a mistake—their father was a shoemaker in Riga and he actually wasn't, he made something else, he made belts—of what possible consequence is that? And if someone says, 'I think I'm descended from a long line of rabbis because the name sounds familiar,' I say, 'Gee, you know, it's possible. Why don't you look it up and see what you can find?'

"My inclination is that if a grandchild of a survivor is able to get enough information—where that survivor says, 'I remember my mother saying they were from Riga originally, and in Riga they were furriers and they imported from the Baltic areas and I heard that my great-grandfather sometimes traveled to Saint Petersburg'—and the grandchild incorporates these snippets and tells a friend, 'Gee, you know, we think we are of a lineage of furriers who trace their lines back to Saint Petersburg,' I say, 'You know what, good for you. Is that how it is?' They say, 'Well, it's as close as I can get it.' You know, for some people that's a lot."

We are interrupted by Marilyn Krell, the doctor's wife, who has ordered a cab to take them to the Castle. They invite me to join their sightseeing tour, and after an initial demurral, I agree. In the taxi, we put our conversation about the Holocaust aside. They ask whether I am married, and tell me about their three daughters. We reach the rococo gates of the Castle just before noon, in time to watch the changing of the guard. The Krells and I make a quick circuit through the grounds of the sprawling complex and take in the highlights: the Viennese outer courtyards, the alchemists' workshops, and St. Vitus's Cathedral. Outside the enormous Gothic cathedral, the doctor stops in front of a statue of Jesus nailed to the cross. "He has no idea of what has been done in his name," Krell says.

From the Castle, we head down a long, sloping promenade, lined with pubs offering tourist menus and souvenir shops selling crystal, wooden toys, scented soaps, and postcards. Marilyn Krell asks me how long I will be in Prague, and I say I would love to stay longer, but right after the conference I'm leaving for Zurich.

"Oh," Robert Krell asks, "will you be interviewing Wilkomirski?"

I tell Krell that I hope to, but it's unlikely. I'm glad Krell asked, because the author of *Fragments* has been on my mind since we left the hotel. I have been wondering how inclusive Krell means to be when he talks about those who experienced the discontinuity of Jewish history. If he includes the grandchildren of survivors, people who left Europe a generation before the Holocaust, and their descendants, would he also include a non-Jew with no familial connection but an enormous identification with the Holocaust?

"If Wilkomirski is inauthentic, and he came clean and said why he did it, that would be very interesting to hear," says Krell. "His motives are not false. Not like that woman from Australia."

The woman from Australia is Helen Darville. In 1993, under the name Helen Demidenko, the twenty-three-year-old Darville published *The Hand That Signed the Paper,* a first novel that she claimed was based on the wartime experiences of her father's family. Most of them had been killed in Ukraine by "Jewish Communist Party officials," she said. The novel, which blames Jews for the brutal transformation of Ukraine under Stalin and uses this libel to justify Ukrainian participation in the Nazi exterminations, was condemned as anti-Semitic, but it also won Australia's highest literary prize, the Miles Franklin Award. Reporters found out that Darville's parents came from Anglo-Saxon stock, and Darville eventually acknowledged she had invented her Ukrainian background.

"I've read about her book, but I haven't read her book," says Krell. "I wouldn't waste my time in that way. She made up a story that is false from a premise that is false, and has something false to say. If Wilkomirski is inauthentic, then it still captures something beautiful about the fragments of memory that child survivors have. And it has to be coming from somewhere. It's like Jerzy Kosinski and *The Painted Bird.* He didn't experience life on the run the way he describes it in that book, but somehow he understood it well enough to write *The Painted Bird.* I know a woman who was an eight-year-old in Galicia in Ukraine, and she told me what she went through and if I wrote it all down it would be *The Painted Bird.* And Binjamin Wilkomirski is the same way. He really expresses something profound about child survivors. And maybe he got it from inner cues."

"You're not looking at anything!" Marilyn Krell chides her husband. She is peering through an archway, mouth agape in wonder at the view. She beckons us, and I pause with Robert Krell to look out onto a patio with a glorious panorama of Prague, even though I'm not in the right frame of mind to appreciate such views.

"You'll have to walk in front to let us know what's coming," Krell tells his wife, and picks up our conversation where we left it. "So he is responding to some sort of cues," he continues. "It could be something that happened to him in multiple foster situations. He might have been abused, or whatever, and he might see what happened to him as his own personal concentration camp."

I ask Krell whether that metaphorical use of the Holocaust to represent an earthly hell, to stand for the worst situation imaginable, bothers him.

"It depends," he says. "When people call abortion another Holocaust, it bothers me very much. When people say they were abused, let's say by their fathers, and spent their own childhood in their very own concentration camp, only it was in a house and they were alone, I don't mind that, because they are trying to find words for something terrible that happened to them. They are trying to find a way of expressing something truly horrible. So when the Bosnians say that what happened to them is like the Holocaust, I—"

Marilyn Krell cuts in again, and takes her husband's hand as we approach the Charles Bridge. As we weave through the crowds on the bustling pedestrian bridge, I wonder how Krell was going to finish his sentence. Is the Holocaust an acceptable metaphor for the Bosnians or not? Is it acceptable for someone suffering from a life-threatening illness like cancer or AIDS? For a person separated from his birth parents and told by his foster parents that his difficult past was all a bad dream? What about the child survivor at the conference who complained to me that the disorganized food service was like it was "back in the camps"?

The Krells pause to look at the pictures for sale on the bridge and at the statues atop each supporting pile. Once again, we pause before a life-size crucifix, ringed in gold by a Hebrew inscription: *Kadosh, kadosh, kadosh, adonai tsvaot*—Holy, holy, holy is the lord of hosts. Our guidebook explains that a Prague Jew convicted of blasphemy had to pay for its construction as his punishment.

On the other side of the river, we part ways. Marilyn Krell keeps sightseeing while the doctor catches a taxi back to the conference hall to lead a session on how Christian rescuers shaped the identity of hidden children.

I MEET UP with Daisy Miller in the Jewish quarter at a community center where some of the conference workshops are being held. After our first encounter, I asked her whether she would be available to talk to me about young child survivors and also about Binjamin. She might have had better things to do in Prague, but she agreed.

Miller seems worn out when she emerges from the Jewish community center. She tells me she has been leading workshops at child-survivor conferences for years, but that this last one was particularly taxing. I propose a cup of coffee, and we walk over to the Old Town Square. We settle in at an outdoor café with a view of the clock tower in the former town hall. Every hour on the hour, little doors open on the fifteenth-century astronomical clock, unleashing a parade of mechanical statues. The crowd of tourists outside the café ebbs and flows with the minute hand, dispersing after the hourly spectacle and gathering in anticipation of the next one.

Miller orders coffee and a slice of apple strudel, and I ask for a hot chocolate. Miller starts telling me about the first meeting of child survivors at Los Angeles's University of Judaism. "At the end of the meeting I said, 'You know, something powerful just happened for me.' I wanted to know if anyone wants to come back specifically to start a child-survivor group, and six or seven people did. So I hate to take all the credit, but it was my question," she says.

As with her Jamesian namesake, there is no great need of walking on tiptoe with this Daisy Miller. She is businesslike but not formal, polished but not phony, media savvy but not guarded. She speaks her mind at a pace that gives her time to form her sentences carefully and journalists time to write them down.

"I was president for many years," Miller says. "We have formed some amazing friendships. For the most part, we are tolerant of each other. I think everyone feels a sense of relief to be around people who understand—I just heard it again today—to be in a room with people who understand, even if their experience isn't the same." Child-survivor gatherings, she says, "give us an opportunity to talk about the consequences of our experience of dealing with our sense of alienation, of not belonging, from whatever country we are in. Most of us are not connected to our country of origin, for whatever reason—and although I am an American, I feel different. I lived in Italy for ten years and I was not an Italian." I ask her for details, and she says, "We can come back to my story if you're interested, but that's not what we were talking about."

Miller says she felt left out in broader survivor groups. "To this day survivors will say, 'You were only a kid,' so there was no great wish to put oneself in such a situation." Even among child survivors, she says, "people jump to conclusions that are very hurtful. People have said, 'You're not a survivor.' We have this hierarchy of pain: 'I suffered more than you did because you were in hiding,' 'I suffered more than you did because you were in hiding with your parents.' I do these workshops, and within these workshops, I try to be as accepting as I can.

"When you are told from a young age that what you talk about is incorrect, when your memories are questioned at the beginning, it only adds to your sense of uncertainty. What I remember is different from what other people remember. And slowly, I began to allow myself my own recollections and allow myself to discover them myself. Memory needs to be honest. It has to come from the individual. We judge in many ways. We are so conscious of being judged and opinions of how we affect people that we are often not honest—and I think it's important to be honest with one's memories, particularly for us, because it is particularly hard on our sense of self. My memories shaped me. They are part of me, they are the flavor and the color of me. So I have come to the conclusion that although it may not be comparable to that of another person, it is still my memory, me, Daisy Miller, and I want to fight for it. Maybe it's not what happened to my sister, but it's what I saw as a three-, four-, five-, six-, seven-year-old. I have come to realize I am very protective of it for child survivors, because I think it's very easy to dismiss them, but it is hard to be confronted with the denial of it. How quickly we make those judgments. How quietly it happens. Yet how damaging we can be in making those judgments."

Miller takes a sip of her coffee and looks at me intently. "You see where I am going with this," she says. "I'm not going to say whether Wilkomirski is true or not, but child-survivor memory has to be allowed. As a child, I was not allowed to speak, I was not allowed to play, I was not allowed to make noise, I was not allowed to be outside. I was not allowed many things. As far as he is concerned, I don't know, but I am not willing to jump on the bandwagon. I'm still sure"—sure that the author of *Fragments* is a child survivor—"but that is not the issue. It is what he represents. If he should be a fraud, let them prove it. But it is the amount of interest this has generated, I find it not only destructive to child survivors and survivors in general, but it's an expression of anger—anger at having to hear so much made of the Holocaust."

We have been sitting for more than an hour, and the waitress comes by and tries to take our plates. There is a little strudel left. "I'm not done," Miller tells the waitress.

"If he in fact is not telling the truth, he's still a human being. I feel for him. I tend to feel sympathy for someone who's in pain. And he's in pain. It's not something you do Tuesdays at 3 P.M. Pain is something you feel all the time. I'm understanding and identifying with the victim. And in either case he's a victim. Others might not see it that way, but as a child survivor, I can relate to the pain of being victimized, of being alone. He is alone against the world, and he's learning to deal with this mass force alone."

The astronomical clock strikes six, and for the second time since we sat down, the mechanical statues move and the tourists scatter. The waitress finally succeeds in getting us to relinquish our table. There is a special service for child survivors that evening at the Jerusalem Synagogue, and Miller and I walk off in that direction. On the way, Miller tells me a little about herself. When she was born, her parents were considering emigrating from Croatia to America, and an aunt had just read an American book with a character named Daisy in it. During the war, her family went into hiding in the Italian countryside. She was seven when the war ended. She spent ten years in Italy before immigrating to America in 1951. In America she married a man named Miller.

Before we reach the synagogue, I ask her about what has been happening in her own group back in Los Angeles. There has been a split, she said, but it doesn't have to do with Binjamin Wilkomirski. I ask about Lauren Grabowski, and Miller won't say anything about her. But when I mention Leon Stabinsky, she lets out a long sigh.

"We're day and night," she says. "I was the one who tapped him for leadership. It was one of my biggest errors in judgment."

CALIFORNIA
SPLIT

When I asked Leon Stabinsky if I would be seeing him in Prague, he scoffed.

"If you look at the program," he told me over the phone from his home in the San Fernando Valley, "it's going to be the same therapists. The speeches will be 'Woe is unto me' and 'We've got to hold hands.' That, to me, is counterproductive. It's a waste of energy. Why do we need a conference every year? Whenever it's in the United States, two-thirds to three-quarters of the people are the same. It's those who can afford it. It's like a gathering of alumni. It's, like, five percent of the population, and they speak for all child survivors."

I can't say I was surprised by his answer. Ever since Stabinsky dug up my home number and woke me up one Saturday morning to share his thoughts about Binjamin Wilkomirski, he had been telling me what a sham the author of *Fragments* was, what was wrong with the support group he had quit. "There's a whole group—mostly women, some of them therapists—who think that child survivors are victims and they need therapy," Stabinsky once told me. "I think we should not consider ourselves victims. I've known some people who have had problems, but there are other orphans, be they Christian or Hindu or whatever. Don't attach a stigma to all child survivors."

Stabinsky hated it when his peers would don the mantle of victimhood, but it seemed to outrage him more when mental health professionals labeled child survivors as damaged goods. "I'm horrified to read the literature of some of these psychologists. With all these post-traumatic disorders, they're making us out to be a bunch of nuts who will never amount to anything."

In particular, he inveighed against Sarah Moskovitz and Robert Krell, who sent out a survey to about one thousand child survivors around the world. Eighty-one percent of the respondents reported being "seriously or permanently affected" emotionally by their wartime experiences, and two-thirds said the physical, social, economic, and educational impact of the war was serious or permanent. Moskovitz and Krell present the statistics in a paper called "Six Roadblocks to Restitution for Young Jewish Child Survivors of the Holocaust," which argues for less stringent restitution guidelines. In a written response to the paper, Stabinsky denounced Krell and Moskovitz's work as well intentioned but shameful. "The conclusions I draw from this study," Stabinsky wrote, are "that 1) Child Survivors are a 'sad' lot, and 2) most of the Child Survivors need the help of a psychologist or psychiatrist." (In his response, written after the Los Angeles support group split, he also claims credit for coming up with the six-roadblock rubric.) When his new group, the California Association of Holocaust Child Survivors, drafted its bylaws, they considered a provision barring therapists from the organization. They didn't, but the group hasn't attracted any.

A therapist might find Stabinsky's vehement resistance to the idea that child survivors need help to be worth further exploration, but he thinks there are more productive ways of coming to terms with the past than therapy. "Where we can leave a legacy is by seeking justice," he says. His campaign to debunk the Binjamin Wilkomirski story and publicize the facts behind it is just one part of his quest for justice. Stabinsky became secretary of the American Gathering of Jewish Holocaust Survivors, a national advocacy group, and he closely follows the negotiations with Swiss banks, insurance companies, and German industry. He has been lobbying for the Justice for Holocaust Survivors Act. The bill, introduced at the beginning of 1999, would under certain circumstances give individual Holocaust survivors the right to sue the German federal government in U.S. federal courts. Stabinsky was hoping to fly to Washington and speak in favor of the bill at a congressional hearing, if the bill ever makes its way to committee. "Whether it passes or not," Stabinsky told me, "it will be a threat."

All the same, it was a shame that Stabinsky did not come to Prague, if only so he could have seen the astronomical clock in the old town hall. Other than his activism on behalf of child survivors, Stabinsky's main passion is collecting antique scientific instruments. He is a member in good standing of the Microscopical Society of Southern California, and since his retirement travels once or twice a year to Europe for collectors' fairs. One of his oldest pieces is an Indian astrolabe from about 1620, but most of the curios he owns date from the eighteenth and nineteenth centuries: field microscopes and sundials, thermometers and barometers, hygrometers and anemometers, calibrated gadgets that take an objective measure of the physical world and leave little room for emotion or subjectivity.

Stabinsky is also fond of at least one modern scientific instrument. With the popularization of the Internet, he has become an avid web surfer, trawling auction sites for antiques to add to his collection and searching for information about restitution and other child-survivor matters. The Internet helped him track developments in the Binjamin Wilkomirski case, and Stabinsky used his computer to explore his suspicions about Lauren Grabowski. The name turned up no relevant pages when he typed it into a search engine. When she first approached the child-survivor group, however, she used a hyphenated name, Lauren Grabowski-Stratford, and searching under the full name turned up a Lauren Stratford who purported to be a child survivor, though not of the Holocaust.

ACCORDING TO *Satan's Underground,* the first of three memoirs by Lauren Stratford, her troubles began at six, when she was raped in her basement by a middle-aged handyman. "Years later, I could only recall that dreadful scene in fragmented images, like a collage of black-and-white pictures in a war documentary," she wrote. She was abandoned by her birth parents and her adoptive father, and her mother treated her more like a servant, beating her, forcing her to do chores, and offering Lauren's sexual favors as compensation to workmen. The mother then handed the girl over to child pornographers, who drugged and brainwashed her. The adults she asked for help did not believe her. She tried running away to her father's house in another state, but she couldn't evade the pornography ring. She graduated to a whorehouse, and her sadistic pimp inducted her into an evil cult. Three times she was impregnated, and each time the baby was sacrificed in a gory ritual to the Prince of Darkness. After a breakdown and a long hospital stay, she finally escaped the world of satanic ritual abuse, guided by her love of Jesus and a therapist who used recovered-memory techniques.

Satan's Underground, Stratford's chronicle of her journey through an earthly hell and into the arms of the Lord, was published in 1988, at the height of the recovered-memory craze. The book became a hit, and Lauren Stratford appeared on mainstream television venues like *Oprah* and fundamentalist Christian programs like Pat Robertson's *The 700 Club*. She began counseling people who reported having been ritually abused.

Because of her high profile, Stratford caught the eye of Bob and Gretchen Passantino, a husband-and-wife team of Evangelical Christian journalists who specialize in evaluating the truth of religious testimony. The Passantinos wondered why the diabolical epidemic Stratford and others described left no physical traces, and whether this lack of evidence was a sign of the omnipotence of evil, as Stratford posited, or spoke to the possibility that the rash of reported abuse was an invention. Moreover, the specificity of the sexual violence she described in *Satan's Underground* was at odds with the dearth of personal, historical, and geographical detail in the book. The Passantinos launched an extensive inquiry into Stratford's past to establish the truth behind her disturbing claims. They spoke to her family and old friends, unearthing stories and correspondence that were at odds with Lauren Stratford's account.

In an exposé published in *Cornerstone*, a magazine affiliated with the Jesus People USA, the Passantinos identified the author of *Satan's Underground* as Laurel Willson, born on August 18, 1941, in Buckley, Washington. Frank Willson, a devout Presbyterian physician, and his temperamental wife, Rose, adopted Laurel at birth. Contrary to the impression given in her memoir that she was an only child, Laurel had an older sister, Willow. According to school records, she was a good student with an aptitude for music. "Her attendance and grades preclude long absences from school such as would have seemed necessary from the extreme sexual abuse described in *Satan's Underground*," the Passantinos wrote. Willow and Rose told the Passantinos that Laurel's childhood was less than perfect, but nothing like what happened to Lauren Stratford.

Laurel Willson's adoptive parents separated when she was nine. In her teens she ran away from her mother's house in Washington and lived with her father in San Bernardino, California, before returning to Washington to live with Willow and her husband. According to Willow, it was then that seventeen-year-old Laurel made her first abuse accusation, this one against Willow's husband. At a Seattle college, Laurel told classmates that she had been molested by college employees, and that her mother had made her work as a prostitute. When confronted, Laurel confessed that she had invented the stories of abuse. At twenty-four, Laurel married. The marriage was annulled two months later. Her ex-husband, Frank Austin, told the Passantinos that Laurel was a virgin when they married and that the marriage was never consummated.

Beginning in the 1960s, the Passantinos explain, Laurel Willson developed a series of relationships with individuals who took pity upon her. Before her marriage, she all but moved in with a Pentecostal family. Laurel had no stepmother, but she told the family that her stepmother molested her. She also feigned blindness in the family's presence. In the 1970s, she joined a gospel choir called Delpha and the Witnesses; Delpha and her husband legally adopted Laurel. She told Delpha she had been abused "in the name of Jesus" and rendered sterile. Another friend from that era recalled that Laurel claimed to suffer from an extremely rare blood disease. In the 1980s, Laurel formed Victims Against Sexual Abuse, a support group in Bakersfield, where there was an ongoing criminal investigation of organized ritual child abuse. It was then that she began speaking of her own abuse at the hands of Satanists; she told one friend she had recordings of her son Joey's ritual murder, but never produced them. Laurel also offered herself as a potential witness for the prosecution in the infamous McMartin preschool child-abuse case in Manhattan Beach, but was rejected because she reported no detail more specific than what had been revealed on television. Her friendships ended badly, the Passantinos say, and often involved a violent outburst on her part.

The Passantinos also established a history of Laurel using popular books as a reference point for her own life story. One friend told them that Laurel's tales—"the torture with enemas, the piano, the whole bit"—were taken from *Sybil*, the landmark tale of Sybil Dorsett's child abuse and multiple personality disorder. Other reference works included *Stormie*, a child-abuse memoir by Stormie Omartian, and *The Beautiful Side of Evil* by Johanna Michaelsen, an occult psychic healer turned fundamentalist Christian speaker who Stratford befriended. Michaelsen wrote an introduction to *Satan's Underground*, and her publisher, Harvest House, added Stratford to their list. Omartian introduced Stratford's next book, *I Know You're Hurting* (1989).

"The story of *Satan's Underground* is not true, but Laurel's emotional distress is real," the Passantinos concluded. "Our prayer is that she gets the help she needs."

At first Harvest House insisted they had evidence corroborating Stratford's story, but they later withdrew her books from the market. Lauren Stratford found a new publisher, Pelican, a small house in Louisiana. In the rest of her trilogy, she combines advice for victims of ritual abuse, accounts of multiple personality disorder and other newly reported afflictions, and a defense of the authenticity of her autobiography.

By the time Leon Stabinsky got in touch with the Passantinos, they had already heard that Lauren Stratford was up to something new. The Passantinos sharpened their pencils and resumed their pursuit of the mythical beast they thought they had slain a decade earlier. The Passantinos published their update on Lauren Stratford in *Cornerstone* in the fall of 1999.

Although she had put on a great deal of weight since her appearances as a satanic ritual abuse survivor, Lauren Grabowski looked like Lauren Stratford, and her handwriting was identical. Lauren Gra-

bowski's application to the Swiss humanitarian fund for needy Holocaust survivors, which requires a signed oath that the applicant is a
Jewish person who lived under Nazi rule, had Laurel Willson's birth
date and Social Security number on it. And Laurel Willson's maternal grandfather, a Polish immigrant to America and a pillar of the
Tacoma Catholic community, was named Anton Grabowski.

In presenting herself as a Holocaust survivor, Laurel Willson
didn't broadcast the history she describes in the Lauren Stratford
books, but she didn't disown it either. She simply placed her Holocaust experiences at the beginning of her litany of woes. She told
members of the Child Holocaust Survivors Group of Los Angeles
and other confidants that her time in Auschwitz was followed by an
unforgiving childhood in an adoptive American milieu. "I was not
kept safe in the camp and I was not kept safe here in the States," she
wrote to German pen pal Monika Muggli. "I used to write about and
speak around the country to judges, attorneys and law enforcement
on the subject of child pornography, child molestation and like abuses
and the long-term effects of the trauma the child suffers well into
adulthood."

During Binjamin's visit to Los Angeles, Lauren told Muggli about
Binjamin and Verena's reaction to her life story. "I didn't want Binjie and her to know, because I knew it would only upset them. But I
needed to explain why I really didn't want to do a documentary that
would possibly be aired in the States. Verena got tears in her eyes
again. And this was at the restaurant over dinner. She said, 'Why do
you have to go through hell in the Holocaust and then go through
another hell here?' She kept hugging me." Lauren never explained to
Muggli that she had been reluctant to appear on the BBC documentary because the BBC had confronted her in 1992 about the lack of
evidence in support of *Satan's Underground*.

As with her earlier personas, Lauren Stratford's transformation
into a Holocaust survivor involved glomming on to a celebrated
writer and folding parts of that person's story into her own. Just as
The Beautiful Side of Evil and *Stormie* had guided her into the world
of satanic ritual abuse, *Fragments* seems to have been her blueprint
for how to be a child survivor of the Holocaust. Her first letter to
Binjamin Wilkomirski in mid-1997 coincided with her first cautious

contacts with the Child Holocaust Survivors Group of Los Angeles, and the mix of vividness and vagueness of *Fragments* presumably enabled her to transpose her fantastic tales of "red fire and blood and candy" from satanic safehouses to Birkenau.

Years before she approached the author of *Fragments* or the Child Holocaust Survivors Group of Los Angeles, Lauren Stratford had already drawn parallels between satanic ritual abuse and the Holocaust. Although in *Satan's Underground* the prevailing metaphor for her experiences is the fiery Christian hell, the Holocaust comes up several times in *Stripped Naked,* which was published in 1993, the year that *Schindler's List* brought the destruction of European Jewry to the forefront of American culture. At one point in *Stripped Naked,* Stratford invokes Claude Lanzmann's epic documentary *Shoah* and the perils of Holocaust denial to support the existence of the Satanist pandemic to which she testifies:

> I would like to take a respectful liberty, if I may, in likening those of us who are victims and survivors of ritual abuse to Mr. Lanzmann's striking expression of the tragic truth of the Holocaust.
>
> We, who are the victims and survivors, had to remain silent for too long. We finally braved the outside world and broke our silence in cautious whispers. Now, some of you are listening to us, and some of you are believing us. But there are many who do not listen, and there are many who do not believe. There are a few of you who do not even believe that we exist! This is a tragedy.

Putting aside the question of whether the liberty Stratford takes is a respectful one, the rhetoric she shares with the Holocaust child-survivor support movement—a defiant insistence on her own memories, an *a priori* acceptance of the memories of her peers, a focus on individual traumas and emotions, an inclusive and collective approach to healing, a wariness of skeptical outsiders and insiders—must have made it easier for her to hoodwink actual child survivors of the Holocaust along with their amateur and professional advocates. And her riposte to the Passantinos in the introduction to

Stripped Naked—"If a survivor is met with disbelief, denials, demands for proof, or even demands for a quick recovery, then the journey to recovery is impaired significantly"—would be echoed years later by Harvey Peskin in defense of Binjamin Wilkomirski and by others in defense of Lauren Grabowski.

At one point Lauren Grabowski participated in an online discussion of who should be deemed a Holocaust survivor. In response to a message on the H-Holocaust Internet mailing list that a Jew who left Germany in 1938 was not, strictly speaking, a "survivor," she wrote,

> People survived horrible traumas who were not in a concentration camp. It seems to me that the question I've heard one too many times of "who is a survivor" only brings division. I think we need to be sensitive to *all* who consider themselves as survivors of the Holocaust.
>
> For myself, the Holocaust is about individual suffering.
>
> I think only the individual can decide if he/she is a survivor.
> . . . And if some call themselves survivors who are not survivors in any sense of the word, does this upset the whole survivor movement? I think not.

Although this can now be read as a clever attempt at self-exculpation, it is also an argument that the Holocaust is an entirely subjective experience. If it is all about memory and individual suffering, documentation is irrelevant. Her comments on H-Holocaust passed muster with the list moderator and impressed someone at the International Society for Yad Vashem enough to reprint the item in its newsletter, *Martyrdom and Resistance*.

Laurel Willson's attempt to assume a Jewish identity was filtered through fundamentalist Christian theology. Some of her linguistic transpositions sound gratingly off-key, even more so than the choice to perform the Kol Nidre in April. Her messages in Internet forums and e-mails were usually signed with "Shalom," the Hebrew word for peace, but her creative usage of the term suggests nothing so much as a Christian state of grace. "May you find true Shalom for yourself. This is my prayer for you," she wrote in her first private

message to Muggli. (Muggli, a repeat visitor to Israel, also used "Shalom" as her regular sign-off.) Later Grabowski asks Muggli, "Do
you ever think I shall find Shalom? Or will my Binjie ever find his
Shalom?" After receiving Muggli's $1,000 check, Lauren Grabowski
wrote, "Beginning to Find My Shalom at Last," as she asks for
$150 more.

As with those who had gotten to know Binjamin Wilkomirski,
Lauren Grabowski's friends reacted to the Passantinos' bombshell in
different ways. Monika Muggli was hurt and furious. She had been
persuaded by Ganzfried that Binjamin Wilkomirski was a faker, and
for a long time she thought her pen pal was being used by the author
of *Fragments*. Now Muggli, who helped Lauren Grabowski out of a
sense of moral obligation and national responsibility, was the one
who felt used. By the time she found out about Lauren Stratford, her
correspondence with Grabowski had slowed to a trickle, so Muggli's
first reaction was to write to Jen Rosenberg, the moderator of the
online Holocaust forum hosted by the Mining Co. (now renamed
About.com) where they met.

"Lauren is a cheat, an impostor," Muggli wrote to Rosenberg.
"Jen, you've been informed about our acquaintance and friendship
from the beginning. You knew Lauren personally, you were (and
are?) friends with her. You remember when I asked you whether I
should send Lauren money to be able to see Binjamin, her alleged
'Holocaust-Brother' again—who also turned out to be a swindler,
what a shame—you remember that you encouraged me to do so."

"She is not a manipulative and lying person," Rosenberg told
Muggli. "She is honest and sweet and caring and probably the most
kind-hearted person I have ever met." Rosenberg still saw Lauren
socially, and trusted her to the extent that she taught Lauren how to
monitor the online forum and delete messages that seemed counter-
historical or otherwise inappropriate. Rosenberg mentioned that
Lauren had told "her full story" to other close friends, and that they
are standing by her. "Lauren has been through a lot in her life and I
fear what these destructive accusations are going to do to her. As far
as I'm concerned, the real Lauren is the one that I know, the one that

I've talked to for nearly two years, the one who opened her heart to both of us. I feel that there is no way that someone could fake such warmth and kindness."

Rosenberg's response mystified and angered Muggli, who posted references to the Passantinos' report on Lauren Grabowski on the H-Holocaust list. Rosenberg wrote to Muggli to say that Lauren had promised to return her money. Muggli said she didn't want it back, and asked that the money be donated to Leon Stabinsky's child-survivor group.

"I see this as a child-survivor thing as opposed to being an adult-survivor thing," Rosenberg told me. By the time I caught up with her, months had passed since the Passantinos' article was published in *Cornerstone* and posted on the Web. She still considered Lauren a friend, and said there was "more information" about Lauren, though Rosenberg didn't have it herself. She suggested I talk to Sarah Moskovitz and the child-survivor group if I wanted to know more. Rosenberg said she was too busy to do her own research about Lauren's past. "My main goal is to educate people on the Holocaust," she said. She explained that she started her site after finding a lot of dubious and intentionally misleading material when she first searched for Holocaust information on the World Wide Web. She wanted her Holocaust education and discussion site "to have real information. I wanted people to know that it is accurate."

What about the links to *Fragments*? And Rosenberg's account of her trip to Auschwitz, where she left a pair of pink plastic shoes in memory of Lauren's friend who died there?

She said she didn't realize she was still recommending *Fragments*, and would take that endorsement down. The report on the pink shoes was another matter. Rosenberg felt loyal to Lauren, and the report, she said, was emotionally honest even if it was based on a lie. "If it isn't real, and if Ana isn't real, there are so many young children and babies who went through that," Rosenberg said. "It really was a metaphor for the children. For Laura it was for Ana. I did it for the children."

"It'll probably come down, since people keep asking me about it. It's not something I want to be involved in," said Rosenberg, who felt that she was unfairly put in the middle of a dispute to which she wasn't a party.

After I published Rosenberg's comments in the *Forward*, the story about the pink shoes disappeared from the Web. So did her Holocaust site.

"I never treated Laura. I'm not qualified to speak about Laura," Sarah Moskovitz tells me over lunch at the Holiday Inn on Sunset Boulevard. It is a hot day, but the white-haired psychologist, who is older than the child survivors she has cared for, is wrapped up in a turtleneck and long skirt. Although I asked to interview her, the grandmotherly Moskovitz asks me the first question, namely, why I want to know about all this—Binjamin, Lauren, child survivors—and I tell her about my Wilkomirski ancestors. She says she doesn't really know much about Lauren Grabowski, and asks me to fill her in. I tell her what I know has been published, but nothing more.

Moskovitz tells me she has been working with Holocaust survivors since 1977 and that, while feelings of uncertainty and inauthenticity are a big issue for her clients, imposture is extremely rare. "If there are six hundred of them and five people are not survivors, I'd say that you're doing pretty good," she says. She does not seem worried about the prospect of one of the five speaking for the others in the future, when there are no living eyewitnesses. Only a few books about the Holocaust will still be in wide circulation fifty years from now, she says, and even though publishers have withdrawn *Fragments*, she hopes Binjamin Wilkomirski's story will be one of those few. "The main thing," she says, "is that the story is well told."

I asked to attend a monthly meeting of the Child Holocaust Survivors Group of Los Angeles, but was told I would not be welcome. A few members did consent to meet with me, including John Gordon, who was involved in organizing Binjamin's visit and still friendly with him; Lya Frank, who had served as cochair along with Leon Stabinsky; and Marie Kaufman, a social worker and child survivor who became the leader of the group after the schism. Kaufman is baby-sitting her grandchild, so we meet in her living room. They warned me beforehand that they had no interest in talking about Lauren Grabowski or Binjamin Wilkomirski, and were no more willing to do so when I arrive. Instead we talk about child survivors and the Los Angeles group. The conversation is stilted, and not only because they seem wary. They use language I have heard from other child survivors and seen in the psychological literature.

The three child survivors tell me their group is still attracting new members, and that their recent experiences with Binjamin and Lauren have not changed their philosophy. "I don't recall the group asking for proof—for any reason, ever," says Lya Frank. "Most of us don't have anything, or we have false documents."

"FOR SOMEBODY who lived in the U.S. to say 'I'm a survivor' is an insult," Stabinsky tells me as we sit in his office among the antique microscopes and Holocaust history books. In person, he looks smaller and gentler than the voice on the phone suggested. He is dressed informally, in a bright blue sweatsuit. His white hair is parted to one side, with a boyish cowlick.

Almost two years have passed since Binjamin and Lauren's concert in Los Angeles, but his anger at both of them is still fresh. "He is a thief. He stole my guts," Stabinsky says. "Since 1945 I have sat up until the wee hours of the night hearing stories of treachery and murder and killing for a piece of food, hearing about the young boys who were sexually molested by the guards, and on and on, and to have someone like this make it up delegitimizes us."

I ask Stabinsky whether he has encountered other child survivors he thought might be impostors.

He winces. "Who am I to ask questions?" Stabinsky says, hurt by mine. "But then people go on acting, with that exaggerated behavior. It's so beyond what I have witnessed in any other child survivors. It didn't ring true."

"The whole Holocaust thing, it's fifty years later and people are writing books. Forgive the parallel, but for some of them it's like a mental laxative," says Stabinsky. "How long do you want to revisit the past? How often do you want to revisit the past? To what end do you want to revisit the past?"

When I ask Stabinsky about his own life story, he hands me a brief autobiography that appeared in the *Journal of the Microscopical*

Society of Southern California. In it, Stabinsky writes about his early-childhood memories: missing his parents when he was in foster care, hearing Nazi speeches on the radio. During the war, he hid in a Catholic orphanage under the name Simon Leblanc, and he explains the convoluted record-keeping system the Belgian underground used to keep track of hidden children while protecting their identities. The article is illustrated with a page from one of the lists the underground kept; Stabinsky was number 1618.

The best record of what happened to him, he says, may be the notes and drawings he remembers making at a Bundist summer camp in Westende, Belgium, in 1946, when he was about twelve. "We were asked to write everything of what we remembered had happened," he says. I ask him where those papers might be now, and he says he has no idea.

AT THE monthly meeting of the California Association of Holocaust Child Survivors, Stabinsky does not revisit the past, or at least not *that* past. "In a former life, with another group, there were no elections for twelve years," he says as a new slate of officers is announced. Stabinsky is the nominee for president once again, but he tells his audience of forty at the Museum of Tolerance that he doesn't want to be president; he would be happy if someone else stepped up. Nobody does.

Next, the head of the social committee, Dorothy Stabinsky, announces a Purim party at a North Hollywood temple; they are hiring a professional square-dance caller. The members discuss whether the group should organize an outing to Catalina or Palm Springs in the summer.

Most of the meeting is taken up with restitution business. Stabinsky hands out a packet of papers summarizing the Claims Conference's progress in negotiating with the Swiss banks, European insurance companies, and corporations that used slave laborers during the war. Someone who doesn't like the Claims Conference compares its Jewish leadership to the Jewish councils in Nazi ghettos that decided which Jews should be shipped to camps. Although it is clear that a couple of the members follow the progress of the negotiations in newspapers, Stabinsky seems to know more than anyone else here.

After explaining what's in the packet, Stabinsky announces that an ad hoc coalition is being formed to lobby the California state insurance commission to put pressure on implicated insurance companies. The child survivors debate whether they should join. One member worries that they are being used to make certain politicians look good, and that the state insurance commissioner can't do anything. Another member expresses discomfort at being in league with organizations like the Five Million Forgotten & Non Jewish Victims of the Shoah and the International Association of Lesbian and Gay Children of Holocaust Survivors. (Nobody complains that the other Los Angeles child-survivor group is also part of the coalition.) Stabinsky acknowledges that the points being made have their merits, but he also says that if they don't join the coalition and go to the meetings, they won't know what is happening.

The talk about restitution goes on for almost an hour. Opinions are aired, and the child survivors are more or less in agreement that they'd like to see a settlement soon, and that the money should go directly to survivors rather than to Jewish organizations. No resolutions are proposed, no decisions are made. Much as Stabinsky can inform his members and pass along their complaints to his colleagues at the American Gathering of Jewish Holocaust Survivors, he has little power to implement their ideas.

As the discussion draws to a close, a man with wispy red hair stands up to make a comment. It is not his first comment of the meeting, and judging from the reactions of the audience when he spoke before, they seem to regard him as something of a pest. If the red-haired man notices their irritation, he is undeterred.

"Every time we come here," the red-haired man says, "we talk about this stupid money that we're never going to get. That's why I'm getting bored. That's why I don't want to come here anymore. I don't know anybody here. I don't know anybody's name."

A silence falls over the room. "You're right," says Stabinsky. "But there are daily developments in these fields. We should have meetings to talk about the money, but we should have meetings to talk about other things."

A few minutes later, the meeting is adjourned. The child survivors walk to the garage, get into their own cars, and drive home through the quiet Los Angeles night.

EFFORTS HAVE been made to reconcile the two groups of child survivors, but Stabinsky says he isn't interested in making peace. At lunch Moskovitz told me it might all be for the best; the two groups have different interests, and this way two sets of people can enjoy the honor of being leaders in their community. She may be right, but after hearing the red-haired man I wasn't so sure. I felt the same way after stopping by the home of Gitta Ginsberg, who was the longtime treasurer of the original child-survivor group before she resigned and became a founder of the new group. On one wall of Ginsberg's den she has a framed picture taken during a getaway weekend with four child-survivor friends. It is mounted along with a poem about their friendship. Ginsberg explains that since the new group formed, she doesn't speak to three of the women in the picture anymore. She had always thought that she would invite the therapist who helped her work through her childhood memories and her divorce and who helped her son overcome a drug problem to her son's wedding, but they stopped speaking during the quarrel among the Los Angeles child survivors.

"The shame of it," Daisy Miller tells me over a bowl of chicken soup at a Jewish deli in the Valley, "is that it broke up this family. Yes, this family was dysfunctional, with major arguments and disagreements and difficult people, but it was a family."

Miller has a slight head cold, but she came to talk to me again, mostly to remind me that the people I have been pursuing in Los Angeles are all child survivors. Each of them lived through terrifying, life-altering events, and for each it is a daily struggle to overcome the war. "Be understanding," she says. "Be kind."

Miller had already made her point to me, though she did not know it. Amid shuttling between the two child-survivor factions and the home of my cousin Susann, who still harbored hope that the author of *Fragments* was a Wilbur, I spent a few hours in the basement of the library at California State University at Northridge viewing the oral history videotapes that Sarah Moskovitz recorded in the early 1980s. I was curious to hear what these child survivors sounded like before they saw themselves as part of a community, before they became part of an affirming subculture, before they came to understand the therapeutic value of testifying. I want to know how their stories sounded the first time they told them, when the idea of videotaping Holocaust survivors was in its infancy. How would they sound different from Binjamin's testimony at the United States Holocaust Memorial Museum?

I began with Miller's videotape, mainly because, of all the child survivors I'd met in Prague and Los Angeles, she had talked the least about her own experiences. Miller says she was born in Zagreb in 1938. "Not a good time to be born," she says with a melancholic grin.

I intended to skip around, watch a few minutes here and there, but Miller tells her story of survival simply and directly, and I am quickly engrossed. I did not want to fast-forward and I could not push stop. For the first time since doubting Binjamin's story, I am opening myself to the story of a child survivor. I don't know why it took so long. Maybe I didn't want to let myself feel anything after being stung once. Maybe I couldn't feel compassion because there were so many stories at hand. Maybe I am one of those people Miller was talking about in Prague who are angry about having to hear so much made of the Holocaust all these years later.

Moskovitz's interview with Miller has the unedited quality of life, not the episodic drama of cinema. She talks about one of the houses where her family hid in Italy, and how she had been spotted in the kitchen by neighbors who were unaware of her family's presence. "It could have cost all our lives. I was close to six by this point," she says, still aware of the weighty responsibility she bore so early. Miller also conveys the constant fear of discovery and the chronic boredom of month after month spent shuttered away. She would invent stories about the ants, she says, to keep herself occupied. There are details she can remember, details she can't remember, and others she doesn't want to think about. At the end of the war, when it is finally safe to emerge from hiding, Miller runs out of the house where she has been kept. She has been cooped up for so long that her muscles have atrophied, and it hurts her to run. At the end of the war, her immediate family is still intact, but her grandfather died in Terezin. Her father dies of an illness a few years later. Life goes on without a triumphant ending.

I tried watching some of the other videotapes, but I couldn't focus. I couldn't stop thinking about Daisy Miller trying to run.

CONSPIRACY
THEORIES

I arrive in Zurich in September. It is a few days before the Jewish New Year, and two years since my first encounter with the author of *Fragments*. I had written ahead to let him know I was coming and to remind him of the invitation he extended over dinner in New York, expressing the disingenuous hope that I would still be welcome at his home in Amlikon. I also mentioned my trip to Riga, and said I would show him the papers relating to the Wilkomirski family that my mother and I found, if only he would meet me. Neither my reminder of his promised hospitality nor my offer of more information elicited a response.

From my hotel I send a note to Verena asking her whether she would sit down with me and try to clear the air. She replies by fax. "I still have very warm feelings for your family," she says, but my coverage of Binjamin's case in the *Forward* had not been to their liking. "I do not wish to meet you again," she wrote. "My main concern is Binjamin's health."

My being a Wilkomirski no longer opened doors into the world of the author of *Fragments*. Perhaps Verena thought I was too close to the story to treat Binjamin fairly, or perhaps my own authenticity posed a threat to his. His government files remain secret, protected by Swiss privacy laws, and his intimates have shut me out. The one time I got his friend and colleague Elitsur Bernstein on the phone from New York, the psychologist told me he does not speak to journalists, even though I knew he already had.

It turns out Binjamin did have a real person in mind when he told the Ortho conference in Washington about Sabina Rappaport, the woman with the magic word repeated in three-four time. When I call Ziona Muller, she says she is Sabina Rappaport, and invites me to come to her home the following Wednesday. Muller explains which trains I can take to reach her small Swiss village, but two hours later she calls me back. "I am not ready to make an interview," she says. I ask Muller whether someone else advised her against meeting me. "I talked to nobody," she insists. "I just don't think it could help me."

She may be right. The Sabina Rappaport on the list displayed at the Ortho conference was a six-year-old shipped from Drancy to Auschwitz in April 1944. According to the *Auschwitz Chronicle*, of the 1,004 people who arrived on that transport, 139 men and women—presumably those deemed fit for labor—were tattooed and admitted to the camp on May 1, 1944; the remaining 865 were sent to be gassed.

There are no signs of life when I go by the clarinet atelier on the Asylstrasse. The formal white-on-black nameplate—bolted to the wall, the sort of nameplate standard in Zurich apartment buildings—says Doessekker. A blue adhesive label with the name Wilkomirski was pasted just beside it. I consider showing up unannounced in Amlikon, but there doesn't seem to be any point since I have already seen the outside of the farmhouse in photographs.

I AM SOMEWHAT consoled by an invitation to the countryside from Daniel Ganzfried, who is holed up at the second home of a friend so he can concentrate on his next novel. Phone calls about *Fragments*, disputations in the pages of the *Weltwoche*, commitments to *60 Minutes* and the BBC, and other bits of Binjamin Wilkomirski business have sidetracked him for the better part of a year. After speaking to anyone and everyone about why *Fragments* is a hoax, Ganzfried has gone into seclusion himself. He is more or less in retreat for the month, he tells me, but will make an exception to see me since I have come so far.

It takes three trains to reach him; the last one, half empty, carries elderly people outfitted with day packs and walking sticks for a midweek mountain hike. Ganzfried meets me at the train station in Nesslau, a small town in St. Gallen, the eastern canton where Paul Grüninger once served as police commander. After picking up some supplies at the supermarket, we hop onto Ganzfried's motorcycle. The road out of Nesslau is empty, but we climb cautiously past lush green pastures, docile tan cows, A-frame chalets with elaborate flower gardens. The exhaust from the motor dissipates quickly in the Alpine air, which is dominated by the scent of cut grass and manure. Vibrant colors and perfect shapes; this is the Switzerland of picture postcards.

We arrive at an isolated cottage high above the town. It is an unseasonably hot day, and Ganzfried suggests talking outside, under the eaves. He brings out a pitcher of water, and sits down at a picnic table with his back to the wall. He faces out on a magnificent valley. Sitting across from him, I get a view of the side of the old house and of Ganzfried, who looks weather-beaten like the wood behind him. He has tousled, graying dark hair, and his suntanned face is distinguished by large brown eyes, an angular nose, and a couple of days' worth of stubble. He is wearing jeans and a plain gray T-shirt.

In the year following Ganzfried's initial exposé, a half dozen investigators with deeper pockets, more time, and greater access to information looked into the identity of the author of *Fragments*. None of them deviated from the three-paragraph biographical sketch that Ganzfried published in the *Weltwoche* back in August of 1998. "I was not wrong at any point that could have spoken in his favor," Ganzfried tells me, peeling off his T-shirt to bask in the late-summer sun. "All the points where I was wrong, it was even worse than I thought."

The only way Bruno Doessekker can be Benjamin Wilkomirski, he says, is if there is still a conspiracy afoot. "An ongoing conspiracy including the Swiss government, including his biological father who paid child support until 1957, including the estate, including the

uncle who knew better but who would not tell, including the authorities in Biel who certify and testify that his files are genuine." A conspiracy so far-ranging and well planned, Ganzfried says, "that I
became the victim of it—if I am not a coconspirator, which might be
possible," he says with an almost straight face, daring me to take his
hypothesis seriously, as anyone who still believes in Binjamin would
have to do.

"This is a fraud—a cold-blooded, well-embedded fraud," says
Ganzfried, thumping the picnic table for emphasis. "He knows very
much what he's doing and he knows very well how to differentiate
between truth and fiction, and lying and not-lying," Ganzfried says.
"He really does things for money," Ganzfried adds, but he also
thinks the author of *Fragments* filled a need. The surviving Jews, he
says, "are tired of speaking to a gentile world about their suffering.
Now here comes a guy, he's willing—he even takes money for it—to
go out to take their task and speak about the Holocaust. 'Look at my
body; this is the Holocaust. Look at me, you don't need to know
more about the Holocaust than seeing my face and my body and my
soul, which I present to you.'

"We have to confront the fact that, this time, fraud and lies are
penetrating not only the side of the revisionists but the side of the
victims. And to my mind, this is worse. Because, much more than
any revisionist, it helps the sound facts deteriorate and erode." In
Ganzfried's view, Doessekker is not the only party responsible. "You
cannot pass a certain degree of wishful thinking—against all facts,
against all evidence, against all logic, and against all common sense—
without becoming complicit. At a certain point, your stupidity does
not prevent you from becoming complicit."

This is the flip side of the message Harvey Peskin relayed to me:
Anyone who is not against Binjamin is for him; there is no such
thing as an innocent bystander. But who is complicit? Is it anyone
who still gives Binjamin the benefit of the doubt? Would it apply to
my Wilbur cousins who still want to think of Binjamin as a relative?

"I do not know your cousins," he says. "Gordon or Peskin, I
would accuse them." In the course of his tirade, he adds others to
the list: Verena Piller, psychologist Elitsur Bernstein, researcher Lea
Balint, Suhrkamp publisher Siegfried Unseld, editor Thomas Sparr,

agent Eva Koralnik, critic Klara Obermüller, and so on. "There was a whole camarilla of people who worked hard to prevent me from publishing." Minutes after ridiculing Doessekker's paranoia, Ganzfried bruits a possible cabal against his own truth-seeking activities. I wait for him to wink, but he doesn't.

Whatever one makes of the alleged plot against Ganzfried, it enrages him much less than the plot of *Fragments*. "This book had one notion: that a victim of the Holocaust is forever a victim. It is forever a child; it is forever sick, not only in its body but in its mind; it is forever the prey of therapists and therapy. Once in the Holocaust, you never get out of it anymore. It explains everything in your life; it explains why your girlfriend left you, why you have a headache, why you cannot have an orgasm anymore.

"The Holocaust victim today is like Jesus. He has on his shoulders every evil deed that was ever committed. We give him some money for it, some public reputation, some respect. So he goes on with his story, I am freed from my guilt, and we all end up in heaven. And this is basically a very cruel and inhuman thing to do. No man, no human being, is only a victim. I never thought that the survivors are the source of our wisdom. They are just the source of the facts."

Ganzfried does value the testimony of authentic Holocaust survivors like his father. "In a little pathetic way," he says, "I did this in remembering my father, who was such a genuine victim, because he was not a victim at all in his own understanding." Ganzfried learned this when he was living in New York and his father paid him a visit. "He was basically a schmuck to me, a boring guy who had nothing to tell in his life and nothing to show off with, and this was perhaps due to the Holocaust, but also perhaps because he was just lazy. He didn't read decent books, he couldn't check into the cinema to see a good movie. When I was with him in New York, he hired a car, which is the most unnecessary thing you could do. Then he stayed in the apartment for the rest of the day. And if he did go out, he just went to drive his car. I thought, What a schmuck, until we ended up on the Empire State Building. I was bored. My first question was, 'Hey, come on, don't you regret the waste of your life?' I thought he would say yes, just to finish the discussion. And he said no. This no was in a way such a pure word, because he said it in a very authentic way: 'No.' So I asked him more, and then comes this story. He sees that his children are healthy, they are okay, and every one had a profession. There's nothing to regret." The conversation with his father inspired a scene in his novel, *Der Absender*.

"My next book is completely different," Ganzfried says. "There is not one single Jew in it, and it plays out in orbit." He gives a brief synopsis: A small, wealthy country tries to build its pride by performing the first live human birth in space. After the launch, however, the spaceship loses contact with home base, and the three-member crew is plagued by uncertainty. They wonder whether they will be rescued, whether their country still exists, whether their shipmates know more about what is going on and won't share it, whether they are really in space or just pretending. "It's very different from my first book, but there is one link," he explains. The spaceship is a partial metaphor for the concentration camp. "It's total isolation from the world," says Ganzfried, who lists the anxieties of his characters: "How do we get out of here? Is there someone who remembers us? If we ever come back, will anyone ever believe us?"

Ganzfried says it has been hard to move on from his investigation of *Fragments*. "I fear that my name will always be smeared with the smell of this dirty case," he says. "You cannot dig so much into shit without getting some on yourself. I knew this in advance—I was not that naive—but the story was kept open so long. People had it in their hands to close it very quickly, but no, they left it open, because they like scandals and they like victims." The crises and mounting uncertainties entered his new novel, he said, only after he got involved with *Fragments*.

"I think Wilkomirski does not exist anymore," Ganzfried asserts confidently. The only thing sustaining him, says Ganzfried, is that Binjamin "is still in a book on the shelf." When Suhrkamp withdraws the book, he says, it will all be over. "What he does in private was never any of my interest. Tomorrow he can go and say he's Jesus Christ; I really don't care." On the other hand, "any testimony of a Holocaust survivor, if it's made public, if it's made as a book, submits itself to the normal rules of public life. He took money on a fraudulent basis. He can be sued for that." The people whose identities Bruno Doessekker absorbed into his own, says Ganzfried, "should just go and sue. I don't think you can sue him for lying in writing the book, but I do think you can sue him for taking public money."

"And you wouldn't want to sue him?" I ask Ganzfried.

"Well, I would be the wrong person, because I haven't been cheated."

After four and a half hours, Ganzfried tells me he must get back to the three characters stranded on their spaceship. Eager to return to his novel, he points out the footpath to the train station and sends me down the hill.

At FIRST hearing, the plot Ganzfried believes to be afoot against him seems as improbable as the constellation of hostile forces that the author of *Fragments* believes acted against him, but then again, many of the unlikely things Ganzfried told me the first time we spoke turned out to be true. Back in Zurich, I try to reach the people there who Ganzfried named as part of the conspiracy. Obermüller does not return my calls. Koralnik tells me she is too busy to meet. (In a later conversation, she tells me the conspiracy described by Ganzfried is "a sheer lie.") Even so, they might not be the main players, and I can't assess Ganzfried's theory without access to the files of Bruno Doessekker and his inner circle. With him ignoring me and with Verena refusing to see me, I call Stefan Maechler. A freelance historian specializing in Swiss refugee policies during World War II, Maechler received a commission from Koralnik's Liepman Agency to investigate the facts behind Binjamin Wilkomirski. Somehow Koralnik convinced the author of *Fragments* to grant Maechler power of attorney so the historian could pore over his governmental files and identify any irregularities supporting Doessekker's claim to be a child survivor of the Holocaust. I know he had never followed through on his promise back in 1995 to produce his papers for Suhrkamp's prepublication inquiry, but still it surprised me that he would agree to such a plan. Did the people who stood by him press him to cooperate? Was there a threat of legal action if he didn't? Or did he simply think that whatever the documents said, they didn't matter, since he accorded primacy to his own memories?

By the time I arrived in Switzerland, the results of Maechler's probe were long overdue. Although he set out to prepare a brief report that would be published as a coda to future editions of *Fragments*, Maechler was so taken with his subject that he went on to write a book-length study, which Koralnik represented. There was no word about when it would be done, though I heard that Maechler was close to finishing. I left several messages on Maechler's answering machine, and the historian asked Ganzfried to pass along a message saying he was out of town.

A FEW WEEKS after I returned to New York, Maechler delivered a draft of his report to Suhrkamp. He did not find anything out of the ordinary in the Grosjean and Doessekker papers, nothing to suggest that Binjamin was anyone other than Bruno Grosjean. With his power of attorney, Maechler was able to fill in gaps in the biography of the author of *Fragments* which journalists could not explain. He presented the first uninterrupted history of Bruno, from his conception through his adoption by Dr. and Mrs. Doessekker.

When Yvonne Grosjean was pregnant with Bruno, she was hit by a car and spent the remainder of her pregnancy in hospital. After learning of her injuries, the father of the child, Rudolf Zehnder, abandoned his pregnant lover. Bruno was born on February 12, 1941, and Yvonne remained at the hospital for some time afterward before mother and child moved to a convalescent home. When she was well enough to work, she took a part-time job with a watch company, but her meager wages and the support payments she received were insufficient to provide for mother and child. Beginning in February of 1943, Bruno was sent to live with a series of foster families in and around Biel: the Schlueps, the Rossels, and then the Aeberhards. Before Bruno had spent a year at the Aeberhard home in the town of Nidau, their eighteen-year-old son, René, implored the local welfare office to place the Grosjean boy elsewhere. "Sometimes my mother is not quite healthy, and in addition the boy is difficult," René Aeberhard told state authorities on February 17, 1945, just after Bruno's fourth birthday. As a result, Bruno was sent to the children's home in Adelboden on March 8, 1945. Yvonne Grosjean was urged to give him up for adoption, and she agreed in May. Despite her brother

Max's desire to adopt Bruno, the boy was assigned to the Does-sekkers in July.

Maechler tracked down Rudolf Zehnder, who was still alive and living in Lucerne. He had never met his son, but pictures of Zehnder as a young army reservist reveal an uncanny resemblance to the teenage Bruno Doessekker; they share the same high forehead, rounded cheekbones, and cocky smile. Maechler also located René Aeberhard, who helped the historian identify moments in *Fragments* which might have their roots in Bruno's stay in Nidau. The layout and environs of the Aeberhard home bore a resemblance to sketches and descriptions of the Polish farmhouse in *Fragments*. René, then a teenager, remembers sledding with Bruno and showing the three-year-old boy his model airplanes; in *Fragments*, Binjamin associates these activities with his older brothers. Furthermore, Maechler suggests that the intimidating woman who banished Binjamin to the cellar and the vicious female concentration-camp wardens might have been inspired by the unstable and occasionally violent Mrs. Aeberhard. It is thus possible, Maechler argues, that real traumas experienced by Bruno Grosjean form the basis of the Binjamin Wilkomirski's Holocaust ordeal.

The facts laid bare by Maechler revealed that the author of *Fragments* seemed not to deserve the benefit of the doubt in any area. It turns out that Bruno Doessekker fought for and secured a share of Yvonne's estate, even though she asked in her will that her biological son not make any claim on it. He exaggerated the seriousness of his medical condition; Maechler says that while Bruno did have several illnesses including a low white-blood-cell count, none of them were life-threatening and he never had leukemia or any other form of cancer. And once the "legal steps" undertaken to resolve his identity led the Swiss authorities to Zehnder, Bruno refused to meet with his biological father's family and told his lawyer to call off the search and see if he could register the name Binjamin Wilkomirski as a trademark. Few people who had come into contact with the author of *Fragments* would vouch for what he said; even Ziona Muller (a.k.a. Sabina Rappaport) told Maechler that the author of *Fragments* overstated his role in her process of self-discovery when he spoke at the Ortho conference. She also told Maechler she may not be Sabina after all.

Despite these many examples of Bruno's duplicity, Maechler stops short of concluding that Bruno concocted *Fragments* consciously. "There is every indication that Wilkomirski found his own narrative true and authentic," Maechler wrote in his report. "Perhaps he did not really believe his story, but he did believe his own telling of it." Nor did Maechler find a broader conspiracy afoot involving Binjamin's friends and business associates, though he says that assessing the responsibility of the agent and publishing houses involved was not part of his mandate.

Upon reviewing a draft of Maechler's results, Koralnik ended her business relationship with the author of *Fragments*. Suhrkamp announced at the Frankfurt Book Fair that, for the time being, it was recalling the book from stores. "After studying the expert opinion, Suhrkamp-Verlag will decide whether and, if applicable, in what form Binjamin Wilkomirski's book will be published again," the October 12, 1999, statement said. It was Suhrkamp's last word on the matter; they offered neither an apology for publishing *Fragments* nor an expression of regret for leaving it on the market for more than a year after its authenticity had been questioned. (Suhrkamp has not republished *Fragments*. Its editors had a first look at Maechler's report but declined to publish it.) In the weeks that followed, the English- and French-language publishers withdrew *Fragments*. "The enormous impact that *Fragments* has had upon its readers must not blind us to the truth about the book," Carol Janeway said in a statement released by Schocken, which went on to publish Maechler's findings together with the text of *Fragments*.

With *Fragments* finally off the shelves, "the Wilkomirski affair has come to an end," Daniel Ganzfried declared in an article in the *Weltwoche* recapitulating many of the thoughts he shared with me in Nesslau. Yet Ganzfried said it wasn't really over. To have proper closure, he said, the individuals and institutions caught up in this "coldly planned fraud" should acknowledge their sins, publicly distance themselves from Binjamin Wilkomirski, give away any income from projects associated with his story to charitable institutions, and accept whatever legal consequences might follow. "The offenses deserve to be punished, imitators deterred," Ganzfried wrote.

In time, the Prix Mémoire de la Shoah, the Jewish Quarterly Literary Prize, the National Jewish Book Award, and the City of Zurich literary prize given to Binjamin Wilkomirski were all revoked. None of the organizations demanded a return of the cash prize. "When the author wants to accept the consequences of his actions, he can return the money," the secretary of the Zurich literary commission told the *Neue Zürcher Zeitung*. The only prize still belonging to Binjamin Wilkomirski is the American Orthopsychiatric Association's Max A. Hayman Award.

The week after Ganzfried's article calling for punishment of legal offenses appeared, a retired Zurich lawyer named Manfred Kuhn filed a criminal complaint with the Zurich district attorney's office accusing Doessekker and unspecified accomplices of fraud. Kuhn, who is not Jewish, has been interested in the Holocaust ever since he covered the Eichmann trial from Jerusalem for a Basel newspaper. He first learned of the controversy surrounding *Fragments* when his daughter interviewed Ganzfried for a Swiss Jewish newspaper, the *Israelitisches Wochenblatt*, shortly after he exposed Doessekker. Kuhn's petition cited Ganzfried's articles and referred to his line of argument, but both men insist that they are not friends and that the lawyer sued Doessekker on his own, not as Ganzfried's proxy.

In his complaint, Kuhn argued that Doessekker could be tried in Zurich courts since the book had been sold by a Zurich agency and its author, who'd spoken in public schools and won a municipal literary prize, had accepted local taxpayer funds under false pretenses. This fraud by Doessekker and company, Kuhn argued, was no benign mistake; it was committed "with a cynicism recalling that of the forger of the Hitler diaries." The maximum penalty for fraud in Switzerland is a ten-year prison sentence.

In addition to the criminal fraud charge, Kuhn filed a civil suit against Doessekker claiming unfair competition under the same law that a mineral-water purveyor might use against a competitor that was bottling sewage and labeling it as the runoff from a mountain spring. To make this argument, Kuhn claimed that *Fragments* has had an adverse effect on the rerelease of his 1980 spy novel *Der Skorpion* (*The Scorpion*), which Kuhn describes as a Middle East thriller "on the level of Irwin Shaw." There is little precedent for the use of the unfair-competition law against a writer who mislabeled a book, but, were the case to proceed to trial, as a plaintiff Kuhn might have permission to view the documents involved in the suit.

Any Swiss citizen can file a criminal complaint, and prosecutors are obliged to investigate every claim thoroughly before deciding whether it should be brought to court. The district attorney's investigation in the Doessekker case has dragged on for more than a year, but the state has access to some information that Maechler did not see. A warrant empowered police investigators to search Doessekker's homes. Both Rudolf Zehnder and Bruno's maternal uncle Max Grosjean submitted DNA samples into evidence, and while district attorney Lucienne Fauquex will not say whether Doessekker did, she did say that a suspect under investigation can be compelled to submit DNA evidence if it is germane to the investigation. The findings of the investigation, including the DNA test, can be made public even if the district attorney decides not to press charges.

If the DNA testing confirms that the author of *Fragments* is, as his papers indicate, the son of Yvonne Grosjean and Rudolf Zehnder (the public will not know for sure until the results are made known), it would seem that this will add a layer of scientific certainty to the documentary evidence. And yet for someone whose faith in Binjamin has not been shaken thus far, it is always possible to remain faithful: to decide that the Swiss governmental conspiracy against him would manufacture a false positive result; to maintain that DNA testing is less than one hundred percent accurate; or to pretend, as the author of *Fragments* himself did that night in the lobby of the Waldorf-Astoria, that the medical experiments to which he was subjected and the resulting leukemia could have altered his genetic makeup.

Whatever further degree of certainty is achieved by the district attorney's investigation, Swiss courts cannot compel anybody to ignore what the author of *Fragments* says he remembers and accept that he is in fact Bruno Grosjean, least of all Bruno himself. When Maechler presented his results in person to Bruno and Verena, the historian told the author of *Fragments* that he'd never been more certain of anything in his life. Maechler suggested ways he might be able to save face while shedding his Holocaust-survivor persona, but Doessekker would have none of it. "I am Binjamin Wilkomirski," he said.

· · ·

WHY DOES he still insist, against all logic and evidence, on being Binjamin Wilkomirski? It would seem that there are two possible answers: either he still believes he is Binjamin, or he is a shrewd con artist. Numerous circumstances—his heel-dragging obfuscation when others wanted to see his government files; his admission to me that night at the Waldorf-Astoria that he never really believed Yakov Maroko was his father even as he asserted that "all the Wilkomirskis are somehow connected"—indicate that he knew he had something to hide. Yet his insistence on being Binjamin suggests that he believes, or needs to believe, he is Binjamin. The truth may well lie somewhere in between. He could be clinging to what Freud would call a family romance, a common type of fantasy in which your actual parents aren't the imperfect, disappointing people who gave you life and raised you; they must have been kings or Gypsies, noblemen or out-siders who, like the parents of Oedipus, Moses, and other heroic or tragic figures, abandoned you for urgent reasons that must remain secret.

I can understand why being a child Holocaust survivor covertly smuggled into Switzerland would be a compelling fantasy, but I'd never thought being a Wilkomirski from Riga would be particu-larly ennobling or degrading. Why not another name, something generic like Cohen, or rhythmic like Rappaport? What made him see being a Wilkomirski as a mark of distinction? According to Maech-ler, the first time Bruno Doessekker came across the name was in March of 1972, on a visit to Katowice, Poland, when he saw a poster for a concert by Wanda Wilkomirska, a well-known Polish violinist from a distinguished musical family that, as far as I can determine, has nothing to do with my great-grandmother Anna and her siblings. A Polish acquaintance who was helping Doessekker obtain tickets saw the posters and remarked that the Swiss visitor was the spitting image of the violinist; the resemblance was so close, he said, that the two must be related. He returned to Zurich with her picture and began telling friends he had a long-lost sister.

Family romances are quite common in children, since they explain how someone who feels unique could have sprung up in ordinary surroundings, but they are usually outgrown. I can imagine why, for an adopted child like Bruno (or, for that matter, Laurel Willson) who knows little about his biological parents and who may have been told to put them out of his mind, a family romance might be that much more cherished and that much harder to dispel. Or perhaps Bruno Doessekker felt his early childhood was so insufferable that he came to think of his life before arriving in Zurich as his own personal concentration camp, and over time incorporated the Holocaust metaphor into his own fragmentary recollections of his time with the Aeberhards and in the Adelboden children's home. After all, when I visited René Aeberhard at his home in California—where he moved from Switzerland in the 1960s to put some distance between his household and his mentally ill mother—and asked him to explain what his home life was like, he told me, "It was hell in our house."

But it is impossible to determine from Bruno's various truths, lies, and silences that any one authentic moment of cruelty—a moment, say, when Mrs. Aeberhard threw him down into the cellar—is the root cause of his Holocaust delusions. It is an intriguing theory that may run parallel to the truth, but such a conclusion comes too close to the false certainties of the seduction theory, the notions about pinpointing childhood trauma which Freud abandoned, and the maybe-means-yes approach of recovered-memory therapy to accept it as proof. One must be careful about putting too much stock in visual similarities between Bruno and Rudolf Zehnder (though they are remarkable), or between Bruno's sketches of the Polish farmhouse and the Aeberhard home in Nidau. And if René Aeberhard thinks his mother may have indeed banished Bruno to the cellar, he may not be an unprejudiced witness, since he also told me, after recounting how the Swiss suffered during World War II, that "about fifty percent" of Jewish survivors are "lying about that Holocaust stuff" because "they smell money."

In my pursuit of answers about the man who calls himself Binjamin Wilkomirski, I have come across all sorts of clever hypotheses, armchair diagnoses, and paranoid plots. He did it for the money; he did it for the attention; he succumbed to his own tentative fiction; he needed to stir up in others the pity he felt for himself; he couldn't help but make himself into the pariah he has always felt himself to be; he was utterly deluded and remains that way; he is, to use the very words he applied to Barbro Karlén, the Swedish poet who claims to be the second coming of Anne Frank, "simply disturbed." One can blame Rudolf Zehnder for abandoning his child, Yvonne Grosjean for her inadequate mothering, Mrs. Aeberhard for her physical and psychological cruelty, the Swiss government for putting wealth before kinship and bypassing Max Grosjean, the Doessekkers for their haut bourgeois Protestant reserve, and so on. They may be responsible for Bruno's troubles, but none of them wrote *Fragments* or spread his story.

What made Bruno believe he was Binjamin is one matter; what made him move from testifying from the treetops or the therapist's couch to the public arena is another. Perhaps he really believed sharing his story with the world would empower and liberate him, or again perhaps he had more ignoble motives. Again, I can't know what he was thinking, but Bruno would not be in his present predicament had Vered Berman not put him on Israeli television when his name didn't appear on any of Wanda's lists and his story "sounded a little fishy" to her, had Eva Koralnik and Suhrkamp postponed publication until after their author had shown them the documents he said he was gathering, or had they consulted knowledgeable, uninvolved experts when they inquired into the rumors about Binjamin Wilkomirski's inauthenticity instead of relying on advocates like Elitsur Bernstein and "Frau Dr. Balint." It doesn't require a conspiracy to hold them responsible for spreading Binjamin's story. Without the momentum they provided and the authority they bestowed, Binjamin Wilkomirski would not have entered the public imagination. If only they had been more careful (and it is not as if his agent and publisher didn't grasp the full implications of the rumors against Binjamin), someone like Michael Mills, the Australian civil servant and skeptical Amazon reviewer, who would go on to volunteer a lengthy brief for Holocaust denier David Irving in his unsuccessful libel suit against Deborah Lipstadt, would not have had the opportunity to put himself on the side of historical truth.

When I wrote to Esther van Messel, the Swiss filmmaker who made *Born a Stranger*, the 1997 documentary screened at the Los Angeles Museum of the Holocaust a few months after Ganzfried's initial exposé, I explained I wanted to interview her because she helped bring Binjamin Wilkomirski's story out into the world. Van Messel replied that I had it backwards: it was Binjamin who had helped tell *her* story.

Her formulation strikes me as the essence of Bruno's confidence game—and it was a confidence game, whether his part of it was intentional or unintentional, calculated or pathological or somewhere in between. Binjamin was a cipher, and the author of *Fragments* offered himself up time and again as a universal placeholder for inexpressible and unappeasable absences. For better or worse, the mass murder of the Jews of Europe during World War II, and in particular the persecution of the children among them, has become a symbol for all sorts of irreversible losses, individual and collective, big and small. Viewing your own bleak situation as a personal concentration camp or identifying with Anne Frank may sound strange or grandiose to some, but for many individuals the impulse to make such a connection is irresistible. To some degree, the impulse that drove Bruno to become Binjamin is an impulse shared by many of us— Jews and non-Jews, survivors and nonsurvivors, Wilkomirskis and non-Wilkomirskis—who identified with Binjamin and saw our own stories through his. Each one of us made use of Binjamin's story in our own way, and in doing so we gave him substance, we made him real.

People try now to read into the elusive Bruno, to sift through his puzzling and often contradictory actions and flesh him out into the fully realized persona of a scheming con artist or a deluded fool or a wronged man. Like him, we crave a complete story most where there can't be one. You might expect him to produce a dramatic ending— a last-minute disclosure, an eloquent confession, an act of self-destruction—but only if you still don't accept him for who he really is. Bruno is a real person, and those who know him through his fictional alter ego cannot provide satisfying or complete explanations of what he did. Nor, with his history of deception, can we rely upon him for an accurate self-appraisal. After years of investigating and pondering the author of *Fragments,* I know little about him. But I have learned that drawing unsupportable conclusions about him is a mistake.

The discussion among his detractors of complicity and sinister conspiracies has done as much to preserve Binjamin as talk of second Holocausts from his supporters. Why Bruno did what he did is a conundrum, but it is not one that I can reasonably expect to solve anymore, nor can anyone solve it with certainty. And to continue wrestling with this question on his behalf strikes me as wrong-headed. From the outset, this sort of speculation has breathed life into Binjamin Wilkomirski. Our interest has sustained him for too long, and it is time to put him to rest.

EPILOGUE

May 9, 2000

It is 11 A.M. and the siren begins.

This is my second day in Israel, and I might have thought the end was near had I not been warned by a friend that there would be a nationwide alarm for Yom Hazicharon, the holiday when Israel remembers its fallen soldiers. Make sure that you are in a public place when the memorial signal sounds, my friend said. I had heeded his suggestion the night before, waiting on a bench on Jerusalem's Ben Yehuda Street for the clock to strike eight. When the siren rang out, the Israeli pedestrians stopped in their tracks and stood in the busy promenade. A few seconds later, other tourists saw what everyone else was doing and politely imitated the stillness of the locals. One minute later, the mechanical wail wound down and everyone resumed his or her own path.

Today, I am not on the Ben Yehuda mall or a crowded bus. I am standing before a bathroom sink in a third-floor apartment on the southern edge of Jaffa, about to sit down to an unexpected late breakfast. At the suggestion of my elderly hostess, I washed my hands a minute ago. I am clutching a clean towel, and my hands are dripping.

The siren lasts twice as long this morning, but it feels many times longer. Though I try to meditate on the losses associated with the noise, I can contemplate only my present awkward situation. I am frozen in a prolonged and semiprivate moment in front of a woman I just met. She is in her own home and her own country, so I am the stranger here.

I stare straight ahead at the pipes that disappear into the plaster wall, but the bathroom door is open and I can see my hostess out of the corner of my eye. She was watching me wash my hands before the siren began, and she is still looking at me, no doubt trying to figure out what to make of the young American reporter who claims to be her long-lost relative.

I don't know what to make of her, either, but I do know more about her than she knows about me. Months after writing to the Latvian State Archive, I received a four-page letter from archivist Irina Veinberga with information about the Wilkomirskis who remained in Riga. The letter contained plenty of bad news. Avram Wilkomirski—my great-grandmother's brother and the man whom the author of *Fragments* used to bolster his own fantasies about his Latvian childhood—lived in Riga with his wife, Baseva, and son, Sima, at Brivibas Street, 125, until they were crossed off the house registry on July 21, 1941. No forwarding address was listed, and their names were not mentioned again in the municipal records. Since the Nazis arrived on July 1, the Avram Wilkomirskis were in all likelihood dispatched to the ghetto, if not straight to their deaths.

However, according to Veinberga, some of my Wilkomirski relatives did survive the war. Hinda Mazo (née Wilkomirski), Avram and Anna's sister who died in 1917, gave birth to ten children, according to the archive, and five survived to adulthood. Hinda's son Moshe Mazo had two daughters, one of whom, Sheina, was born in Riga in 1927 and left for Israel in 1972. Sheina had a grandson, and his wife had also written to the Latvian State Archive to research the family tree. In her letter, Veinberga included an address and telephone number for a woman in southern Florida. When I called, she told me how to reach Sheina in Jaffa.

I first met Sheina at the bus stop near her house. She asked me to stand still as she examined me. I looked at her warm, tanned, oblong face, which seemed familiar, but only in the sense that I wouldn't be surprised to see her walking out of Loehmann's. After studying me,

Sheina said tentatively, "There's something there"—a similarity between my facial features and those of her family in Riga. I took this as a sign of welcome, but it reminded me that when Binjamin was in New York, someone said he looked just like me.

I have been in this situation once before, meeting someone who seemed to be my long-lost cousin, but this time the roles are different. Sheina, the host, is playing my mother's part, and I have taken over Binjamin's. Of course, with the information provided by the Latvian archives, there may be more to go on this time than physiognomy and wishes.

THE SIREN stops, and I sit down to a plateful of silver-dollar pancakes served with honey from a renowned kibbutz. Sheina plies me with unfamiliar treats. I am less taken with the bonbons from Riga than with the fresh Israeli loquats and a juicy, softball-sized melon she carves and shares with me. Sheina's hair is dyed a bright orange-red; tufts of gray remain at the temples. She is wearing a thin blue sweater and, around her neck, a golden charm with a blue iris to ward off the evil eye. As I eat, we make small talk. I explain how I took two buses from Jerusalem, which is a little more than an hour away. Sheina tells me that in her three decades in Israel, she has been to Jerusalem three times.

By the Hebrew calendar, it is Memorial Day in Israel, but for Sheina today is a doubly significant occasion because it is also the anniversary of the Allied victory in Europe. V-E Day still reverberates strongly for former citizens of the Soviet Union, since much of the war was fought on their soil. Sheina turns on the television and flips between Hebrew and Russian channels. Coverage of Yom Hazicharon takes a somber tone; for the victory over the Fascists, the Russians carry on lively celebration. Beyond the military parades and the reminiscences of veterans, there are recordings of Russian popular songs sung by famous wartime entertainers, celebrities as familiar to her as Bob Hope or Glenn Miller would be to an American septuagenarian. Also shown are snippets of old films about World War II.

Footage of the Battle of Stalingrad comes on, and Sheina starts telling me how she spent the war years. She was thirteen in the summer of 1941 when the German armies declared war on the Soviet Union. At the end of June, days before the Nazis took Riga, Sheina fled eastward with her parents, her younger sister, and other relatives. Her father was in uniform, she tells me; he made the rest of them march single-file, as if he had arrested them. The authorities at the Riga central station told them to go home because the trains were full, but her father insisted that they stay and eventually they found a way to leave. Moving slowly and at night, they crossed into Soviet Russia. In Pskov the family was treated fairly well, but they could not linger because of the approaching German army. From Pskov they continued to Yaroslavl, and when the Nazis threatened Moscow they moved on to Gorky, where the streets were crowded with refugees, rations were smaller, and bread was scarce. Winter was coming, but her father sold his fur hat for food. From Gorky they traveled along the Volga, ending up near Astrakhan. Here the family split up. Her father was called to service and disappeared in unknown circumstances during the Battle of Stalingrad; her mother ended up in a hospital, sick with hunger; her aunt and cousin made their way to Central Asia; Sheina and her sister headed to the Ural Mountains. She worked twelve hours a day, seven days a week on an assembly line. She can't remember what the factory made, she says. Following the German retreat and just before V-E Day, she slipped back into Riga.

In Riga she married a Jewish man who also managed to flee; they'd had their eyes on each other even before the war. They had a son and settled into a life that was materially secure but in other ways uncomfortable. Her son became a target of anti-Semitism in school and among his playmates. The last straw came after the Six-Day War, when a drunkard accosted her in the center of Riga and blamed the Jews for all of society's ills. The family applied for a visa; her husband lost his job. In 1971 their departure was approved. They arrived in Israel, and Sheina went to work in a supermarket, where she moved up from the cleaning crew to the cash register as she struggled to master Hebrew. She worked five hours in the mornings, four hours each afternoon. Her husband died in 1981, and she retired more than a decade ago.

· · ·

"Let's see the pictures," Sheina says. I have brought copies of my mother's old family pictures of Wilkomirski ancestors who lived in Riga. I have with me about twenty pictures, the same ones Bruno Doessekker saw.

Sheina examines the pictures. She does not recognize my great-grandmother Anna, or my aunt Miriam or her brothers, or Avram or his son, Sima, though here and there she notes certain physical similarities. Then she comes to a studio portrait of a man and a woman on the verge of adulthood. The high-foreheaded, slick-haired young man stands tall and a bit stiff; a white handkerchief is tucked into the pocket of his double-breasted dark suit. His companion, seated on a tapestry-covered bench beside him, wears a jacket, a skirt hemmed at the knee, and high heels. Her bobbed hair is parted in the middle, and her full lips are slightly open, revealing her teeth but not yet forming a smile.

"Where did you get this?" Sheina asks urgently, as if I have taken something from her.

"From my mother," I say, and explain that my mother probably got the picture from her grandmother who came from Riga, but that I really don't know. Of the twenty pictures I brought, it is one of the few my mother couldn't identify. On the back of the photograph there is a stamp from a Riga photo studio, and a Yiddish inscription that Sheina translates for me. The picture, dated 1929, is addressed to Anna's family. There is a playful message, the gist of which is an apology from the people in the photograph for not looking so good. This is reflexive self-deprecation; the pair is stylish and modern, much more so than the people in the other family pictures.

"Where did you get this?" Sheina asks again, this time less in anger than in disbelief. She reaches for her own pile of photographs, which is smaller than mine, and pulls out a photograph of the same man and woman in the same modish outfits taken at the same studio that same day. The only difference between Sheina's photograph and my mother's is that in hers the woman in the picture is facing the man, whereas in the one I brought she faces forward. My mother's copy has been safely kept in New York City since 1929, while Sheina's

has had a tumultuous journey from Riga to the outskirts of Tel Aviv, though it is not much worse for wear. They were once a pair, but here they are side by side again after seven decades.

MY TRIP TO Israel has just begun. After my day with Sheina, I will meet Vered Berman, who will tell me over coffee about the follow-up television documentary she wants to make, a story that will nail Bruno once and for all. I will visit Lea Balint, who will repeat her fervid defense of Binjamin and plead with me to help him just as

Zola aided Dreyfus. I will keep after psychologist Elitsur Bernstein, who does not return the messages I leave at his home and office. I will look around at the archives at Yad Vashem, but I find nothing new. Elsewhere on the grounds of the memorial is a sandstone labyrinth devoted to the lost communities of European Jews, a place I recognize because Bruno posed there mournfully for the television cameras. When I find the section of this maze devoted to Riga, I will think not of Binjamin—he is not real and no longer helps me tell my story—but of the actual Wilkomirskis who were stricken off the house register in 1941: Avram, his wife Baseva, their son Sima, and many of Hinda's children and grandchildren.

Sitting silently with Sheina, on the other hand, seeing her broad smile and her teary eyes, I have found what I came to Israel for, what the Wilburs have been looking for all along. The author of *Fragments* offered us a European counterlife, a story we could use to imagine our origins. In the process, he made us aware of names and faces of not-so-distant relatives caught up in World War II, and even though he isn't one of them, I am forever grateful to him for that. Sheina is a Wilkomirski, however, and her account of her wartime odyssey presents the Wilburs with a scenario that is much less speculative than Binjamin's. If Anna Wilkomirski hadn't left Riga and her descendants had survived the Nazi occupation, my mother could have had a life like the one Sheina, her second cousin, just described for me.

And yet when I hear Sheina tell her story, I now know that it is not the Wilburs' story, and that it can tell me only so much about myself. Hers is a typical story in certain respects, an example of what happened to those Jews who managed to outrace the Nazis' eastern advance, but she does not speak for anyone but herself. Sheina's story is also missing some information, but I now know better than to expect a story complete enough to satisfy my curiosity about the Wilkomirskis of Riga, or one that moves me enough to allow me to come to terms with what happened to relatives who remained in Europe, their neighbors, and the many other communities that were also destroyed. There is no story that will fill the void created by the Holocaust.

I have not come to collect Sheina's testimony. She invited me over so that we could become acquainted. I cannot demand that Sheina bare her soul, nor would I expect her to. Though I have convinced her that I am a relative, I am still a relative stranger.

AFTER A LONG silence, Sheina identifies the couple in the photograph. The man is her uncle Shmuel, and the woman Shmuel's sister Sora—the very same Sora whom Aunt Miriam mentioned back in New York, the Sora who, three years earlier, the cousins gathered in my parents' living room tried to merge with a Sonia Wilkomirski (*Sora, Sonia. Sonia, Sora. Maybe like a nickname?*) from Vilna who was mentioned by Binjamin. After the war, Sheina says, Sora gave birth to a daughter named Marina, who lives just ten minutes away by car. Sheina telephones Marina, who arrives with her husband within the hour.

Marina marvels at my sudden appearance and at the paired photographs, but what intrigues her most is the family tree I have brought. Compiled by my mother on her computer, it is a list in genealogical-outline form of Wilburs, with page after page of names in small print. Before my arrival, Sheina and Marina thought they had only a few living relatives: Sheina's sister in Riga and Marina's half brother in Toronto. Marina can't really read English, but she pores over the list carefully, slowly assimilating the idea that her family extends into dimensions she perhaps hoped for but never expected to find.

As shaken as she is, Marina can't quite comprehend why I have bothered to come to Israel looking for distant relatives when I have so many in America whom I have never met. I try to explain to her and Sheina about Binjamin Wilkomirski and *Fragments,* but the story doesn't mean much to them. Neither of them had heard of the book before—despite his appearance in *Wanda's Lists,* Binjamin wasn't such a big story in Israel, neither as a child survivor nor as an impostor—and Marina didn't even know that her grandmother's maiden name was Wilkomirski.

When I return to Tel Aviv a few days later, Marina picks me up at the central bus station to show me around town. She takes me to the Museum of the Diaspora, to Old Jaffa, to the plaza where

Yitzhak Rabin was assassinated. We stop for refreshments in a mall just off Rabin Square, and Marina starts asking me about her American relatives. She and her husband have long wanted to take a monthlong tour of the United States, she says, and now that she knows of the Wilbur clan, they have an added incentive to visit.

I hope they come soon. A few weeks before I left for Israel, I had brunch with my mother and a handful of her Wilbur cousins. I told them about Sheina and how we found out about her from the archives in Riga, but mostly they wanted to talk about Binjamin: how they were angry at him for misleading us, how they were holding on to admittedly unrealistic hopes that he was still a relative despite all the evidence. Perhaps a face-to-face encounter with Marina, an authentic cousin, will allow the Wilburs to leave Binjamin behind once and for all.

I tell Marina my mother wants to add her to the family tree, and I ask her for genealogical details about her immediate family. She tells me the names of her three children and when they were born. I also ask her about Sheina's family. When I pressed Sheina for details about her father's death, she demurred, so I decide to ask Marina if she knows what happened to him during the war. Marina asks me what I've heard, then tells me that Sheina misinformed me. Marina says she knows exactly what happened to Sheina's father. For that matter, Marina says, so does Sheina.

For a moment, it feels like everything is beginning again. The suspicion to which I have become so accustomed from chasing after Binjamin flows back into my veins. But I decide not to ask any more questions, at least not right now.